Midfielder's Moment

Cultural Studies Series
Paul Smith, Series Editor

Midfielder's Moment

Coloured Literature and Culture in Contemporary South Africa

Grant Farred

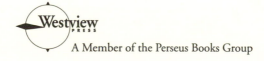

A Member of the Perseus Books Group

Cultural Studies Series

Copyright © 2000 by Westview Press, A Member of the Perseus Books Group

Published in 2000 in the United States of America by Westview Press, 5500 Central Avenue, Boulder, Colorado 80301-2877, and in the United Kingdom by Westview Press, 12 Hid's Copse Road, Cumnor Hill, Oxford OX2 9JJ

Library of Congress Cataloging-in Publication Data
Farred, Grant.
    Midfielder's moment : coloured literature and culture in contemporary South Africa / Grant Farred.
        p.   cm.—(Cultural studies series)
    Includes bibliographical references and index.
    ISBN 0-8133-3514-0
    1. South African literature (English)—History and criticism.   2. Politics and literature—South Africa—History—20th century.   3. South Africa—Politics and government—20th century.   4. Rive, Richard, 1931—Criticism and interpretation.   5. Nortje, Arthur, 1942–1970—Criticism and interpretation.   6. Davids, Jennifer, 1945—Criticism and interpretation.   7. Sports—Social aspects—South Africa.   8. Racially mixed people—South Africa.   9. Racially mixed people in literature.   10. Race awareness in literature.   Title.
PR9355.2F37   1999
820.9'358 21—dc21   99-045372

10   9   8   7   6   5   4   3   2   1

This book is dedicated to my mother, Julia Farred:
For her humor, faith, and love

Contents

Acknowledgments

There is a story about Sigmund Freud's work habits that is, in all likelihood, apocryphal. It is, however, appropriate for describing the process of writing *Midfielder's Moment*. Freud, the story goes, used to have two desks in his office: a big one for his main project and a smaller one for his secondary task. My own intellectual projects have been, over the past decade, bifurcated, split not between two desks but rather between work in cultural studies—generally speaking—and a focus on issues South African. Political, literary, and cultural developments in South Africa have consistently occupied me, even in those moments when I was researching Bob Marley or "New Jack" cinema. In place of the two work spaces I have had (and continue to have) parallel desks, projects that were (and are) of equal import but one of which assumed priority on the basis of immediacy, intellectual urgency, or current interest.

Midfielder's Moment is an attempt to address what I consider to be a crucial political and cultural issue in contemporary South Africa: the experience of being coloured, the occupation of the racial interstices, the condition of hybridity in a society marked by a penchant for polarity. This book is neither an apologia for a nascent, vague, and politically inefficacious "coloured nationalism" nor a condemnation of "colouredness." It represents nothing so much as an effort, as I elaborate in the "Introduction," to take the coloured community's politics, cultural practices, and (to a far lesser extent) voting tendencies seriously.

This book has benefited from the suggestions, readings, and critiques of several friends and colleagues, all of whom gave generously of their time. Their support, intellectual, political, and personal, was invaluable in the writing of *Midfielder's Moment*. I would like to thank Paul Smith, who encouraged this project from the first, kept faith with it throughout, and made my relationship with Westview Press an enjoyable one. Paul's friendship and professional advice pales for me, appropriately (given the title of the book and my own obsession with the English Premier football league, and the fortunes of my beloved Liverpool F.C.), in light of his greater accomplishment: his loyalty to Southampton F.C., a club that tests the nerve and courage of its fans every season, or so it seems.

Special thanks to Adina Popescu and Andy Day, my two remarkably insightful and patient editors. They both trusted me implicitly, cajoled, made (vague) threatening noises when deadlines approached, and, most important, supported me throughout. This book could not have been completed without them.

Stan Ridge read every chapter of the manuscript and commented, via regular mail, e-mail, and in occasional conversations, in the most astute terms. He probed firmly when it was necessary, asking just the right question, always with an underlying generosity. *Midfielder's Moment* owes him a considerable debt. Brinda Mehta kept me honest, always providing a sense of the importance of gender and the postcolonial—both within and outside its South African instantiation—as I worked through the chapters. Her friendship was a boon, her sense of humor just cutting enough.

My friendship with Thomas Kohut developed remarkably in the course of writing this book. His reading of the sports chapters was invaluable (though his literary sensibilities, I hasten to add, are exemplary too), and his obvious pleasure in my stories about Liverpool fandom enabled me to look more closely at the complicated politics of township football, nonracial cricket, and the exploits of South Africa's postapartheid cultural heroes. My other Williams colleagues, "Mick" MacDonald, Chris Pye, and Geoff Sanborn were unstinting in their support. They read various drafts of these chapters with insight; their suggestions were unfailingly useful; their good cheer in the Berkshire snow providing more sustenance than they could imagine. Thanks also to David L. Smith, who provided support and assistance as both dean and friend at crucial junctures.

Andrew Ross encouraged me many years ago to conceive of a book on South Africa. His ideas resonated at key moments in the writing of *Midfielder's Moment*. I am also grateful to the editors of *Social Text* (Toby Miller) and *Polygraph* (Jason Middleton) for permission to reprint "The Nation in White" and "Theatre of Dreams" respectively.

If I adhere to the "two-desk" approach to intellectual life, then I also live the life of a bicontinental academic, teaching in the United States while spending my Northern-Hemisphere summers in the Cape Town winter. Family and friends in Cape Town have been tremendously helpful in this project. My mother, to whom *Midfielder's Moment* is dedicated, has always been remarkable. She has sometimes turned her eyebrows up at my work habits, but she has never been anything less than completely supportive. My older sister, Karen Hector, has always demonstrated intellectual acumen and a wonderfully detached political criticism; my younger sister, Helga Farred, has always been a model of support and creativity. I am thankful to my brothers, Glenn, fellow Liverpool supporter and keen political critic, and Glynn, who came back at salient moments in the writing of this project. My work in Cape Town was made immeasurably easier by the helpfulness of my sister-in-law, Soraya Farred, who faxed, gave me access to e-mail, and printed drafts with only a hint of exasperation. Betty Young has been inimitable—full of banter and witticisms. Mark Fortuin offered a mildly cynical—and not always funny—view of the world. I am grateful to "the boys," my nephews Brent Hector (the gifted but occasionally reluctant spin bowler) and Dylan Farred (the youngest Liverpool fan in the family), for their laughter and their sense of fun.

Hassiem and Judi Bardien have been everything one's oldest friends should be: unqualifiedly supportive, hospitable, occasionally befuddled by my bicontinental lifestyle, always generous. Brian and Irene Anthony have been consistently wonderful, always ready to lend a hand and a vehicle. Francis Johnson was an enthusiastic, kind, and considerate presence. Eugene and Evelyn Agulhas have become wonderful friends—considerate, fun, and helpful to the hilt. To S.A.: for many things, including being a fount of generosity and support. Nathan and Mary Adriaanse: Thanks for always being up for a party. Andre Marais has been a good friend, always pushing me to undertake one more writing assignment on things South African. I am grateful to Karen Marais and Jerome Jacobs, the SAMWU (South Africa Municipal Workers Union) folks who provided that much needed administrative and technical support. Thanks to Roger Ronnie for turning a blind eye.

Thanks to Cynthia Young, who read every draft of every chapter and supported me through it all with a combination of good humor and incisive critique; she never lost patience, even though she had many an occasion to. I am deeply grateful to her. Most important, I suspect that she likes the academy more than she is willing to acknowledge.

To my daughter, Andrea Farred: a child of rare courage and fortitude, a ten year old with tremendous powers of discrimination. This book is a gift that I hope you will in time come to appreciate. I love you so much.

Midfielder's Moment is my tribute to Richard Moore Rive: friend, mentor, intellectual. Without Richard's encouragement and faith I may never have left South Africa; without his model of what a disenfranchised intellectual was, I might never have conducted the inquiries I do in this book. Yours, Richard, was a voice that was silenced too early, too brutally. You were a victim of South African homophobia—it was not only two young men who killed you, but an entire society that made it difficult (impossible, even) for you to reveal that most intimate side of who you were. *Midfielder's Moment* has many points of origin, one of them most assuredly your study where you acquainted me "personally" with Chinua Achebe, Wole Soyinka, Amos Tutuola, Zeke Mphahlele, Ingrid Jonker, and Arthur Nortje.

Grant Farred
Williamstown, MA

Acronyms

ANC   African National Congress
ICC   International Cricket Council
NP   National Party
SACB   South African Cricket Board
SACBOC   South African Cricket Board of Control
SACOS   South African Council on Sports
SACU   South African Cricket Union
SAMWU   South Africa Municipal Workers Union
SANROC   South African Non-Racial Olympic Committee
UCBSA   United Cricket Board of South Africa
UDI   Unilateral Declaration of Independence

Introduction:
Occupying the Interstices

The Problematic of the Middle

So they forgot her. . . . Sometimes the photograph of a close friend or rela-
tive—looked at too long—shifts, and something more familiar than the dear
face itself moves there. They can touch it if they like, but don't, because they
know things will never be the same if they do.

—Toni Morrison, *Beloved*

In nations that function according to the law of racial absolutes, the interstices is a precarious, embattled, under- and (frequently) unrecognized
space. The contestation between black and white, often coded as "oppressed" and "oppressor," enjoys an ideological primacy that overwrites
(and undermines) the struggles of groups whose racial identity is more
vexed and complicated. Privileging polarities serves to vitiate the already
compromised political agency of those who occupy the racial interstices
because this group is less enfranchised—or more disenfrachized—than
those constituencies whose identity is more clearly marked; "blackness,"
then, has a greater political saliency than "mestizo-ness." Through hierar-
chization, racial absolutism produces its own restrictive (and restricted)
discourse, a sociopolitical vocabulary that thrives on binaries; this
rhetoric is founded on a set of polarities that are understood as "natural"
opposites—"black" versus "white," "indian" versus "black." Binaries are,
however, not so much different as they are codependent, polarities that
inform, inflect, and (inversely) reflect one another.

Invoking the Hegelian dialectic, Helene Cixous argues, "Thought has always worked through opposition,"[1] one set of ideas articulating itself in relation to another—one mode of thought feeding off another. Racial absolutes, in this regard, keep each other ideologically solvent: The one

enables and sustains the other; one can survive without the other, but it would lose a considerable amount of its appeal and rhetorical efficacy. However, binaries also derive considerable value from oppositionality: One of the two philosophical poles has to be devalued for the other to acquire meaning, and vice versa. Patriarchy, for instance, functions by undermining women—socially, politically, economically, and intellectually[2]—in much the same way that whiteness "invalidates" (to overstate the case) blackness.

The fiction of racial purity, the "undilutedness" of blackness and whiteness, is especially strong in societies, such as the antebellum American South and colonial Africa, founded on these binary oppositions. So much so that the in-between, the psychic and political domain of the hybrid subject, is a place that can only be occupied with considerable difficulty because of the ambiguous racial history this mixed body represents—it cannot fit into the existing social categories. Because their racial identity negates (or complicates) any notion of "purity," it also attenuates the mixed, mestizo, dougla,[3] or coloured claim of national belonging. By virtue of being labeled racially mixed, the hybrid subject cannot be a full member of the nation, in either its black or its white instantiation; for the coloured constituency there are all too few differences between white rule and black governance. Within a discourse grounded racial purity, coloured affiliation remains problematic, qualified; the marginal or marginalized national outsider. Partial enfranchisement, or partial disenfranchisement, is frequently the apogee of national belonging for those who are mixed; they may identify with the nation, they may name themselves as members of it, they may even participate in its triumphs and failures, but this does not mean that they can ever fully belong to it. (The hybrid body marks a problematic third option, the point at which the nation suffers disintegration, the symbolic—and temporary—breaking apart of national identity. Here the interstitial constituency makes the self-conscious—or unreflective—decision to situate itself outside the body of the nation.)

This is not to suggest that hybridized constituencies are incapable of momentarily—and, for some members, permanently—situating themselves fully within the "body" of the nation. Rather, it is to recognize how fraught with "racialized" obstacles such an identification is, how slight and contentious the claims to national belonging are: Full membership has to be demonstrated through transcending hybridity. "Mestizo-ness" or colouredness, which can be read as the Othered, liminally black subject, is a condition that has to be overcome for national belonging to be possible; here self-affirmation is predicated on self-negation—the historically willed "black" self ideologically liquidates the "hybrid" self. The hybridized self has to split itself off from itself, it has to undergo an imaginary "division": It has to imagine itself as unqualifiedly "black" or "white," a self-representation only achievable through the denial of that body's "blackness" or "whiteness." In this mode (and moment), the mixed race subject has to show what it is not: National belonging depends upon partial negation, a denial of an integral self that is difficult to accomplish because the subject is the product of an interracial sexual exchange. The hybrid body cannot disentangle itself from itself. This is a community for whom, in Kobena Mercer's terms, the notion of an "imaginary unity" is difficult to achieve—in place of singularity there is plurality, at best a duality, of identifications that have to be negotiated. Mestizoness signals at once the incorporation—the experience of living with—both black and white, yet being neither one nor the other. The hybrid body speaks of a historic entanglement that does not allow the easy dissociation of black from white.

Neither does the hybrid subject facilitate the repression of the violence, psychic and physical, innate (and intimate) to the production of the mestizo or coloured subject. Hybridity results, the coloured body reminds us, from the violent, sexual encounter between the colonizer and the colonized, the oppressed and the oppressor; its origins can be traced to a power discrepancy that allowed the colonizers to fulfill their sexual desire as easily as they were able to assume control of the colonized's economy or bureaucracy. (Power, of course, is primarily what distinguishes the oppressor from the oppressed: The former could more easily fulfill their desire than the latter.) Hybridity is simultaneously the most subtle and obvious articulation of the colonizer (and neocolonizer) or the oppressor's power. It is, in this way, an expression of the violence integral to the colonial project: Hybridity marks the appropriation of the colonized or the oppressed's culture, the ability to transform it into something either recognizable or unrecognizable from its original shape; it is an expropriation of their economic resources. And, finally, hybridity speaks of the power of the colonizer to create "new" physical communities, "new bodies" (pigmentations, textures of hair, or physiognomies previously unknown to the colonized and possibly even to the colonizer) out of the sexual encounter between the "West" and the colonized.

As hybrid communities reproduce themselves and produce their own (abbreviated or expansive) histories, their violent origins are subsumed by the larger struggle of making, or maintaining, their marginal place in societies where "racial purity" holds sway. In its struggle to deal with the mundane, the "mixed" subject makes itself vulnerable to the erasures and eradications of history: The determination to forget, eradicate, reinscribe, or fetishize the origins of hybridity. Through the everyday (though not unexceptional) workings of history, the hybrid becomes a commodity, not a subject—in both senses of the term—with a severed and truncated past (the hybrid self can only re-create itself in fragments, by piecing together an array of narratives, or elements of narratives). The history produced through physical violence becomes, in the contemporary instantiation, a history misrepresented by the violence—both subtle and brutal—done to memory. Violence becomes, in the terms of Morrison's *Beloved*, that aspect of hybrid life that is all too frequently "forgotten"—banished from public memory—because it evokes a disturbing recognition. The coloured body sparks a historic confrontation, a meeting of the black and the white selves in a form that is at once physically different but hauntingly recognizable. This is the white self "distorted," the black self "refigured," but always insufficiently different. Both black and white can "see," that is, identify itself, sometimes through a physionogmic lens that refracts, "dilutes," but does not eliminate "whiteness" or "blackness." As Morrison says, "Sometimes the photograph of a close friend or relative—looked at too long—shifts, and something more familiar than the dear face itself moves there." Morrison's "something more familiar" is, of course, the white or black self identifying itself in the "dear coloured face." It is not, in this instance, that the racial absolutism cannot "touch" the coloured body (it is precisely because they "touched" so intimately that there is a coloured body), but that they cannot acknowledge their own presence in its visage. Conversely, in constructing themselves as an identifiable community, the coloured constituency sometimes strives to replicate this tendency: They do not speak, or they determinedly mute, the presence of the black (more often) or white body in their physiognomies. However, once the white colonizers "touched" the colonized blacks, things could never again "be the same," racially or otherwise. In producing "new" bodies, they were also reproducing—albeit in a form not quite mimetic but still eminently recognizable—themselves, a familiarity they have denied far more often than they have claimed it. Being confronted with the coloured body represents, in Judith Butler's terms, a meeting with the "phantasm of the original"—the "original" that at once recognizes, denies, and is unable to identity itself in an Other self that is disturbingly similar; the coloured body is the hybridized, "blackened," white self; alternatively, it is the black body "whitened." When the white—or black—body does acknowledge itself within its coloured counterpart, it is frequently for expedient political purposes.

Within the context of both apartheid and postapartheid society (though more problematically so with the latter than the former), the struggle to inhabit—sometimes with the intention of liquidating—the interstices is the experience of coloured South Africans. A product of the early encounter (from at least the fifteenth century on) between European colonialists and indigenous southern Africans, coloureds have historically occupied a marginal role in the nation's body politic—a community that belongs fully neither in one place nor the other because it has substantive (and biological) links to both. From the perspective of coloured South Africans, some might validly argue, postapartheid society is all too reminiscent of, if not indistinguishable from, its apartheid predecessor. Ambivalently located during the National Party (NP) government's rule, awkwardly situated between the ruling white minority and the oppressed black majority, the coloured community once again finds itself idiosyncratically marginalized within the nation's reconfigured body politic. The coloured community was politically disenfranchised by a white apartheid regime with which some of its key constituencies, rural and huge sections of the urban, working class coloureds, shared a language (Afrikaans), religion (the austere Protestantism of the Dutch Reformed Church), and culture (a common passion for certain sports, cuisine, and social practices). In postapartheid South Africa, coloureds appear to be as riven by ambiguity in their efforts to delineate their relations to the new African National Congress (ANC) government. They find themselves torn between their commitment to a political party that spearheaded the antiapartheid struggle, an organization with which many of them have openly identified (as many of them continue to do), and a fear of how they are understood (and understand themselves) as liminally "black." Coloureds also fear being dominated (or "discriminated against") by the Africanist majority; coloureds see themselves being subjected by blacks who are of "purely" African descent, though that is a designation also claimed by certain "progressive" sectors of the coloured community.

Unlike their Africanist counterparts, coloured South Africans have played an uneven and problematic role in the struggle against white minority rule. This community has, for much of its history, been fully supportive of the black liberation movements and, at others, it has made common cause with the rulers of the white state. In the antiapartheid moment, coloureds participated in the Defiance Campaign of the 1950s,[4] in the school boycotts of the 1970s and 1980s, and in the insurrections of the 1980s.[5] Coloureds participated fully in the historic Congress of the People in 1956 (when the ANC adopted its Freedom Charter, still its guiding political document) and were instrumental in founding the United Democratic Front in the early 1980s. And yet, as long ago as 1924, "coloured votes helped bring the NP to power. . . . During that campaign, General Hertzog had promised that the NP would draw white and coloured people together as 'civilised' people against the 'native.'"[6] Some seventy years later, with the first democratic elections in postapartheid South Africa, a majority of coloured voters again returned the National Party to power. These vastly different commitments demonstrate a contradictory political tendency that marks coloured electoral thinking. At still other moments, coloureds have resembled a gymnast on the parallel bars: precariously balanced between the two dominant groups, tenuously linked to both but with a firm "grip" on neither; their "hold" on whiteness and blackness is politically slight, which means the interstices is, in effect, the only place they can occupy.

Coloureds represent, to amend Gloria Anzuldua's term, an interstitial "borderland":[7] the alienated, peripheral community that occupies the political in-between rather than the margins of society; coloureds are geographically in the postapartheid society but not wholly—that is, ideologically—part of it. Consequently, this constituency recognizes itself as "coloured" before it identifies itself as "South African." Many members of this community would echo Richard Rive's memorable phrase, "'I could not say with full conviction that I am a South African.'" Unlike Rive, who is split between his desire to announce his "South African-ness" and the disenfranchisement of apartheid that delimits (legally forbidding) his citizenship, a substantial number of coloureds would hesitate before affiliating themselves with postapartheid South Africa. National belonging, "South African-ness," is a condition this community can achieve, reject, or partially accept. The coloured sense of national affiliation depends on the identificatory possibilities South African society allows them, on their commitment to "overcoming" hybridity; coloured interpellation is contingent on how this community sees itself being addressed, spoken to, or spoken for; or, how they see their particular needs being disregarded or ignored. In Rive's phraseology, coloureds have to be "convinced"—as much by others as by themselves—that they are truly national subjects. It is a "conviction" that does not come easily, nor is it consistent (or even reliable).

South African colouredness is, arguably, best understood as a quasi-ethnic identity: a racially indistinct—including in its ranks several different physical "types"—community bound together by cultural practices, mores, values, and traditions, all of which have evolved in the face of racist white hostility. In the absence of an autochthonous black culture or an imported (and amended) white European culture, coloureds have had to forge a set of cultural practices out of disparate racial experiences—East Asian slaves, indigenous African communities, European influences. (Colouredness, however, is different from ethnicity in that it is without the kind of narrow racial overtones that usually gird such a description, which is not to say, of course, that it is not conscious about race.) Overdetermined by what we might term "negativity," coloureds are not white, they are not black; colouredness assumes primacy in this community because it marks their distance from the South African nation; it speaks most complexly of this constituency's ambivalent location within the body politic. They are that part of the nation that is only partial, or tangential, to the South African political imaginary. Regionally defined and confined by their historical status as the oppressed majority in the Western Cape (in other parts of the country, blacks constituted the disenfranchised majority), their geographical containment marks them as liminal and symbolically integral to the nation. (Coloureds also live in other regions of the country, but because the Western Cape is home to the greater majority of this community, it has become the psychic lodestar for coloured difference.)

Numerically peripheral to the nation, though not so unimportant that their voting power can be discounted in the region, their existence serves as a physical reminder of apartheid's colonial antecedents. Contemporary Cape Town, not incidentally named the "Mother City," marks the region where Portuguese explorers Bartholemew Dias and Vasco da Gama made contact with the local African people. Coloureds are, in a historically perverse way, the quintessential "South Africans": They are the articulation of the modern (and postmodern) South African nation, neither African nor European. Coloureds symbolize the hybridity of the postcolonial condition, even if they cannot signal a "postracial" discourse. This community has no history outside South Africa because they were produced in the (then not-yet) nation: They may not be its original inhabitants, but their existence marks—and enunciates—the site of original contact; without colonial exploration and desire, without the indigenous presence, there would be no coloured community. They do not so much belong to and in South Africa, as their existence is completely contingent upon its political formation: Their very existence depends on someone else; they are inconceivable—and the pun is intended—without someone else's imperial or sexual desire.

Bereft as they are of a prelapsarian (that is, precolonial) or European past, coloureds are completely grounded in South Africa. Unlike the autochthonous Africans, they belong only to the site of that first encounter between the colonizer and the colonized, not to other social formations such as the Khoi or the San or the Xhosa, tribal entities that continue to have considerable purchase in the new nation. Unlike the European colonialists, they are rooted in this part of Africa, without connections to the metropole; the Netherlands or Britain is not a space that coloureds can claim as "home," however precarious that affiliation might be for whites. Paradoxical as it might seem, it is not surprising that these quintessential "South Africans" have not had their national identity endorsed either by blacks or by whites, nor have they themselves embraced it; marginality has been accepted, transformed into the dominant coloured subject position, as much it has been imposed from without. Hybridity is a sign of difference, of racial, cultural, and ideological impurity; a marker of alienation, hybridity is not read as a measure of integration into (and centrality to) the nation. It is certainly not understood as emblematic of the nation—

racial fictions sustain themselves precisely because they ignore, disregard, rationalize, or overwrite hybridity. Produced from that long ago
union of a white father and a black mother, coloureds dominate the
"Mother City," but they cannot stake a claim either to creating—"mother-
ing"—or to representing the nation. The "future" of global culture may
very well, as Stuart Hall has observed, "belong to the impure,"[8] but the
South African body politic certainly does not. Racial impurity does not so
much disqualify as it signifies a perpetual symbolic disenfranchisement, a
marginalization that cannot be transcended. No South African community is better versed in the vagaries and contradictions of the politics of
the impure than coloureds.

The Peculiar and Demanding Condition
of the South African Hybrid

*Honor is accorded by taking . . . ideas seriously and debating them, extend-
ing them, quarreling with them, and making them live again.*

—Stuart Hall, "C.L.R. James: A Portrait"

By taking "seriously" the condition of colouredness in a postindustrial,
increasingly globalized economic moment when the very concept of the
nation-state is in question, this hybrid community offers the opportunity
to reflect upon the contructedness of both nation and race in South Africa.
Midfielder's Moment marks an engagement (predominantly cultural) with
the term "coloured," not the denial, valorization, or unqualified endorsement of this racial appellation; it is not, as I said earlier, an apologia for an
obviously fanciful coloured nationalism but an attempt to speak to that
discourse, to interrogate the terms on which that notion is founded. (The
problematic and contested nature of this designation, a term many
coloureds themselves reject, is signaled by the use of the small "c" rather
than the capital "C" of apartheid classification.) This project does not represent the unproblematic embracing of the term "coloured"; nor is it a jus-
tification for a nascent coloured separatism. Rather, it is a cultural investigation into why the term has resonance, why huge sections of this hybrid
community has adopted "coloured" as an identity, and how it functions
for these people. If we do indeed, as Marx suggests in *The Eighteenth Bru-
maire of Louis Bonaparte*, make history under conditions not of our own
choosing, then *Midfielder's Moment* wants to explore the kind of history
the coloured made during the apartheid era and wants to glean the kind
of history this constituency might make in the postapartheid moment.
The concept of "colouredness" and its effects, the ways in which it in-
forms the thinking, political responses, the voting tendencies, the cultural
particularities, the divided, bifurcated racial consciousness, of this South

African constituency can only be understood if it is publicly "debated," "extended" (in the sense that it is subjected to a demanding intellectual interrogation), and "quarreled" with over and over again. The experience and history of being coloured is, in Hall's terms, all too "alive"—coloured memory is vibrant, its understanding of itself often contorted and conflicted but also intensely self-aware. Colouredness, understood here as the dynamic accumulation of this hybrid community's unique experiences, history, culture, and traditions, cannot be erased, ignored (though some might think that possible), or incorporated unproblematically into "blackness" or "whiteness." Colouredness can no more be disregarded in the postapartheid era than it could be overlooked in the apartheid moment. *Midfielder's Moment* marks the attempt to demonstrate how this community constitutes an indelible, and richly entangled, part of the South African cultural and political landscape.

It would, in any case, be politically shortsighted to ignore this community or its complicated past. If postapartheid South Africa is to produce itself as a nation out of disparate, conflicting racial (and raced) histories, out of different narratives of "arrival," out of a black community divided both by apartheid legislation and its own history into distinct, often warring, "tribes," then no community offers a more instructive instance of "construction" than coloureds. If the "new" South Africa is to achieve a symbolic or rhetorical "wholeness," a national identity, then it has to understand how it is the consequence of historically different migrations—"diasporic" movements that speak of very different motivations for their presence in South Africa. Blacks from central Africa moved south during the sixteenth century Difakane; white ethnic communities have for five hundred years come there from Europe, some in search of religious freedom, other seeking economic prosperity; and, inspired by the Pan-Africanist thinking of the Jamaican Marcus Garvey, black Caribbean intellectuals and activists made the transatlantic journey (the reverse Middle Passage, one might say) early in the twentieth century to locate themselves within the struggle to liberate the motherland from colonialism—even as the Caribbean itself was still subject to colonial rule. In the face of multiple deracinations, of having families torn apart by apartheid legislation (where siblings were separated from each other and placed into distinct racial categories because their physiognomies were different), and disenfranchisement, the coloured community has survived. Through a combination of resilience, borrowings from other cultures, ingenuity, and creativity, coloureds have produced practices distinctly theirs: a body of literature, a set of tropes, metaphors, a collection of metropolitan cultural affiliations, and, in Hall's allusive phrase, "repertoires of representation" that are marked and understood as "coloured." In overcoming the affects and effects of apartheid, South African society will have to engage in a

process of nation making that will require some of these skills and ideological strategies.

After the manichean politics of apartheid, where racial binaries dominated, the demands of the postapartheid moment are more "impure," an
instance where the values of hybridity are likely to be more efficacious
than the absolutist fictions of the NP era. The "new" South African nation
will have to be, much like the coloured community has repeatedly been,
produced out of difference; a series of differences that postapartheid society is, understandably, reluctant either to recognize or to engage.
Apartheid, after all, was little more than the racist—and divisive—invo-
cation of difference—coloureds were "different" from both blacks and
whites, that is, racially superior to the former and inferior to the latter.
Ironically, the only to way to counter (and possibly overcome) the cynical
and destructive deployment of (racialized) difference is to confront the
residual—in Raymond Williams's rich conception of the term—effects of
apartheid. Continuing in the Williams vein, some might argue (and not
without a certain validity), that the terms of the apartheid discourse are
not so much residual as they are mutedly dominant, refracted now
through the postapartheid, ANC lens. The Nationalist's policies "consoli-
dated," in both the offensive and defensive sense of the phrase, the
coloured community. It gave this constituency legislative standing, a
process that articulated its "differences" from the other South African
communities; those conceptual differences have had real political consequences, effects that continue to have ideological purchase for coloureds
in the postapartheid dispensation.

The 1994 elections, a signal moment in and for the coloured community, may have marked the formal end of apartheid and the inauguration
of the postapartheid state, but it was also a forceful reminder of how the
majority of coloureds—many of them working class—enunciated their
"difference." Coloureds are always considered a "swing" constituency, a
grouping whose hybrid racial identity meant that they would not automatically vote for Nelson Mandela's party, and it was only because of
coloured support that the NP (now renamed the "New National Party")
was able to win power in the Western Cape in the first democratic elections;[9] it was one of only two regions, the other being Kwazulu Natal,
where Mangosuthu Buthelezi's Inkatha movement was elected, where
the ANC did not win a majority. Although the outcome of the election in
the Western Cape was not totally unexpected, the pivotal role of coloured
voters was met with disapproval by the (predominantly black) leadership
of the ANC.

Enfranchisement became, for coloureds, an opportunity to articulate a
distinct kind of political oppositionality, a moment to align themselves
against the "black"-identified ANC. The outcome of the 1994 elections in

the Western Cape also constituted a form of disenfranchisement because the coloured community was read as, not surprisingly or without a certain validity, "antiblack," "anti-ANC," and strongly opposed to the new status quo. Coloureds were, once again, effectively if not formally, disenfranchised, consigning themselves to (and implicitly consigned to) the margins: The "new," ANC-led nation was loathe to tolerate this determined marking of "difference," this breaking the ranks of an expansive, inclusive (but uncritical) "blackness." All that the events of 1994 made apparent, however, was the problematic and the tenuousness of coloured "blackness." Affiliating with blackness or whiteness, out of political strategy, fear, "racism," or even expedience, is the best option available to coloureds—they cannot ever *be* black or white, complex and fictitious as these terms are.

Vacillating between these different racial affiliations, between black and white, apartheid compelled coloureds to recognize how the apartheid regime positioned them differently—that is, marginally better—in the racial structure from blacks. Coloureds had to, in response to this relative racial privileging, negotiate a way to oppose and undermine the NP's attempts to divide-and-rule the disenfranchised—they had to, in other words, learn how to situate themselves as "black" despite the tactics of the apartheid rulers. Coloureds had to engage their apartheid "privileges": how, among other things, their slightly better economic and educational opportunities (they were not subjected to the humiliation of the "pass" system, an apartheid law that required blacks to carry an identification document on their persons at all times, especially when they were in white areas) and their access to marginally better housing and healthcare (though this was often not the case) affected their relations with their black counterparts. This community had to understand how their "blackness" was being "artificially" abbreviated by the white regime. In the anti-apartheid moment, these differences—small but not insignificant, considering the functioning of the apartheid state—were "temporarily" set aside as coloureds took their place in the ranks of the South African disenfranchised. The enemy, it was presumed in these campaigns, was common, apartheid; the cause a shared one, a commitment to a democratic, nonracial society. In 1994, the political landscape was less clearly marked, ideological fissures and fault lines more difficult to discern, and the place of the coloured community in the nation's body more complicated—alternately invested in and removed from the "new" society, in some moments (mainly cultural) coloureds identified with the nation, at others they saw themselves subjected to a "raced" disenfranchisement.

The result of the first democratic elections in the Western Cape also reminds us that the coloured role in the antiapartheid struggle only complicated its relations to white South Africa; it did not sever those connections. Remarkably, as the outcome of the 1994 election in the Western Cape demonstrates, the memory of coloured affinity for and with whites survived the violences and traumas of the apartheid years; a remembering, or imagining, of racial ties to whites complicated by a fear of a black, ANC-dominated society that speaks of an undercurrent of racism in the coloured community; the publicly unspoken, or rarely speakable, coloured belief in its racial "superiority" over a now politically hegemonic black group. To paraphrase, coloureds see themselves not only as racially distinct, "We are not black," but more disturbingly, as racially superior, "We are better than black." In the townships of the Cape Flats, this last sentiment found widespread, if not uncontested, articulation in 1994 as the coloured "working class"—which includes in its ranks large numbers of unemployables—feared that the "black" ANC government would not be as attentive to it as it would be to its "own" Africanist constituency (ies). The demands and ethics of the antiapartheid movement were such that it did not, could not, would not give those sentiments public utterance; coloureds, in that moment, may not have been unqualifiedly black, but they were certainly disenfranchised. Where it was acknowledged, coloured "difference" could, in the NP era, be explained by the apartheid hierarchy—they were interpellated differently, occupying a nominally but symbolically "higher" rung in the race (ist) system. However, this discourse has become unavailable in the postapartheid paradigm where disenfranchised "unity"—under the auspices of the ANC—is a powerful fiction. Because national "reconciliation" (between the historically enfranchised and disenfranchised) constitutes the dominant narrative trope, Nelson Mandela's party presumed a certain unproblematic support for the ANC—the disenfranchisement of apartheid was expected to translate into electoral support from the entire "black" populace.

When the majority of the coloured "working class" voted their "fear" in 1994, the ANC government, the coloured left, and various other commentators were compelled to speculate on this event, unsurprising as it was to this constituency itself. Coloured electoral "fear" represents the anticipation of what they understand to be a different form of disenfranchisement: marginalization by the new "black" government. Expecting this, coloureds (who keenly felt their vulnerability) gave utterance to their racial (sometimes difficult to distinguish from a racist) unconscious. Unlike whites, they were without the historic benefits of apartheid and the skills valuable to the postapartheid nation (coloureds do not have the academic and technical training that was routine for apartheid-era whites); unlike indians (South Africans of Asian descent), they did not constitute an identifiable, fairly well-resourced community; and, unlike blacks, they could not anticipate the future as a symbolically and physiognomically integral component of the newly dominant group. They were, as always, faced with the question of ideological allegiance. For coloureds, it was not just a matter of voting for a political party, but that their vote would be racially construed: If they voted ANC they would mark themselves as "black"; if they threw in their electoral lot with the NP, they would be labeled (sympathetic to) "whites."

Predictably, coloured ideological loyalties wavered. This uncertainty, however, is not (only) a sign of political expediency or unarticulated racism, but rather marks a peculiar uncertainty: the problematic of mobile affinities, of unresolved, irresolvable dual linkages, of negotiating between racial identities that cannot adequately accommodate the hybridized body, of being "neither black nor white, yet both."[10] The ideological middle represents, in this instance, a fluid, contestatory, shifting political domain where the capacity for radical ("black") and moderate ("white") alignment jostle dynamically, and sometimes unpredictably, with each other.

Writing Colouredness

Inside him the confusion has not settled.
—J.M. Coetzee, *The Master of Petersburg*

It is not surprising that, despite its political significance, no event has undermined the complexities of the middle as much as the 1994 elections in the Western Cape. This moment has captured the political imagination of the South African populace—an analytical mode that has repeated itself in the wake of the 1999 results.[11] After all, how could a community previously oppressed and deracinated by apartheid legislation vote for the party that crafted such a series of racist policies?

With the exception of the final two chapters (and then frequently in a refracted, cursory, circumspect fashion), an examination of the ways the young coloured sportsmen Paul Adams and Benni McCarthy have been represented in the media and claimed by various communities, *Midfielder's Moment* will not directly engage these issues—let alone provide answers. This is not to suggest that the project is unconcerned with these issues. It is, but from a historical distance: With the exceptions of "The Nation in White" and "McCarthyism Township Style," this project interrogates "colouredness" as a cultural and political phenomenon retrospectively. *Midfielder's Moment* represents the long view, a series of essays attuned to the contemporary questions that have accrued to "colouredness"—but engaging these issues mainly through the cultural practices and literature produced in the apartheid era. The politics and culture of coloureds in contemporary South Africa cannot be fully grasped without understanding how a hybrid sense of self and community has marked this grouping—an ideologically entangled sense of belonging (and unbe-longing) as evident under the NP regime as it is today.

Midfielder's Moment is a collection of essays (three on coloured literature and three on coloured sport) that offers a sense of how the complexities, ambiguities, and ideological uncertainties of the coloured community be-came manifested during the forty years of the antiapartheid movement. This project demonstrates how colouredness is, as befits its hybrid subjec-tivity, an uneven experience, characterized by several contestations that emerge as much from within as from without; every facet of coloured cul-ture is subjected to external scrutiny and to intracommunity tensions, de-bates, and conflicts. The problematic of coloured identity, what it means, how it should be read, what political allegiances it implies, how it marked a "black" or "white" political subjectivity, is salient and fought over in the work of the three creative artists engaged in the first section of *Midfielder's Moment*: This project sets up a dialogic conversation among the novelist and short story writer, Richard Rive, and the two poets, Arthur Nortje and Jennifer Davids. All three of these authors approach the question of "colouredness," so far as they acknowledge the term and its apartheid overtones, from different ideological positions and with different invest-ments. Rive and Nortje both engage the coloured experience explicitly, though for distinct purposes and from varying physical locales; and colouredness is such a surreptitious, disguised presence in Davids's verse that it raises the question of whether Davids should be recognized as a coloured poet at all.

More than any of the three authors, Rive's work is preoccupied with transcending colouredness and achieving an incorporative blackness. The oldest (born in 1930) and most productive of these writers (both Nortje and Davids's literary output was limited to a single volume of poetry),[12] Rive offers a paradigm of blackness that is based on "nonracialism," a construct designed to invalidate "coloured" as a political identity but that paradoxically brings it more into focus. Rhetorically, if not always politi-cally because it did not win widespread support in the disenfranchised community, nonracialism was the most incisive counter to apartheid: Nonracialism constituted not only an opposition to apartheid, it refused the very philosophical grounds on which this system of white racial supe-riority rested; the concept of race was denied by nonracialism, removing the very epistemological basis of apartheid. (This political philosophy was developed in the late 1940s by the Unity Movement, a political orga-nization with which all these authors—though Rive more than either of the other two—were acquainted; much of nonracial thinking was influ-enced by the anti-Nazi critiques of race produced by the European left in the wake of World War II.) The philosophy of nonracialism also provided, as the essays in the sports section will show, the ideological foundation for the South African Council on Sport (SACOS), an antiapartheid movement with which Rive was involved as an athletics administrator; this philosophical link is made most obvious in the name of SACOS's international wing, the South African Non-Racial Olympic Committee (SAN-ROC), an organization dedicated to isolating white South African sport globally. Another poet, Dennis Brutus, was a key member of SANROC. (Brutus was Rive's friend and contemporary, and Nortje's mentor when the young poet was a high school student in the Eastern Cape city of Port Elizabeth.)

Founded in the late 1940s with the publication of work by the black writer Ezekiel Mphahlele (*Down Second Avenue*) and the coloured author Peter Abrahams (*Tell Freedom: Memories of Africa*), Protest writing marks the first generation of urban disenfranchised literature. It was an attempt by "black" writers (in the inclusive sense) to break with the largely rural, mission school-inflected representations of disenfranchised life and to give voice to the new experiences of a rapidly urbanizing populace. Protest Writing coincided with the ascension of the apartheid to power and much of its focus in the 1950s and 1960s was aimed at depicting in literature (mainly short stories) the anger, tribulations, small triumphs and hopes of black people trying to make their lives in cities such as Johannesburg and Cape Town under a repressive NP regime. Mainly black and based largely in Johannesburg, there was also a Western Cape Protest School. Rive (who along with James Matthews, and Alex La Guma comprised, as I delineate in Chapter 1, this branch of the Protest movement), was a leading member of this "black" literary School and its ideology informed much of his approach to the issue of "colouredness."

Influenced by his involvement in the Protest movement, Rive was critical of race both as fiction and as a divisive (apartheid) social construct. As a Protest writer, Rive rejects the concept in favor of a "blackness" that can accommodate all the disenfranchised South African communities—Africans, coloureds, and indians. (Coloured becomes, in this epistemological paradigm, a form of antiessentialist, "black-based racelessness"—it eradicates apartheid's racial categories in the cause of a larger disenfranchised unity. In place of apartheid's divisions, nonracialism recalls Mercer's "imaginary unity"; this antiapartheid concept is the South African equivalent—and predecessor—of the 1980s definition of "black Britons," a term that could accommodate British subjects of the African, Caribbean, and Asian diaspora.[13] Neither of these notions excludes difference, but both focus on the shared experience of disenfranchisement, systemic racism, and oppression—all of which involves violence against marginalized communities.) Because nonracialism does not recognize the biological foundations of race, because it is founded on the Enlightenment principle of human equality, it contains within it the ideological possibility of making common antiapartheid cause with enfranchised white South Africans who resisted the racist status quo. The poet Davids implicitly, though never articulately, shares the novelist's views on nonracialism because she too was fairly well versed in Unity Movement thinking.

For all his commitment to nonracialism, Rive not only recognizes the discursive value of "blackness" as a political catalyst, but also that these two concepts perform different functions in his intellectual oeuvre. Nonracialism constitutes the ideological girding, symbolizing the idealized democratic society; "blackness" is the rhetorical strategy, a way of situating himself as integral to the experience of the majority of (disenfranchised) South Africans. Rive was fervently opposed to any notion of race or racism, but his work is attuned to the unique resonances of "black" as a political moniker. As a thinker deeply influenced by the Harlem Renaissance, a writer involved with the postcolonial movement in sub-Saharan Africa, and alert to its mobilizing capacities in the Black Power movements in the United Sates in the 1960s, Rive understood how "blackness" could unite disenfranchised South Africans and align his native community (or communities) with international movements dedicated to "black" liberation. It is precisely because Rive subscribed to this complex and uniquely qualified notion of "blackness" that he, the coloured author who refused to acknowledge the apartheid state's racial designation, found himself in such an ideological bind in his fiction. Any attempt to "overcome" colouredness and write himself into "blackness" is an implicit acknowledgement of his status as coloured subject. For the hybrid South African intent on achieving blackness, colouredness is a transient moment; however, blackness is unachievable without understanding the "limitations" of colouredness.

Located in the chronological middle of the literature section, linking the work of the elder statesperson of coloured letters and the largely unknown Davids, Nortje's writing throws Rive's conception of colouredness into sharp relief. Nortje is the only one of these writers who "accepts," in the most contorted and even disabling sense of the term, colouredness as an identity. Unlike Rive, an author always already liquidating colouredness, Nortje embeds his work in it; unlike Davids, who can never bring herself to even say the word, Nortje is sometimes so overwrought by hybridity that it becomes a key term in one of his most important poems, the aptly—and disturbingly—titled "Dogsbody half-breed": "And I hybrid, after Mendel, / caught between the wire and the wall"[14] he writes, demonstrating the depth of his intensely painful, and ultimately tragic, grappling with his status as coloured South African; the problematic, and exacting, occupation of the middle was a condition that Nortje could never come to terms with, not during his stint as teacher and student in Canada or in his brief stay as a graduate student at Oxford University in England.

The experience of being hybrid, the son of a Jewish (which he configures as white) man and a coloured woman, animates Nortje's poetry with an anguish that is at once lyrical and unsettling. The intensity of colouredness in his verse, however, serves as an effective counterpoint to Rive—whose political eye is focused on transcending—and Davids— where colouredness is erased, in the Derridian sense (colloquially transcribed, for everything we say we leave several things unsaid). Nortje's writing provides the opportunity to plumb the coloured psyche, to examine the painful effects of the experience, and to explore how colouredness cannot be overcome through deracination or exile. If Rive is intent on evacuating the (coloured) middle, rendering it ideologically bankrupt and unusable, then Nortje demonstrates the psychic costs of living in the racial interregnum. It is not so much, Nortje's verse suggests, that coloureds belong in the middle, but that they do not belong anywhere else. They are ideologically landlocked "between the wire and the wall" because neither the barbed "wire" nor the unscaleable "wall" will accept them. Coloureds are not so much "caught" in this space as they are permanently "trapped" there—occupants of an interstitial middle that cannot be expanded, transformed, or appropriated, except for political expediency. The middle is, however, too contested a space to be "owned," even by those who inhabit that space.

As much as Nortje's poetry is explicit about colouredness, so Davids's is elusive. As much as the male coloured poet's work is characterized by intensity, so his female counterpart demonstrates a measured remove from the identity. Where Rive and Nortje both engage colouredness, albeit from entirely different locations, Davids is Wildean about racial categorization: This is the identity that will not speak its name, not even to itself, not even in its own rhetorical space. If colouredness is obvious in the work of the coloured men, it has to be "discovered," recovered, unearthed, and searched for in Davids's work. Her writing provokes a series of inquiries: What does it mean to be coloured? How much does being coloured depend on an acknowledgement of that identity? If the coloured body is an unreliable marker of hybridity, how can colouredness be read from the miscegenated body? Is colouredness unacknowledged colouredness eviscerated? Can colouredness be overcome through silence? What are the values of encoding colouredness? Why do Davids and Nortje take up the question of exile, so central to both their work, so differently? Why is the coloured woman silent where the men are ideologically boisterous? What is the relationship between race and gender for a coloured South African woman who appears determined to not own her hybridity? How do questions of gender affect the work of these authors? How do we read the different ways Davids and Nortje explore women and patriarchy in their poetry?

Davids's reticence about her racial identity can stand as a metaphor for the experience of the coloured community itself: Colouredness has to be, and has always been, constructed—every experience of this community is an artifact, produced from and in the face of racist hostility, indifference, and ignorance; colouredness is an act of intellectual, cultural, and political labor. Coloureds are autodidacts with a difference, a community that had to learn not only how it was racially different but had to understand the various implications of that difference; and, most important, that coloured racial difference was fluid, that it registered distinctly from one historical moment to the next.

Davids's poetry requires that most treacherous and challenging of political acts, reading for an identity that the text itself works so diligently to disguise, mute, and silence. By disavowing her racial identity, Davids implicitly voices the negation of her own status. Paradoxically, because colouredness is silent in her poetry, it becomes a spoken condition. Because she is so reluctant to "name" herself coloured, her slim volume must be read against itself for the reader to discover how her text is coded, the poetic means through which it subtly approaches colouredness, at once enriched and complicated by her gender—the female poet being read alongside two men who are nothing if not vocal about their identities and the ways colouredness is central to their writing. However, for all her distinctness as woman and poet who stands at a remove from colouredness, Davids also shares with Rive and Nortje a literary locale (the Western Cape is often the backdrop to her poems), an affinity for the Western canon (perhaps more so, in moments, than either of the men), and a commitment to a transformed South African society. Her reluctance to represent herself as coloured, however, renders those similarities provocatively disjunctive: She relates to Rive and Nortje from an odd literary and ideological angle, making the conversation amongst these writers all the more engaging dynamic. The very concept of colouredness is at stake in this dialogue because these three authors offer us a sense of the variegation, the expansiveness, and the complications of their community's identity. They all represent different ways of being coloured, none more emblematic than the other; Davids's multivalent "silence" speaks to and about Rive's desire for "blackness," and both are, sometimes despite themselves, in conversation with Nortje's predilection for hybridity. Within the context of *Midfielder's Moment*, colouredness is constantly being reconfigured, its multiple meanings and identity formations negotiated as Davids's verse engages Nortje's, amplifying and amending Rive's short stories; setting up the conversation amongst these authors demonstrates how colouredness is jostled over, redefined, and rethought, even as the writers reject or embrace the term, grappling with the ways apartheid has inscribed it and influenced—or abbreviated or enabled—their own use of it.

The Politics and Culture of Coloured Sport

How special it must feel . . . finishing off a career in this fashion, it must feel like a culmination you could only dream of years ago, growing up without a role model, without a high school on a hill.

—Don DeLillo, *"The Rapture of the Athlete Assumed into Heaven"*

As seriously as the debate about colouredness is conducted in the literature section of this project, and as much as the readings of Rive, Nortje, and Davids set the ideological tone, the title of the collection is symbolically derived from the second half of the book. Because this project marks the attempt to read the culture of sport, and the ways these cultural practices are politicized, so the title also metaphorizes the role of the midfielder in football (soccer). In football, midfielders represent the link between defence and attack, much as the coloured community constitutes the physical connection between black and white South Africans; football games, the pundits say, are won and lost in the midfield, that area of the field where the contest (and the contestation) is most fierce, competitive, and intense. It is here that the battles are most searing, the tackles most crunching, where decisions about defence or attack have to be made quickly and adroitly; it is here where the complexion—if you'll excuse the pun—of a game can change most rapidly. Midfielders, like all footballers, have only a moment to make up their minds, and the fate of a contest depends upon their decisions.

Midfielder's Moment is written from and about the precarious center of South African cultural and political life. This project represents an attempt to briefly shift the debate from the perspective of the binaries to the interstices, to change the angle of focus, to look from and at the experience of racial polarization from those who have historically stood—and lived—in between. In other words, what does South Africa look like from that place on the football field where respite is infrequent and the entanglements many? The middle here constitutes not some "centrist" location nor an attempt to resolve conflict with a minimum of ideological offense. Rather, it marks the interrogation of South African politics and culture from a space where the contestation between the disenfranchised and the enfranchised is played out, where the grounds for debate is constantly shifting, where racial or ideological certainty has to be achieved (again and again), where cultural traditions have to be crafted, invented, reinvented, where meaning is constructed (reconstructed and deconstructed), not given.

The essays in the second section broadly map the trajectory of coloured sport from the experience of Group Areas deracination, signaled here as "1970," when most coloured families were forced to move from the fringes of the now "white" city to the townships or the suburbs, through to the contemporary moment. The highly politicized role of sport in South African society has always been recognized as crucial, especially in terms of the efforts to isolate apartheid codes (rugby and cricket in particular) conducted internationally by SANROC and internally by SACOS. *Midfielder's Moment*, however, engages coloured sport as a series of cultural practices where pleasure and politics complicate each other, where the memory of cultural opposition shows itself to be precarious (in the political vanguard in one historical moment and almost completely forgotten in the next), and where the racism of apartheid is stringently opposed but an imported metropolitan racism is implicitly tolerated. *Midfielder's Moment* reads sport as a social practice in which the politics of representation reveals at least as much as it conceals and where the burden of black overrepresentation is borne unfairly by individual sportsmen—it is always gendered male. Girding *Midfielder's Moment* is the recognition that sport's practices replicate patriarchy; in township sport women are predominantly assigned domestic roles—they wash the football kit, they provide support from the sidelines while often tending to the children at the same time, and sometimes they even perform secretarial duties, but they are generally "peripheral" to the game even though they are central to the organizational structure of the football club. There are clear echoes in South Africa, and countless other places around the globe, of football manager Ron Atkinson's proclamation about women in sport. For the ex-Manchester United coach, a woman's place was anywhere but in the game itself: "In the kitchen, in the discotheque, but not in football." The antiapartheid football and cricket struggle could not reconfigure the place of women in sport; it could not think of them outside of those overdetermined, heavily gendered spaces—the "kitchen" and the "discotheque." Ironically, although the "kitchen" remains—despite changes in gender roles—a largely female space, the "discotheque," that archetypal '70s arena, was more often coded gay than female, which is certainly not Atkinson's intention.

Midfielder's Moment demonstrates how nonracial sport resisted the strictures of apartheid by reaching outside the geographical boundaries of South Africa to the football culture of the English metropolis. It also reads politics back into sport in the postapartheid moment when the discourse of "reconciliation" has crept insidiously into this cultural practice; the postapartheid dispensation has made it difficult—if not impossible—

to critique the residual consequences of racism, the memory of SACOS's principled opposition lost in the melee that is cultural nationalism. The nation at play has become, not unexpectedly, a symbol of unity, the arena where the effects of apartheid can be overcome, even though those racially-based discrepancies continue to make themselves felt—certain constituencies remain infinitely better resourced than others. For this reason, the myth of the nation playing itself into oneness, if only for the duration of a rugby or cricket or football match, has such resonance in contemporary South Africa.

Bookended by the two essays on football, the chapter on cricket is the pivot of this section, marking the transition from SACOS to postapartheid sport. One of two previously published essays (the other is "Theatre of Dreams"), "The Nation in White" is about the costs of that transition: Through a critique of the racism that girded apartheid sport, this chapter demonstrates how the replacement of the SACOS discourse of oppositionality with the narrative of postapartheid inclusion, sponsored by both white sport's administrators and the ANC government, has insidiously eradicated the politics of sport. Although sports officials continue to pay lip service to the historic inequities that still mar South African sport, the radical imperative—the insistent linking of sport and access to resources, the relationship of success on the field to health issues such as nutrition (or the lack of it), inadequate or overcrowded housing—has been lost. Sport has become an important rhetorical tool in the narrative of postapartheid nation-building and racial "reconciliation," a cultural weapon used to demonstrate how successfully this "rainbow nation" can play together. To recall the rhetoric of antiapartheid struggle, sport has been "depoliticized" because it has been appropriated as a cultural language indistinguishable from that of the dominant discourse.

Written in 1997 as a critique of the continued (postapartheid) domination of whites in cricket, I have only "updated" the chapter in a few places so as to keep it current (substituting names, for example; or amending the argument via footnotes where significant developments have taken place) without losing the rhetorical intent of my intervention. Taking up the issue of depoliticization, "The Nation in White" focuses on the deeply raced nature of all South African sport, showing how the white domination of cricket has continued largely unabated. So much so that cricket has become a sport in which the singular coloured body of the young spin bowler Paul Adams has been made to represent racial integration. (For a brief moment the black fast bowler Mhkaya Ntini shared the spotlight with Adams, but subsequent legal problems have dimmed his prospects.)[15] Adams's role, however, is problematic not only because of his singularity but because his "integration" into the predominantly white team has publicly obliterated the sociopolitical force that motivated

SACOS sport. The inattention to history, the sense of sport as an arena of cultural struggle, a consciousness of race and racial injustice, and an explanation for Adams's singularity are all issues for which SACOS provided a politicized narrative. An oppositional cultural history, so crucial to coloured sport's identity over the past two decades or so, has been sacrificed in the writing of the new nation's history: It looks forward into the postapartheid future with little self-reflexivity, or consciousness, of the contestations and battles of the past. SACOS's cultural past, the kind of politics it enabled, has no place in a future where the discourse of national reconciliation—which stands here for the selective remembering of anti-apartheid history—has triumphed soundly over a politically inflected, integrated understanding of culture. To invoke the feminist credo of the 1970s, the political is cricket (and football and rugby), cricket is nothing if not politics; antiapartheid resistance is embedded into the very fabric of SACOS cricket; cricket and football are only, in the most nominal and reductive renderings, sport.

As "Theatre of Dreams," the opening essay in this section shows, however, the oppositional tendencies of coloured sport are often encoded in surprising ways. This chapter is an exploration of the unique trans-Atlantic link between the working class coloured townships on the Cape Flats and English football clubs, a connection not shared by any other South African constituency, enfranchised or disenfranchised; the chapter also accounts for the existence of the metropolitan-perpihery nexus and reveals how political resistance can assume unexpected forms. The chapter demonstrates how the deracination occasioned by the Group Areas Act compelled the residents of the newly constructed Cape Flats to make a new cultural history for themselves. Following the destruction of their established communities on the fringes of urban white spaces in the mid-to-late 1960s, working class coloureds drew on the footballing culture of the British metropolis in their efforts to re-create a set of traditions and social practices that could counteract the debilitating effects of the Group Areas Act. Resisting the apartheid regime meant, in this historical instance, finding new ways to produce a community. "Theatre of Dreams" shows how a politics of resistance turned as much on a cognizance of apartheid injustice as it did on a capacity for ingenuity, the capacity to re-make community by borrowing from a geographically, but not culturally, distant model. Drawing on the metropolis provided a template for working class coloured survival, an instance where the "foreign" was crucial to the construction of an internally cohesive, "native" community. "Theatre of Dreams" demonstrates the complicated, myriad, and multivalent forms in which sport articulates its politics: as resistance, as pleasure, as desire, as necessity, as understanding of historical circumscription and the determination to transcend—if only momentarily, in some cases—the limitations imposed by apartheid. Sport is not so much always already politicized, though it is certainly that because it compels us to attend to the nuances and disguised expressions of football (or cricket), as it is a series of political articulations.

The final chapter in *Midfielder's Moment* is, ironically, not about a midfielder but about a young coloured striker and the ways his racial identity is both recognized and denied. (The striker, however, derives some of his currency from a comparison to a midfielder.) A product of the coloured township of Hanover Park, the young striker who grew up without DeLillo's "role model" or his "high school on the hill," Benni McCarthy went rapidly from obscurity to national (and international) prominence. A forward with a penchant for poaching goals, McCarthy has gone on to become a national hero, the most recognizable—if not the best or even the most talented—player on the team, the player who has inspired "Benni mania" among countless generations of South Africans; his is an adoration that transcends racial boundaries, even if it does not invalidate them. Born and raised during the apartheid era, McCarthy represents not so much the "culmination" of the SACOS "dream" as the transcending of that moment and movement; SACOS's "dreams" were restricted by the paradigm of apartheid, whereas McCarthy is about the reinscription of the township footballer as national hero. This essay, however, explores the disjuncture between McCarthy's generic (black) South African-ness, the narrative means by which he has been positioned as the symbol of racially nonspecific blackness, and the ways his colouredness is publicly denied yet publicly visible.

"McCarthyism Township Style" is a demonstration of how, in strategic moments, colouredness is susceptible—we might even say vulnerable—to appropriation both by whiteness (the 1994 elections) and by blackness (McCarthy). Whatever public understanding or acceptance there is of the Hanover Park striker's racial heritage, it cannot be articulated within the context of postapartheid football. In this instance, when the goal-scoring dark brown body represents the aspirations both of the nation and of the national team, his difference has to be subsumed, the blackness of his brownness has to be emphasized; the reverse would be not so much intolerable as a bad fit with the ideological tenor and demands of the moment. The new South Africa is no less politically expedient than the old, appropriating, reinscribing, eliding, or exaggerating racial sameness or difference as is ideologically useful. This is not to suggest that the new society is indistinguishable from the old, but to bring into focus the ways they resemble each other, draw on the same rhetorical strategies, use the hybrid body.

Benni McCarthy—or the symbol he has become—speaks of the complicated positionings of the coloured community. The capacity to give voice to colouredness, to enunciate its racial complications, to announce its racial identity in public, and the predilection to deny or transcend this condition, is as prevalent in the representation of the young Hanover Park striker as it is in the work of Richard Rive or Jennifer Davids. There is a crucial difference between the authors and the sports figures, however, that stems from the distinct ways they relate to the community. Rive, Davids, and Nortje are concerned with the relationship between the individual and the community, with the struggle to producing an independent voice that is nonetheless representative of the coloured experience. Often this voice leads to alienation, and in the case of the poets it results, literally, in exile. The second half of *Midfielder's Moment* is about the ways the community claims the individual sports hero—how it makes Benni McCarthy or Paul Adams its representatives. If the artists demonstrate the dangers of literary remove, then the sports figures show how overinterpellation makes McCarthy and his ilk vulnerable to appropriation and, possibly, to political and ideological misrepresentation. As difficult as it is to claim to speak for a community, so it is equally problematic to find yourself spoken for, to be represented even as you represent the ("new") nation.

The struggle to produce a voice that can articulate the complexities of colouredness as a political condition, a series of experiences, a set of cultural traditions and practices, which has been struggled with, over, and for, is the core of this project. Colouredness is invariably about difference, not only the different appropriations of this community but the different senses of self that exist within it. Colouredness, *Midfielder's Moment* shows, is a mode of being in South Africa that will continue to be subjected to several contestations, both from without as well as from within. *Midfielder's Moment* represents an attempt to take that conflicted understanding of self and community seriously, to grapple, with, over, and for it because it is the multivalent voice of a constituency whose sense of itself is fluid, multiple, pliable, flexible, and yet resilient. Colouredness should be taken seriously because no other South African community has had to remake itself so frequently, under so many different conditions; no "natural" constituency has had to deal with a difference that is at once recognizable and difficult to articulate, a difference that is simultaneously salient and ignored, silent yet voluble.

Notes

1. Helene Cixous and Catherine Clement, *The Newly Born Woman*, trans. Betsy Wing (Minneapolis: University of Minnesota Press, 1986), 63.

2. In *The Newly Born Woman*, Cixous and Clement's major oppositionality is gender-based; they map the historic inequity of patriarchy.

3. Douglarization is the process of racial intermixing between indians and blacks in the Anglophone Caribbean. "Douglas" has historically been a pejorative term applied to this group, a synonym for "half-castes" or bastards. Recently, however, "douglas" have politicized this appellation and transformed it into a movement that struggles for the recognition of a hybrid culture—music, art, dance, and so on.

4. For a history of this period see, among other works, Leonard Thompson's *A History of South Africa* (New Haven: Yale University Press, 1995); Thomas Karis and Gail M. Gerhart's *From Protest to Challenge*, vol. 5, *Nadir and Resurgence, 1964–1979* (Bloomington: Indiana University Press, 1997); Tom Lodge's *Black Politics in South Africa Since 1945* (Johannesburg: Ravan Press, 1987); and George M. Frederickson's *Black Liberation: A Comparative History of Black Ideologies in the United States and South Africa* (New York: Oxford University Press, 1995).

5. See Thomas Karis and Gail M. Gerhart's *From Protest to Challenge*, vol. 5, *Nadir and Resurgence, 1964–1979* (Pretoria: Unisa Press, 1997).

6. Robert Mattes, Hermann Giliomee, and Wilmot James, "The Election in the Western Cape," in *Launching Democracy in South Africa: The First Open Election, April, 1994,* ed. R.W. Johnson and Lawrence Schlemmer (New Haven: Yale University Press, 1996) 110.

7. Anzaldua's conception of the term in *Borderland/La Frontera* is a rich, complex, and insistently gendered (female) one. In drawing metaphorically on Anzaldua's understanding of the interstitial in this specific instance, this particular usage is not as reliant on her feminized deployment of the "borderland."

8. Stuart Hall, "Subjects in History: Making Diasporic Identities," *Race Matters*, ed. Wahneema Lubiano (New York: Vintage Books, 1998), 299.

9. See, among others, Mattes et al.'s "The Election in the Western Cape"; Sandile Dikeni's "How the West Was Lost"; and DSA and Idasa's "Building a Democratic Culture in the Western Cape: The Present Terrain" for a review of coloured voting patterns in the 1994 elections; in *Public Opinion Service Reports*, no. 8 (May 1996), an Idasa publication.

10. Werner Sollors, *Neither Black Nor White Yet Both: Thematic Explorations of Interracial Literature* (New York: Oxford University Press, 1997).

11. See, inter alia, my essay "Better the Devil You Know? The Politics of Colouredness and Postapartheid South African Elections in the Western Cape," *Souls: A Critical Journal of Black Politics, Culture, and Society* 2, no. 2 (April 2000) for an engagement with the issue of coloured voting patterns in the 1999 elections.

12. As I argue later, Nortje produced a "second" volume that was largely a replication of *Dead Roots*.

13. Stuart Hall, who has written extensively on this subject, remarked in the mid-1990s about the dissolution of this expansive "blackness": "They called themselves black. . . . It was a very important moment politically in Britain. It isn't the moment we're in now. That significance has gone. It is partly dissolved into a variety of new, more ethnically specific signifiers. People now call themselves not only Asians, but Indians, Bangladeshis, Pakistanis, and indeed, South Indians. Things have now moved into a new kind of ethnicized politics of difference" (Hall, "Subjects in History," *The House That Race Built*, 295).

See also Paul Gilroy's *There Ain't No Black in the Union Jack: The Cultural Politics of Race and Nation* (Chicago: University of Chicago Press, 1991) and *Small Acts:*

Thoughts on the Politics of Black Cultures (London: Serpent's Tail, 1994) for a discussion of that "earlier moment" of British "blackness."

14. Arthur Nortje, *Dead Roots* (London: Heinemann, 1973), 104.

15. In 1999, Ntini was sentenced to six years in jail for raping a woman, an event that once again brings into focus the relationship not so much between sport and violence, but that complicated nexus between stardom and the sexual license presumed by athletes, musicians, and other public figures. Ntini's experience is not exceptional, resonating as it does with the echoes of ex-heavyweight champion Mike Tyson; what is unusual about the fast bowler's imprisonment is that cricket is a sport not associated with this kind of behavior. Gambling, drugs, and illegal bowling actions are more the norm in this most "gentlemanly" of sports.

1

Writing in a Twilight Zone: Richard Rive, the Making of a Coloured Artist and Intellectual

Ah, the people who are neither black nor white but live a twilight existence— half free, half slaves to the whims and laws of apartheid.

—**Don Mattera,** *Sophiatown*

The Formation of a Coloured Thinker

For Lukacs realistic characters are distinguished from those in other types of literature by their typicality: they stand, in other words, for something larger and more meaningful than themselves, than their own isolated individual destinies.

—**Frederic Jameson,** *Marxism and Form* **(original emphasis)**

Richard Moore Rive stands as and for a specific kind of coloured intellectual. Born in Cape Town's District Six in 1930 and the victim of a gruesome murder (in his own home) in 1989, Rive is one of the preeminent figures in South African letters. A gay man whose work is remarkably silent about his sexual orientation, Rive was killed in his suburban home by two young men after he had gone "cruising" and picked them up late one evening. His was a publicly repressed gayness, a sexual orientation that was, as I have discussed elsewhere,[1] understood, intimated, hinted at, but never really openly discussed. The silence about Rive's gayness is understandable and disturbing. His reticence was explicable because his literary and political focus was, quite deliberately, race and not sexuality, a political privileging not unprecedented in anticolonial or antiracist strug-

27

gles. Rive's sexual silence was, in a complicated way, produced by and commensurate with the homophobia of South African society.

Rive's sexual orientation—important as it is—does not, however, constitute the focus of this chapter because it was not the major component of a literary career that spanned some three decades. During his literary life Rive achieved a formal education rarely matched among his disenfranchised South African contemporaries and produced a rich and substantial oeuvre. Internationally trained, Rive obtained degrees from a local South African university as well as from major American and British institutions. Although his fictional work and his university research were seldom coterminous (he only wrote a few short stories in the time that he was a—fairly mature—graduate student), he did start producing his first short stories in the 1950s, the initial moment of his tertiary—and political—education. A leading member of the Protest School, Rive went on to write three novels and a range of essays; he also occasionally experimented in poetry and drama. His literary forte was, undoubtedly, the short story. His final works, a play adapted from his novel *Buckingham Palace, District Six* and a novel titled *Emergency Continued*, were performed and published posthumously.

Rive's status as South African intellectual, however, derives in the main from the way he positioned himself primarily as a "black" or disenfranchised author, a writer whose work speaks resonantly of a complicated relationship to his identity as a coloured. Rive belonged to the first generation of coloureds assigned this designation and the problematic, contentious identity it signaled. Much of Rive's work, and that of his fellow Western Cape Protest writers, James Matthews and Alex La Guma, was a response to the consequences of the social label imposed upon them by the Population Registration Act of 1950. "Writing in a Twilight Zone" sets the tenor and maps the ideological terms for the literature section of *Midfielder's Moment*, demonstrating—paradoxically—that Rive both outrightly rejected and tacitly embraced the appellation "coloured."

This reading of Rive's work is grounded in an exploration of him as an intellectual. Rive constructed himself as a creative artist profoundly concerned with formally educating himself, a commitment that occupied him so intently that it explains, in part, why his intellectual activities took precedence over other crucial aspects of his life, such as sexual orientation. By investigating various models for oppositional intellectuals, ranging from Antonio Gramsci to Bertrand Russell, and how these figures function in oppressive societies, from cultural activist to public transcriber, this chapter will delineate Rive as a radical thinker. The following section will take up these questions: How did Rive conceive of himself as an intellectual? Why was he so concerned with acquiring a formal education? What were the consequences of a coloured writer pursuing degrees within apartheid South Africa? Does advanced education necessarily mean alienation from the intellectual's originary community? How do intellectuals resist? What form does that resistance take? and, What weapons, tools, and platforms do they use?

In the second section of this chapter, the discussion of Rive as intellectual is focused on and refracted through the ways his education enabled him to view the coloured experience differently from his fellow Western Cape Protest writers. Rive's status as intellectual is due in part to how closely he defined himself in relation to the academy and its auxiliary institutions (scholarly conferences and publications, a world in which Rive was deeply invested), a positioning shared by neither La Guma nor Matthews. Despite their discrepant levels of education, the work of these three writers represented an important moment in coloured literature. From their base in the Western Cape, they crafted a series of short stories, novellas, novels, and essays that constructed a distinct body of South African letters. As is always the case when engaging Rive's work, these issues must be considered within the context of how race mediated, impacted, influenced, or debilitated his understanding of himself as an intellectual.

Alf Wannenburgh, the Protest writers' one-time collaborator (Rive edited a collection of stories by four Western Cape writers, called *Quartet*, which included work by Wannenburgh, La Guma, and Matthews), summarized Rive's ambivalent position with an allusive aptness. "One of the ironies of Rive's position—one that he was aware of—was that he gained recognition as a writer," Wannenburgh writes, "largely because he was seen as the very thing that he most vigorously repudiated: a 'coloured' writer, a 'coloured' intellectual."[2] Rive was caught in an epistemological bind, one he could not resolve—the "'coloured' intellectual" who wrote primarily about the "coloured condition" simply wanted to be recognized as an "intellectual." This ideological quandary did not prevent him from trying to overcome and negate the very identity that afforded him public prominence. "Coloured" was a racial designation Rive struggled with throughout his career, a political condition he sought to transcend.

Although, as this chapter will show, his struggle to invalidate coloured as an apartheid category was largely unsuccessful, it did not debilitate him as an artist. Instead, he used this intellectual conflict, his intimacy with and insights into this community, generatively: It animates all his writing, from his critical essays to his drama to his novels. Whatever his discomfiture with (and resistance to) his public reception—and recognition—as a coloured artist and an intellectual (or apartheid-induced "misrecognition," he may have argued), it did not prevent him from concentrating his creative energies on this community. As much as Rive distanced himself from the appellation "coloured," his act of disclaiming, invalidating, and opposing apartheid terminology did not turn upon the rejection of the coloured community. He wrote not only from a sense of familiarity with this constituency, but out of a political and artistic commitment to the coloured experience.

However much "'coloured'" may have implied a tacit acknowledgment of apartheid's racial categories, Rive's deep-seated investment in this community impelled him to investigate its cultural practices. By writing only about the coloured experience, Rive reveals how much it is indeed "his" constituency; and, as important, how distinct it is from the other South African disenfranchised groupings. His fiction and his autobiography *Writing Black*, in particular, demonstrate various kinds of engagements with "coloured" as a racial appellation; consequently, his creative focus never strayed far beyond the racial confines of this community. Although the depth and extent of Rive's grappling with the political valences of colouredness are unusual, the struggle in his short stories and novels is not: The District Six native's oeuvre is representative—or "typical," in Lukacs's sense—of his community. Rive's work is metonymic of a common dilemma, it stands and speaks for and of "something larger and more meaningful" than the Protest author "himself." (In taking up his position as intellectual, Rive demonstrates the tension between speaking "for" and "of" a community—some of the difficulty is attributable to his academic positioning and some of it can be traced to the issue of representation. Who gets to speak in a community's name? What do those public articulations mean? How, and for whom, do they resonate?) At its most incisive, Rive's work captures the ambivalence of coloured belonging and unbelonging to the disenfranchised community that constitutes the core of his community's experience. The particularities, and peculiarities, of coloured disenfranchisement so central to Rive's writing is, following Jameson's reading of Georg Lukacs's "realistic characters," symptomatic of a social condition that exceeds the author's own "isolated individual destiny."

Refracted through a coloured (and communal) lens, Rive's writing explored the pain, pathos, courage, pleasure, humor, and the resilience of District Six, the community he viewed as his primary "home." The penultimate section addresses the (omni-) presence of District Six, that most emblematic of coloured communities and a protagonist that figures prominently in Rive's writing. This "metaphoric" home, the place Rive left in his late teens, is the space he not only continually returns to in his fiction, but which he is compelled to re-create after the Group Areas Act evicted his community, leaving in its wake a psychic devastation the Protest writer attempted to counter through his short stories and novels.

As the final section of the chapter will demonstrate, apartheid legislation not only destroyed District Six, it threw into question the very notion of "who" was "coloured." By determining every South African's racial categorization, the Population Registration Act left the coloured community especially vulnerable to the dictates of "racial interpretation": The wide range of physical types who constitute this grouping made them subject to the whims and fancies of apartheid bureaucracy. Because they resemble both blacks and whites, because they are so racially indistinct, Rive's work shows how coloured families were torn apart by this Act. In addressing the consequences of the Population Registration Act, Rive's work converts the understandable bitterness of the District Six community into a poignant indictment of apartheid's viciousness.

The Radical Intellectual as Fighter

We have a responsibility not only to ourselves but also to the society from which we spring. No one will ever take the challenge until we, of our own accord, accept.

—**Steve Biko,** *I Write What I Like*

The relationship radical intellectuals have with the disenfranchised community they belong to is complex. Characterized by a tension between belonging and apartness, intellectuals are ambivalently situated: They shift, some more than others, between a transient integration and a momentary but intense alienation. Although commitment to the political struggle symbolically (and substantively) connects intellectuals to the oppressed group, their very status as "intellectuals" marks them as anomalous subjects—as our discussion of Rive will show—within the ranks of the disempowered. Politically disenfranchised or oppressed, they nevertheless possess a cultural capital that separates them from their community. The ways individuals are defined as intellectuals may vary: academic achievement (the "degreed" Rive), artistic talent (the fierce lyricism of Matthews), or political acumen (the ideologically committed La Guma). In all these instances, the radical intellectual enjoys a form of enfranchisement that contrasts sharply with the oppressed group's more general lack of access to public platforms. Fluidly positioned, radical intellectuals such as Rive can sometimes "invalidate" the oppressor-oppressed, enfranchised-disenfranchised binary, constantly negotiating a space that can accommodate the complications (or contradictions) of political commitment, academic alienation, and ideological interstitiality— that unsettling sense of belonging simultaneously in—and to—more than one place and no (existing) place at all.

Empowered within and by their own community, oppositional thinkers are in a position to represent the struggle of the disenfranchised in and through their intellectual practices. Through their activities, with varying degrees of subtlety, stridency, and a sense of political commitment that is occasionally ambivalent or unexpectedly critical, intellectuals adopt the cause of liberating the oppressed group; this process requires and demonstrates the strategic importance of those ambiguous intellectual skills. Radical figures perform significant political functions in that their work challenges the ruling group on its own intellectual terms, and most often on hostile ideological terrain. Familiarity with the dominant discourse enables oppositional thinkers to engage, disarticulate, intervene in, and disrupt the governing bloc's political landscape. Intellectuals occupy a signal position within their society: Trained in the terms of the dominant ideology, they share originary (and sometimes organic) links with the disenfranchised community. At same time, these links are often—and almost inevitably—strained by the degree of interpellation into the hegemonic discourse. Straddling two worlds that are in ideological conflict, these intellectuals are invariably compelled to privilege one set of concerns, pursuits, or interests over another—to frequently make choices that would, in a nonantagonistic political context, be entirely artificial and maybe even irrelevant.

However, these dual—and competing—allegiances explicate the complicated location of the radical intellectual. Politically opposed to the dominant regime, these oppositional figures are also estranged—as Rive will show, sometimes more self-reflexively than others—from their originary community by the very skills that enable them to combat the ruling group. Possessed of a rare class mobility, these figures have acquired an economic (and commensurate cultural) capital that propels them socially upward, away from the very community in whose name they so fervently speak. For some oppositional intellectuals, however, their multifaceted "marginality" offers not so much a debilitating but an enabling alienation, a critical distancing from both the dominant and the oppressed constituencies;[3] their peripheral relations allow them to make—or not make—interventions from a location that is strategically unique within their society.

Whatever the complications, hesitancies, and ambivalences of his position, Rive is unique among the Western Cape Protest writers in defining himself so self-consciously as an intellectual. Rive was most unlike his fellow Western Cape Protest writers in his formal education. Alex La Guma was a high school graduate and James Matthews had only, as Rive wryly observed in *Writing Black* the "merest rudiments of a secondary education."[4] The District Six native, on the other hand, was "supremely educated" (*Writing Black*, 10). Describing himself as a "compulsory degree-taker," Rive's master of arts at Columbia University in New York and his doctorate at Oxford were preceded by several degrees—a bachelor of arts, a bachelor of education, and a master of arts in English, comparing the South African Protest writers to the Harlem Renaissance—at the local University of Cape Town. More formally educated than any other coloured writer before or since (short story writer Zoe Wicomb is perhaps the only other coloured author to approach Rive's academic accomplishments), he rendered the coloured community, and particularly District Six, through a singular intellectual vision.

Most important, Rive's relationship to this community was retrospectively enabled because most of his writing was produced years after he had left District Six (just as he acquired his tertiary education after leaving District Six). Reconstructing his links allowed him to conceptualize—or to "imagine," in Benedict Anderson's sense of the term—District Six in the years after he had left it. This relationship was therefore filtered through the complicated lens of advanced education and personal reinscription. On the one hand, his education signaled an upward social movement that substantially altered the novelist's relations with District Six, essentially a poorly educated, coloured working class community. "Because of my education," he writes, "I was able to take my first shaky steps into the ranks of the 'Coloured' middle class" (*Writing Black*, 10). Automatically propelled into a higher social class by his diplomas and degrees, his education substantively altered his ability to align himself ideologically with District Six. "I was," he writes in his autobiography, "a teacher with a Bachelor of Arts degree . . . I now lived in Walmer Estate" (*Writing Black*, 10,11). Transforming Rive into a (relatively) privileged member of the coloured community, his education positioned him to escape the "slum life" that was District Six and move to neighboring, middle-class "Walmer Estate" (*Writing Black*, 4). On the other hand, Rive's newfound social mobility was not without political contradiction:

> But paradoxically I also became more aware [after moving into Walmer Estate] of my own position as an unenfranchised, Black noncitizen. I started producing my first, raw, angry prose, which was accepted for publication by left wing magazines and those catering for an emerging Black readership. These were the only outlets prepared to publish the protest fiction we were producing. (*Writing Black*, 10)

Education performed a dual, dialectical function in Rive's life: It altered (and elevated) his social status while simultaneously radicalizing his political consciousness. He became, in the process, only secondarily a member of the coloured middle-class; he was primarily transformed into a writer, an intellectual intent on voicing the experience of District Six, a community he laid increasing claim to during his career. His work enabled him to symbolically integrate himself into "the District," to achieve a literary connection—an "organicism"—with a community he no longer physically belonged to.

Within apartheid South Africa, racism was both singularly demanding of and hugely influential in the formation of a radical disenfranchised intellectual. Regardless of their (varying) ideological tendencies, their appetite for oppositionality at any given moment, or their capacity to be efficacious spokespersons for their community, apartheid race law yoked intellectuals to their racial constituencies. This created an incommensurability between the apartheid state's (in)ability to control radical thinking and its capacity to restrict the basic freedoms—the franchise, the right to live where one chooses, the right to basic health care, education, and housing—of these figures and their communities. Oppositional figures were raced subjects before they were intellectuals. Although the Nationalist Party government was less successful (but no less interested) in placing ideological constraints on these figures, it was able to legally restrict the potential of the oppressed for upward social mobility. Even if black or coloured South Africans acquired an advanced level of education or achieved some artistic success, the various "capitals" they garnered could not exceed the narrow realms of their geographically circumscribed community. The terms of Group Areas Act of 1950, which assigned living spaces according to race, enforced their physical location within the ranks of the disenfranchised.[5]

Ironically, as Rive's links to District Six demonstrate, the laws of apartheid inadvertently strengthened the relationship between disenfranchised intellectuals and their community—even after the intellectual removes himself or herself from the physical site of the community. Explaining the intellectual's bifurcated position both within and outside his or her community, Rive argues, "the writer is the articulate black man in the ghetto and is therefore better able to express himself through words. Otherwise he is indistinguishable from the non-writer, and what is more, he is treated no differently by the authorities."[6] Girding Rive's conception of the writer is a rich and conflicting representation of the intellectual: The well-trained thinker stands at once as a member of the "internal (oppressed) elite" and an oppressed everyperson. The policy of apartheid functioned, at one level, as a great leveler: It undermined the usually elevated academic and artistic status of the intellectual, making him or her racially "indistinguishable from the non-writer" (although these bonds were not without tensions). Apartheid laws, such as the Group Areas Act, the Population Registration Act, and the Prohibition on Mixed Marriages Act, ensured that intellectuals maintained a strong bond with their community. "Organicism," in the Gramscian sense, was less a political option than a lived experience for disenfranchised intellectuals such as Rive in the apartheid era. The Group Areas Act meant that the intellectual was subject to the same geographical circumscription as the working class or even the wealthy members of their community: They could not live outside the "areas" set aside for their "group." (Geographically bounded, these areas were stratified by class, with the suburbs for the middle class and the townships housing the working class, although these neighborhoods frequently border each other. In this way the apartheid regime fermented class tensions, thereby creating intracommunity strife. All this, of course, was intended to distract the disenfranchised from resisting the regime.) Intellectuals could not transcend racial boundaries through material acquisition because the Population Registration Act fixed, permanently and irrevocably, their identities: Classified "Bantu," "Indian," or "Coloured" by this law, their mobility was confined by race, not class. Finally, intellectuals were compelled to interact "socially" with members of their own race. (The Prohibition of Mixed Marriages Act rendered illegal any marriage between members of different race groups: The Immorality Act, which proscribed interracial sexual relations, girded the Mixed Marriages Act.)

Within the racially delimited paradigm of South Africa, Rive's relationship to the community was of necessity not only a more integrated, but also a more overtly political experience. For the oppositional South African intellectual, there was no way out of the race conundrum. To be a "voteless" South African was, as Rive puts it, to recognize the intensity of the Althusserian political condition: You were always already hailed as "black" or "coloured." Intellectuals from these communities were invariably positioned as antiapartheid spokespersons, thinkers expected to hold forth on the question of race (and racism), required to give articulate voice to the experience, commitments, and visions of black disenfranchisement. "Voteless" South African intellectuals were always, though probably more so abroad than at home (where the nuances, complexities, and shortcomings of their positions were more incisively understood), speaking to, for, or against race(ism). Apartheid rendered any other political debate secondary at best, inconsequential at worst.

A Generation of Coloured Protest Writers Emerges

These contingencies—of language, rhetoric, power, and history—must now be openly confronted in the process of writing.

—James Clifford, "Introduction," *Writing Culture*

When the National Party came to power in 1948, communities from District Six in Cape Town to Marabastad in Pretoria and Sophiatown in Johannesburg, had to contend with deliberate attempts by the state to destroy their community. District Six, for this very reason, represents a crucial moment in the experience of Western Cape coloureds. The Group Areas and the Population Registration Acts constituted the most substantial threats to District Six. The former aimed to raze the area in the name of "slum clearance," the latter threatened to divide families in the cause of "racial purity." That Rive, Matthews, and La Guma started to write about the coloured community in the early 1950s is important for another reason: These three young men represented the first generation of urban, coloured Western Cape writing. Through their writing about this community during the Protest era, they were constructing a tradition of coloured (Western Cape) literature at a moment laden with historical tension. The trio worked at a juncture when coloured politics, in the Western Cape and nationally, was transforming itself. For the first half of the century, coloured politics had been a largely nonconfrontational practice dominated by an elite whose "aim was amalgamation into the white society, not its destruction."[7] Intent on protecting coloured privilege through maintaining close links with white politicians, this class of coloured leadership found itself increasingly displaced in the 1950s. In a decade characterized by large-scale disenfranchised resistance, the traditionally conservative political strategy of coloured politicians was supplanted by a mass-based movement that aligned itself with ANC-led campaigns. In the bus boycotts,[8] the Defiance Campaign,[9] and the widespread protests against the apartheid regime during that era, coloured politics—and the community as a whole—adopted a more radical, black-identified outlook.

Rive and his literary cohort were charged with the responsibility of establishing a tradition of Western Cape writing while dealing with the radical political transformation of their community. Rive, La Guma, and Matthews had to produce in a dynamic and turbulent environment. Their first works were written during the battle between the antiapartheid protesters and the state's repressive machinery. However, to create this broad, nonracial political front to oppose the apartheid regime, the ANC's Congress Alliance used the four racial categories of apartheid's Population Registration Act. Rive had to negotiate between the challenges of integrating his community into the broader black struggle and of maintaining a sense of the coloured community as a political entity. Caught in an ideological bind, he found himself working within the divisive parameters of apartheid rhetoric to overcome it—the very apartheid ideology he was struggling to eliminate first had to be employed as a political weapon. Aware of this peripheral location, and committed to addressing (and redressing) this alienation, Rive had to, in Audre Lorde's terms, "use the master's tools to dismantle the master's house."

Rive recognized that the apartheid designation rendered the coloured community politically unstable. Motivated by the desire for a more secure ideological location, Rive strives to write his community unproblematically into the disenfranchised South African experience. Borrowing from the Harlem Renaissance poet Langston Hughes, Rive proclaims with a grandiloquent flourish in his 1979 autobiography, "I am Johannesburg, Durban, and Cape Town. I am Langa, Chatsworth, and Bonteheuwel" (*Writing Black*, 23). A great admirer of the Harlem Renaissance poet laureate, Rive uses phrasing in *Writing Black* that echoes a self-description in Hughes's own 1940 autobiography, *The Big Sea*: "I was Chicago and Kansas City and Broadway and Harlem,"[10] asserts the American. In *Writing Black*, Hughes's "Chicago" has become Rive's "Johannesburg," the Negro's "Kansas City" has transmuted into the South African's "Durban," the American's "Harlem" (his home) finds its equivalent in the Protest author's "Cape Town." In announcing himself an urban Negro poet, Hughes was expressing more than his intent to sing the blues for all of the African American experience—he wrote with equal alacrity about "Chicago" and "Kansas City," although he had a decided preference for New York's "Harlem." More important, Hughes was using his autobiography to write back to and against his white patron, Charlotte Mason—unnamed but so clearly present in *The Big Sea*, who wanted the poet's work to be more "primitive."

Inspired by his personal links to black Protest authors (such as Ezekiel Mphahlele and Nat Nakasa) and Hughes's grand vision of the "Negro" condition, Rive wanted to write for the "universal" disenfranchised South African condition, to make himself figuratively—and literally—a part of that experience. However, Rive stakes a political claim that rests—unlike the Renaissance poet's—on unstable ideological ground. Rive constructs himself as the single manifestation of the disenfranchised struggle. He wants to speak not only for the urbanness[11] of the disenfranchised, "Johannesburg" and "Cape Town," but also authoritatively for the experiences of black ("Langa"), indian ("Chatsworth"), and coloured ("Bonteheuwel") South Africa. All these communities signify, to some extent, Group Areas social arrangements because they were created after disenfranchised South Africans were deracinated by apartheid law. This declaration of his multivalent "blackness" is Rive's attempt to make himself metonymic of the spectrum of disenfranchised South Africa. He is, in this moment if not in this text, implicitly writing out the substantively different experiences that distinguish coloureds, blacks, and indians. This is Rive's universalist representation of disenfranchisement, a reductionist, essentialist (colouredness can only become "blackness" if it forswears colouredness), and contracted conception of blackness. This, then, is black South Africa writ singly, writ urban, and writ large; it marks an ef-fort by Rive to produce a singular black experience—if not a single black identity—despite the fracturing and division wrought by apartheid.

This subtly envisaged unity of experience that girds Rive's claim that the suffering, deracination, and poverty that are common to Langa and Chatsworth and Bonteheuwel is valid, but could not by and of itself tran-scend the racial, cultural, and political barriers that divided these con-stituencies. In this moment, when Rive's racial hybridity and his desire for black political unity are engaged in an awkward dialectic, Samuel De-laney's reflections seem apropos: "So, I thought, you are neither black nor white / . . . And you are that most ambiguous of citizens, the writer."[12] Confronted by the ideological schizophrenia that is colouredness, in pos-session of an "ambiguous citizenship" peculiar to those who are "neither black nor white," Rive strives to overcome this debilitation by becoming the "ambitious citizen": the coloured South African writer who proffers an envisioned unity, an imaginary wholeness that has historically proven unachievable.[13]

Among the coloured Protest writers, Rive was an artistic anomaly, in-tellectually distinct from both La Guma and Matthews. Like Rive, La Guma was a District Six fiction writer—producing novels and short sto-ries—while Matthews was a short story writer and a poet. However, un-like the Communist Party member La Guma, political activism was not pivotal to Rive's conception of himself as an intellectual. Matthews, too, was in moments more politically active than Rive; so much so that he was imprisoned by the apartheid authorities in the mid-1970s for his involve-ment in the Soweto uprising. In his essay "Writing or Fighting?," which is a moving tribute to Arthur Nortje as well as Rive's most accomplished re-flection on the role of the antiapartheid artist, the District Six native re-veals a preference for the scholastic model of the intellectual. Founded on two provocative lines from Nortje's poem, "Native's Letter,"

> *For some of us must storm the castles*
> *Some define the happenings.*[14]

Rive uses these metaphors to outline his own position as a disenfran-chised South African: "Although the emphasis is at present on storming castles and less on defining the happening, it is essential that [the writer] be allowed to fulfill his main function, which is to define and record. He is an articulate memory of his oppressed people."[15] Uncomfortable in and unwilling to assume the La Guma mode of activist-intellectual (in part because he lacked the communist's convictions motivating La Guma's fic-tion and could find no home in a political movement), he crafted a differ-ent, more traditionally Western model for himself.

Rive represents the thinker most at home as a politically committed writer, an intellectual grounded in, familiar with, and committed to the oppositional politics of his moment but who invariably situated himself at a critical—and creative—remove from the actual "happenings." Rive is emblematic of the intellectual as outsider, a figure who understood the conflicting, exacting political demands of his moment but preferred his peripheral location. He was sympathetic to (and even endorsed) the ANC's mass-based, activist politics and the more rarefied philosophical debates and principled stances of the Non-European Unity Movement, a largely professional organization (lawyers, doctors, and teachers dominate the membership) that Rive was loosely affiliated with for most of his life. The class composition of "Unity Movement," as this grouping is commonly known, is unrepresentative of the coloured community. In the main, Rive eschewed unambiguous, formal political affiliation in favor of writing.

The District Six writer is a complex, hybrid intellectual, a disenfranchised South African who blends the love of scholarship so vital to Julien Benda's *clerc*, the transformative political vision of a C. Wright Mills or a Bertrand Russell (the artist not simply as scholar but as a self-conscious, articulate political spokesperson), with a Gramscian organicism particular to a coloured creative writer in apartheid South Africa. Rive always attempted to situate himself, if only symbolically and not always literally, within the coloured experience; through his writing he showed how integral, how central to his fiction the experiences of his community were to him even though he was physically removed from their living conditions. He "took," the South African Nobel laureate Nadine Gordimer writes of Rive's contradictory relationship to District Six, "unashamed if not defiant pleasure in getting physically as far away as possible from the ghetto, though his best writing remained rooted there." The intellectual trying to overcome and transmute his outsiderhood through his fiction; the outsider endeavoring to become, however metaphorically, an "insider" through the "fiction" of organicism.

As an intellectual who for many years played a leading role as a spokesman in the antiapartheid sports movement, SACOS, Rive did not dislike political combat, but he preferred his "fighting" to be of the *clerc*—or the literary, at the very least—variety. Rive's intellectual metier was that of the writer as transcriber, the "organic" novelist who keeps "oppressed memory" alive and in a good state of artistic repair; it was in his role as author that Rive thrived, though he did sterling work as a nonracial athletic administrator and coach; he believed firmly in lending his intellectual skills to the development of nonracial sport and to ensuring the international isolation of apartheid sport (an intellectual model that had been pioneered by Rive's fellow Protest writer Dennis Brutus, a figure instrumental in founding SANROC, SACOS's international wing). Because "defining the happenings" through writing was for him a form of "storming the castles" of apartheid, Rive implicitly rejected the polarized choice that Nortje's poem offers.

Whatever its rich, romantic resonances, Rive did not want to "write or fight." Rive was a thinker who, unlike many South African intellectuals of his (and our) day, was distrustful of binaries: "Some insist that the black South African writer must both write and fight; others say that he must write while others fight; and we also have a third variation which claims that a literary state can be so desperate that it can demand that writing ceases in order to allow the political problem to be resolved."[16] Whatever the "political" logic that girded these three positions, they were all equally untenable to Rive. He was too distrustful of political jingoism to choose between "writing or fighting"; he was too conscious of the value of an "organic" connection to the coloured community, too aware of his own political responsibilities as an intellectual to situate himself as the writer who wrote while others fought and died. Finally, he could not "cease" his writing, although in the 1970s his fiction gave way to academic pursuits when he attended graduate schools in the United States (Columbia) and England (Oxford). Rive always wrote in one form or another; he could fight only by writing.

His very sense of himself was bound up in his status as an oppositional writer. In this regard, Roland Barthes's argument about "The Death of the Author" offers a subtle counterpoint to Rive's construction of himself as a disenfranchised subject through writing. "Writing," according to Barthes, "is the destruction of every voice, of every point of origin. Writing is that neutral, composite, oblique space where our subject slips away, the negative where all identity is lost, starting with the very identity of the body writing."[17] While Rive certainly did not conceive of his writing as the "destruction" of his "voice" or the negation of his "identity," his commitment to transcending colouredness was such that he disguised—even he did not quite destroy—his "origins." Rejecting his categorization as a coloured subject, his writing became that "oblique space" where he could recompose himself as "black," where his "identity" could be "lost" in the cause of the larger disenfranchised struggle, where his "body" could be misread or reread. Rive did, in some fundamental way, want to "lose" himself in and through his writing. However, even though Rive the writer wanted to construct himself as a different political subject, apartheid law prevented his immersion into that Barthesian "loss." A "loss" that represented, for Rive, the ideological disenfranchised position par excellence because he could submerge himself into a "blackness" that his very "point of (racial) origin" rendered inaccessible to him—unlike Nortje's poetry, Rive's prose does not linger overly long on the problems of biracial "origin," the very reason for his hybrid identity. Through his (ultimately unsuccessful) striving for this "literary loss," Rive is, finally, expressing the desire to compensate for the "lacks" that mark his political identity.

It is, in part, because of the rich Barthesian complications that inflect Rive's status as author that his is such a complex intellectual formation. (His very construction of himself as a "black" author reveals, ironically, the unachievability of that location.) Rive's was a model that did not so much privilege the *clercs* over the activist, though there is more than a touch of that predilection, as it refracted the commitments of a Bertrand Russell through the solitariness of a Benda scholar. Toward the end of "Writing or Fighting," Rive subtly acknowledges the limitations of his own position. The writer "opposes," he holds, "in the way that he can do best, by writing about it and revealing injustices." This is Rive's definition of himself as intellectual: Always respectful and admiring of the activist, he is a writer first, it is what "he can do best"; as such, he is a thinker who recognized the restrictions of his own position. Rive is accountable to the antiapartheid struggle, but his contribution is specific: He is the articulate author able to "reveal injustices." If there is a hint of apology at the conclusion of his seminal essay, it is because Rive is aware of how his model of the intellectual made him vulnerable to the charge by antiapartheid activists that "writing" was not "fighting."

Claiming "The District" as Home

The reconstruction of the past as legacy . . . for new and critical geographies of the history of struggle, must eventually develop alternative directions and directives, contending with the "broken chains", covered tracks and inter- rupted narratives.

—Barbara Harlow, *After Lives*

Situated on the fringes of downtown Cape Town, District Six is a community inscribed in Western Cape public memory as a loaded political symbol. Home to the coloured community for many decades, District Six became an ever more inscribed sign—some might say overburdened and even romanticized—when the Group Areas Act declared "the District" white. Its very name became a sociopolitical palimpsest onto which was written the lost freedoms, political defiance, and cultural creativity that flourished before the apartheid bulldozers began the work of physically destroying a community. In the wake of deracination, District Six came to stand as a metonym for the coloured community: District Six as the community, predating its razing in the mid-1960s and as the model for all future social collectivities; "the District" as the organic social unit. That wholeness was sometimes idealized, but more often District Six served mainly as a potent reminder of coloured loss, a testament to a seldom acknowledged powerlessness against apartheid legislation, a symbol of the psychic effects of dislocation and relocation to the townships. Uprooting coloureds from District Six also had material consequences: They moved from proximity to the urban center to the nondescript, squat houses and the low-rise tenement blocks on the Cape Flats that were without adequate public transportation, or, in those traumatic initial moments, sufficient schools, medical facilities, or places to shop. Of all the "slums" cleared by the Nationalists, however, District Six represents an instance of unique empowerment for the ex-residents. After the physical destruction of the buildings and the deracination of its coloured inhabitants, it stood barren, unpopulated and underdeveloped. It became an unsightly "scar on the face of Table Mountain," as Rive once remarked, a reminder of the violence done to a community in the name of racist greed; the place that District Six occupied in the Western Cape—and, to a lesser extent, the national psyche—could not be erased as the homes of coloured inhabitants had once been bulldozed. In its ghostly, post–Group Areas Act emptiness, it became an even more potent and resilient symbol of public loss, a site that would not allow its past to be written—or built—over. It became an uninhabitable, "haunted" space, reminiscent of the house at "124 Bluestone Road," that abode that contains so fantastically the private and public memory of African-American slavery in Toni Morrison's *Beloved*. From District Six, the disenfranchised coloured majority in the Western Cape were forced to take occupancy of those soulless houses on what Rive describes as the "sandy wastes of the Cape Flats." As a native of the District, Rive produces work that participates, as an act of political resistance, in the creation, critique, and preservation of that public memory of a lost coloured community.

From his earliest short stories in the mid-1950s to his 1986 novel *'Buckingham Palace', District Six*, the dominant protagonist in Rive's work is District Six. His writing is so preoccupied with the District (even his autobiography, he points out, grew out of a 1979 academic paper that had its roots in "Caledon Street and District Six") that one could argue Rive was artistically fixated, unable to write beyond the razing of his birthplace. Even that fragment of his fiction that is not located in District Six is either vicariously connected to that community through the protagonist's histories or is engaged with issues that resonate with the feel of District Six. Providing more than a clue to his psychobiography, these continual revisitings constitute his artistic and his political agenda: the continual recreation of District Six as the physical site of an ideal community. Rive's work is, in Morrison's terms, an act of "rememory":[18] It is the "re-membering," the putting back together, the public reassembling of District Six.

From shards of memory, fragments of loss, insistent nostalgia, and historic opposition, District Six is given a renewed and politically charged public life by (as well as in and through) Rive's fiction.

Rive's investment in District Six as an "organic" community, a self-sufficient social construct, unveils a contradiction at the core of coloured history. It was at once a racial artifice, a community fabricated into existence by an ideology of racial separation that predated apartheid (though the Nationalists lent it a special legal credence), and a constituency that showed itself capable of developing a sustaining set of cultural practices. As the erudite, Rive-like narrator of Buckingham Palace remembers:

> And in the evenings we would stand in hushed doorways and tell stories about the legendary figures of District Six, Zoot, Pretty-Boy and Mary . . . or just talk about the ways of white folks and how Cissie Gool was fighting for us and showing the white people a thing or two. . . . The young men went to parties or bioscope, and the older men played dominoes and klawerjas on the stoeps, holding the huge boards between them on their laps, and when they banged down the dominoes or the cards, hordes of flies would spin up and then settle down again. The young girls waited for the men to fetch them, all coy, demure and made up in the latest fashions. The older housewives came out with their wooden benches and sat apart from the men and gossiped the mild evening away.[19]

Borrowing again from Langston Hughes (*The Ways of White Folks* is the title of the American's collections of short stories), Rive demonstrates how the nurturing social practices, the "dominoe and the klawerjas"[20] games, the older people "gossiping the mild evening away," and the "young girls" expecting their dates, all signify a coloured cultural continuity. A community that incorporates and constitutes a wide range of physical types, District Six represents the triumph of cultural coherence, the point where the experience of marginalization within the racially polarized body politic is overcome by a historically and internally produced cohesion. Forced to occupy the racial interstices, coloureds have, through their various cultural practices, made themselves into a community: Physiognomically indistinct, devoid of an essentialist racial identity, they are a constituency made through and sustained by culture.

From one generation to another (from the "older housewives" to "demure" young women), a whole range of traditions is forged and, more important, passed on. In their alienation from both black and white communities, their ingenuous way of perpetuating a coloured identity produces an enduring, if precarious, sense of self. Obscured by the dynamic cultural practices are the activities of "Cissie Gool" (who was "fighting for us and showing the white people a thing or two"), a champion for disenfranchised rights who came from a well-known political family. Her struggle is shown, in this evocative sketch, to be integral to the lifestyle and thinking of District Six. This tableau from *Buckingham Palace*, however, is dominated by a representation of working class culture that gives us a sense of (imagined) generational succession: The young men on the way to the "bioscope" (cinema) will become the older men who play cards and board games; the young women expecting their dates will in time become the "housewives" who "gossip." District Six enables the perpetuation of the coloured community, and *Buckingham Palace* shows how these people function as a distinct social organism. So much so that when District Six was razed, coloureds had to refashion the community; predictably, the model for this process in townships such as Hanover Park and Heideveld was "the District."

This is why "District Six" is such a loaded symbol in this community's history. It represents a telling instance of coloured political vulnerability and a rare moment of psychic stability, that place and occasion when coloureds functioned most normatively as a social unit. After District Six was bulldozed out of physical existence by the Group Areas Act, "District Six"—its metaphoric, nostalgic instantiation—had to be reclaimed repeatedly; District Six became *the* memory of social cohesion, a social arrangement to be achieved again and again in those townships coloureds were relocated to against their will. (So powerful a metaphor was "District Six," however, that it could never be re-created: It became, as time went by, an ever more romanticized, evocative symbol of loss. Its very eradication made it tantalizingly irrecoverable.) What is frequently undermined in the remembering of "the District" is that, as a disenfranchised community, District Six was made impotent by the legislation that devastated it. The Group Areas Act expelled its inhabitants to the townships of "Mannenberg and Heideveld, and a wind-swept area which with almost malicious sarcasm has been named Hanover Park" (*Writing Black*, 4).

The inability of District Six residents to resist the effects of the Group Areas Act registers the extent of the coloured community's political disempowerment. The Nationalists believed that by relocating the inhabitants of District Six and bulldozing the physical buildings they were destroying a preapartheid past, an eclipsed white political system that had permitted coloureds to inhabit a neighborhood that bordered urban "white" space, a physical proximity that would not be tolerated by the apartheid regime. The Group Areas Act was, after the 1913 Land Act (designed to force black farmers off their land, "forcing them into already crowded reserves,"[21] and, not least important, into the service of the understaffed mining industry), the second major redrawing of the map of South Africa. However, whereas the Land Act "urbanized" the black community (the earliest incarnation of a tribalized hostel system for black men), the Group Areas Act wanted to reverse that process by reordering the country's geographical landscape. Coloureds, blacks, and indians were forced out of the cities, which the Act reserved for whites, and into the "desolate" townships—far removed, naturally, from white living spaces; some of these had until recently been occupied by disenfranchised South Africans.

The terms of the Group Areas Act included an especially potent dimension, the power of naming, an aspect Rive was all too aware of. The coloured author correctly points out that "malicious sarcasm" was involved in the naming of "Hanover Park," a Cape Flats township that sadistically invoked the memory of Hanover Street, the cultural and economic hub of District Six. The "Hanover Park" to which deracinated coloureds were relocated in no way resembled the bustling nerve center that had been "Hanover Street." This act was not only insensitive to an oppressed people's past, it was committed to destroying it. In *Buckingham Palace* Rive writes most poignantly of the psychic and physical violence wrought by the Group Areas Act:

> They had taken our past away and left the rubble. They had demolished our spirits and left broken bricks. They had destroyed our community and left dust and memories. And they had done all this for their own selfish and arrogant reasons. They had sought to regulate our present in order to control our future. And as I stood there I was overwhelmed by the enormity of it all. And I asked aloud, "What men have the moral or political right to take away a people's past? . . . For the past will not be forgotten" . . . And the people on the bleak Flats whisper and remember what greed and intolerance have done to them. And they tell children and their children's children because it must never be forgotten. (*BPDS*, 128)

Rive's determination to keep alive the dignity of the disenfranchised, preapartheid past, his preservation of the memories of District Six ("tell the children and their children's children") despite the perniciousness that motivated its demise, recalls Frantz Fanon's critique of colonialism in *Wretched of the Earth*. In this text Fanon argues that an oppressed people's history is always a target for colonialist "revision": "By a kind of perverted logic, [the colonial power] turns to the past of the oppressed people, and distorts, disfigures, and destroys it."[22] The Nationalists routinely engaged, as *Buckingham Palace* so vividly demonstrates, in the "disfigurement" and "distortion" of black South Africans' "past"—District Six was a "past" that spoke of a different history, a societal arrangement that could be neither countenanced nor tolerated by the regime. All traces of "the District" had to be eliminated. The Group Areas Act stands as the reinscription of the country's urban geography, a mode of social reorganization that was central to the Nationalist's attempt to rewrite South Africa as an a priori apartheid society; the Act ensured the society's urban planning conformed to the logic and vision of apartheid. In the Nationalist's terms, racial separation was an absolute, perhaps especially so for a community that was the product of racial intermingling; the hybrid body could be legally acknowledged, but interracial living spaces—and the physical traces of it—had to be outlawed.

The Nationalists reserved, in this "malicious" project, a special viciousness for the destruction of those sites—District Six, Sophiatown, Marabastad—that had a history of opposition to and defiance of their segregationist policies. The apartheid government believed, erroneously (if arrogantly) as it turned out, that when District Six was razed so was a people's past. They intended to leave nothing, as Rive says, but "dust" and "memories." "No White authority," he writes, "ever bothered to ask me whether they could take my past away. They simply brought in the bulldozers" (*Writing Black*, 5). The Nationalists underestimated, in their physical devastation, the power of "memory" to sustain a community, to keep alive its sense of a past so that it could reimagine a postapartheid society where District Six could be, if not physically reconstructed, then certainly used to animate that future. Rive's work is, in this regard, an eloquent and moving response to a brutal act of deracination, capturing the spirit of District Six by reproducing its experiences as fiction again and again; always exhorting his community to "never forget" the cost of "greed and intolerance" (*Buckingham Palace*, 198). Rive's penultimate novel makes evident how the recreation of a public memory of the community was the central political commitment of his oeuvre.

In metaphorically confronting the bulldozers of apartheid, however, Rive was doing considerably more than protecting District Six's past: he was also trying to relocate himself within the community's experience. Though Rive was wary of romanticizing District Six ("In truth the slum was damp, dirty and dank," as he so bluntly puts it in his autobiography), the community represented the closest approximation of an organic and self-supporting structure in his experience (*Writing Black*, 4). Ambivalent as he was about his District Six roots because of his education and literary achievement, and spared the trauma of deracination that resulted in the relocation of the inhabitants to the townships of Heideveld and Hanover Park, he sought to situate himself in those experiences through his writing. He sought, in this moment, to achieve Lukacs's notion of the "typical": He wanted to represent, through his fiction, "something larger and more meaningful than himself"; he attempted to not only exceed his "own isolated destiny" but to integrate his future—his sense of himself— with that of the ordinary District Six resident. Rive wanted to become, like his characters, "typically" District Six, and this is why his writing (especially his fiction) is so crucial to him: It enabled him to mediate between the social privilege he had achieved and the struggles of District

Six that had shaped his early life. He was rewriting his own history and reconstructing his sociopolitical umbilical cord, determined to reclaim District Six for himself and for his community.

The tensions created by this project, as *Quartet* collaborator Wannenburgh points out, reveal themselves most clearly in the "stilted" and "contrived"[23] language of Rive's protagonists. This criticism is, to varying degrees, as valid of his 1964 novel *Emergency* as it is of 1986 work *Buckingham Palace*. Part novel, part drama, *Buckingham Palace* takes its name, ironically, from the home of British royalty. This work depicts a "single" day in the life of District Six, morning, afternoon, and evening, analogues for the "rise," "noon," and "demise" of the lives of itinerant, charmingly disreputable, and respectable residents who live in a row of rented cottages in this community. Discursively (and linguistically), *Buckingham Palace* is divided between the manicured, dulcet tones of the Rive-like, unnamed, narrator's voice and the quotidian, vernacular speech of the ordinary inhabitants of District Six. (The main protagonist, Zoot, also has moments in which he resembles Rive's way of speaking and thinking. Most of the other characters, such as the ex-convict Pretty Boy and the bordello madam, Mary, use only working class District Six speech.) A telling instance of this "contrived" speech occurs towards the end of the novel where Zoot's final critique of apartheid, delivered against the backdrop of District Six ruins, is deeply inflected by the rhetoric of the Holocaust. Here Zoot deconstructs the Nazi concept "untermenschen" in a language ill-suited to him: "The greedy people who have taken away our homes will soon have to answer to us. They thought that they had reduced us to untermenschen but they lied. We are living proof that they lied" (*Buckingham Palace*, 197). As articulate as the irascible Zoot is (an author of doggerel verse whose given name is "Milton," after the poet, no less), this vocabulary belongs not to him but to the political rhetoric of the Unity Movement, a political movement dominated by bourgeois intellectuals with whom Rive was loosely affiliated. Rive's deployment of "untermenschen" in this speech is ill advised, a term that disrupts rather than enhances Zoot's critique, serving only to emphasize the gap between the writer and his community.

Crafting a vocabulary that can represent the dialogue of District Six residents presented Rive with an intricate ideological conundrum. How could a writer who is, as Wannenburgh claims, "suspicious of any concession to the vernacular of the Cape Flats" hope to create convincing protagonists when he is hostile to their speech patterns? In truth, however, what Rive rejects is not the patois but the way the dominant culture is able to exploit and undermine the "vernacular of the Cape Flats" through the perpetuation of negative coloured cultural stereotypes. Rive was loathe to participate in that depiction of "the District" characterized by what he called the "over-raucous twang of guitar strings and the over-loud bursts of carnival costumes."[24] The challenge that confronted Rive was to reclaim the "vernacular" and invest it with the verve, dynamism, and spunk of its native speakers. (Politically explicable as Rive's aversion to the "over-raucous twang" is, it also marks the ways he differs from Hughes, a poet who invested the speech of "Negro" Americans with a verve and resonance that enabled him to become the voice of the black popular classes.)

In his work *No Respect*, Andrew Ross carefully delineates the difficulty that intellectuals have in negotiating their relationship to popular culture, which is instructive for understanding Rive's relationship to vernacular speech:

> The status of popular culture—what is popular and what is not—is also an unstable political definition, variably fixed from moment to moment by intellectuals and tastemakers, and in this respect, is often seen as constituting, if not representing, a political identity for "popular classes."[25]

As both an "intellectual" and a "tastemaker," Rive was concerned with how the stereotype of the "happy, carnival-loving coloured" was deployed against his community, how coloured popular culture was used by the regime to represent a denigrated, crudely populist political identity. As a member of the (coloured) intellectual class, one who was committed to the struggles of working-class District Six, Rive took it upon himself to ensure that coloured political identity was not reduced to—or reducible to—that of the "'popular classes'."

Because of his ambivalent relationship to the average District Six resident, Rive struggled to capture the vibrancy of this working-class hybrid of English and Afrikaans. The District Six patois was for him not only a vicarious linguistic experience, even though he would have encountered it as a teacher and a sports administrator, but also the very symbol of a language the Oxbridge-trained scholar was not always—or even especially—comfortable with. District Six-speak was a culture that Rive sought both to embrace and distance himself. In the interstices of political commitment and public articulation, Rive grappled repeatedly with the ideological implications, affect, and effect of language. In attempting to fashion a dialogue that was authentic but untainted by the dominant stereotypes, Rive invariably found himself producing a vocabulary that bore traces of his own (relative) social privilege, a class location that undermines his literary goals. Rive was always negotiating between his middle-class existence and the pressures of the social commitment of his work, between the memories of District Six that sustained him artistically and his desire to escape it; between the vocabulary he remembered and the academic one he had acquired. These are some of the central tensions

Rive engages with as a writer. It may be that in his final published novel *Buckingham Palace* (*Emergency Continued* was issued posthumously), Rive, who was sensitive to criticisms about his dialogue, tries to circumvent this problem. He experiments by introducing each of the three sections with a prologue so that the background is provided by the narrator, thereby paring the amount of dialogue. The narrator leaves the protagonists free to engage in sharp and witty dialogue. As a result the humor is spontaneous and the dialogue breaks down only when the residents of "Buckingham Palace," especially Zoot, become politically didactic about the legislation that destroyed their community.

Who Is Coloured?

As coloured woman defines a boundary that is at once inside and outside, the insider's outsideness. The stillness that surrounds her, the gaps in her story, her hesitation and passion that speak between the self and its acts—these are moments where the private and public touch in contingency.

—Homi Bhabha, *The Location of Culture*

The promulgation of the Population Registration Act in 1950 was arguably the most traumatic historical and psychological event Rive had to grapple with as an intellectual. This Act at once divided families, friends, and communities, and constituted the coloured community as a politically and geographically—if physionogmically disparate—constituency for the first time. Together with Dennis Brutus and Bessie Head, Rive, and the Western Cape Protest writers represented the first generation of coloured writers who had this racial categorization thrust upon them. An appellation that had for preapartheid generations signaled an indeterminate, shifting, and ambiguous racial identity, the term now contained within it "hierarchic implications, implying inferior to Whites and superior to Blacks" (*Writing Black*, 2). The Population Registration Act translated a fluid identity into a fixed, legally determined category. Before this law came into effect, some "coloureds" who had the physionogmic means or the will to "transcend" their "race" had been able to "pass" as "white" (or, "for white," as the common expression in the coloured community goes) and thereby acquire access to the white world of power and privilege.

The Population Registration Act lends Fanon's injunction that the "native . . . strip himself naked to study the history of his body," a particularly poignant resonance (Frantz Fanon, *Wretched of the Earth*, 211). Inscribed onto the coloured body is the history of colonialism, racism, and sexual and economic exploitation. Miscegenation produced the coloured body, but apartheid rendered it the most vulnerable of South African so-ciopolitical constructs. In "Resurrection," one of his earliest short stories that deals with a coloured family's experience of the Act, Rive captures the divisive and devastating consequences that follow apartheid's racial classification. Mavis, the only "black" child in her "mixed" family nar-rates this short story about how the Population Registration Act placed social relations under unnatural pressures, tearing unmercifully at the fabric of the coloured family. She is bitter about the implications of her racial classification: "You made me black!"[26] she yells at her mother in an especially traumatic exchange. Mavis's anger is impotent and, most im-portant, misdirected—her mother is responsible for her birth, not for the derogation attendant to being labeled "coloured"—not "black," as Rive claims. Apartheid law has stratified not only society but the coloured family, discriminating against Mavis while affording her "white" siblings the benefits of enfranchisement.

Mavis, however, is at least able to confront the cruelty of apartheid real-ity. There are in her story, as Bhabha would have it, fewer "gaps" and "hestitations." She is able to transform the "private" space that is the home into a forum for the discussion of intensely "public" matters; she demonstrates how the Population Registration Act has made the "private and the public" entirely "contingent upon one another." Her mother, transformed into an "outsider" to her other children by this Act, is unable to comprehend the invasiveness—the psychic contortions—wrought by this legislation; she, unlike her daughter, believes that the "boundary" separating the public from the private still holds. The mother simply can-not understand that while a parent's love is colour blind, the law in South Africa is not:

> "Mavis, why do they treat me so? Please, Mavis, why do they treat me so?" Mavis knew the answer and felt the anger welling up inside her till her mouth felt hot and raw. . . .
>   "Because you're black. You're black, Ma, but you gave birth to white chil-dren."(Rive, "Resurrection," 31)

Through his dramatization of the psychological and emotional effects wrought by the Population Registration Act, Rive demonstrates that the law's consequences far exceeded the material. Classification as "white" or "coloured" involved more than access to or denial of access to power and privilege. Often, as in this instance, biological and personal ties were bru-tally severed, families were destroyed. The coloured past is indeed a frag-ile historical construction. It is a past, and therefore a present and future, always vulnerable to the dictates of apartheid.

Despite the aggressiveness with which Mavis describes herself and her mother as "black," Rive knew that his experience of being "black" was qualitatively different from that of other disenfranchised South Africans. His experience did not coincide precisely with that of his "less fortunate Black brothers in the location; those who carry passes and those who are made bachelors although they have wives" (*Writing Black*, 214). Through the title of his autobiography, *Writing Black*, Rive gestures toward effecting greater symbolic unity among disenfranchised South African writers. The use of "Black" in the title is an attempt to overcome the consequences of apartheid's artificial, but strategically successful, policy of group and ethnic divisions. However much he rejected this imposed and fabricated identity, Rive implicitly understood that his being a coloured South African meant that he had recourse to a unique set of cultural traditions, practices, and institutions: a culture that grew out of the urban coloured experience, a culture that was typical of modernity, shaped as much by the influence of Western rationalism as by the social practices of the indigenous black community. Rive was a man who not only straddled but bridged disparate cultures, in possession of a body that symbolized the intersection of Europe and Africa, the hybrid product of these two civilizations. He could consequently claim, with authority and conviction, "I am buses, trains, and taxis. I am prejudice, bigotry, and discrimination. I am urban South Africa" (*Writing Black*, 23). When Rive insists upon his urbanness and rejects the "palm fronds and nights filled with the throb of the primitive" in *Writing Black*, he is speaking for the broader community of disenfranchised South Africans and, as significantly, postcolonial Africans. Unlike most of the Protest writers, Rive was close to sub-Saharan writers such as the Kenyan Ngugi wa Thiongo and the Nigerian Chinua Achebe and he acquired from his contact with them a disdain for the romantic icons of imperialist ideology. Rive was, in the words of Jakes Gerwel, "a singular cultural phenomenon: he was the one nonexiled black South African writer to be part of the postcolonial African literary experience in the Sixties. For a long time he represented our one living link with African literature and also the body of exiled South African literature."[27] Rive was not, as Wannenburgh unfairly described him, the "African who does not like Africa." Rive was simply a (not quite) postcolonial African writer who recognized himself less in "palm fronds" of colonialist mythology than he did in the complex of "prejudice, bigotry and discrimination." Rive understood that he was not so much "discriminated" against as that his South African-ness was liminal, preventing him from saying with "full conviction" that he was a "citizen" of his native land. His South African-ness was always truncated, disabled, despite his deep commitments, by his racial hybridity.

Paradoxically, in making these grand claims for blackness (in both its South African and sub-Saharan instantiations), Rive only draws attention to his own peculiarly abbreviated "blackness." Rive was, in fundamental ways, hiding his own difference behind a critique of imperialist fantasy. "Palm fronds" were indeed alien to him, but then again so was a fuller, less embattled notion of blackness; this is why his articulation, "I could not say," is actually a double negation. It is not simply that he "could not say, 'I am a South African'," but that he "would not say," as his work does with a rich complexity, "I am a coloured South African." Rive is unable to recognize how the incompleteness of his articulation is founded in a fundamental denial, even a misrecognition of the self. The writer who can depict, celebrate, and act in lyrical defense of his community, the novelist and essayist who strives to integrate himself into his originary community, is finally unable to see how his identity is inextricable from theirs. Richard Rive, champion of District Six, cannot fully take his place in that coloured body politic because he is unable to voice his own colouredness. Recognizing his hybridity, Rive seems to suggest, implies a repression of his blackness, a political condition unacceptable to him; a subtle thinker, Rive was too invested in an ideologically explicable, but nonetheless essentialist, "blackness" to understand that his hybridity was multivalent, that it could be lived and experienced in a variety of ways. Consequently, although apartheid prevented him from staking full claim to his South African-ness, it was his own political convictions, his admirable (if unreflective) belief in nonracialism, that inhibited his capacity to name himself—and his racial identity—accurately.

Notes

1. This is an issue I explored briefly in an earlier essay, of the same title, on Rive. See Grant Farred, "Writing in a Twilight Zone: Richard Rive, Coloured Artist & Intellectual," *New Contrast* 19, nos. 2 and 3 (1991): 74, 75.

Rive's sexual orientation is rarely discussed in South African literary circles; it was especially evident at the time of his murder, when the mainstream press did its best to portray his murder as a "robbery" rather than a hate crime. At that moment in 1989, Rive's public reticence about his sexuality and the homophobia of his society converged to "protect" the author in death; a death, of course, that was facilitated, in part, by the culture of silence.

2. Alf Wannenburgh, "Death in Cape Town," *Guardian* (Manchester), 7 February 1991.

3. See, for a fuller discussion of this issue, Edward Said's *Representation of the Intellectual: The 1993 Reith Lectures* (New York: Pantheon Books, 1994).

In this series of lectures, which turns on a dynamic coupling of Julien Benda and Antonio Gramsci, the Palestinian thinker Said delineates the complications that attend to the role of intellectuals, both those who are and who are not expressly motivated by political commitments.

4. Richard Rive, *Writing Black* (Cape Town: David Philip, 1980), 10.

5. It was, of course, because of their antiapartheid position that a range of intellectuals gained recognition abroad, a status that translated as notoriety for the apartheid authorities and enabled them to overcome the physical limitations of geography. Most prominent amongst these oppositional figures were exiled writers such as Ezekiel Mphahlele, Bessie Head, Alex La Guma, Dennis Brutus, Bloke Modisane, and artists such as Gerald Sekoto; political exiles such as Oliver Tambo, Ruth First, and Joe Slovo enjoyed this same status; of course, none of these intellectuals rivaled the standing of that most famous of antiapartheid icons, Nelson Mandela, a man revered for decades both within and outside the country, by very different antiapartheid constituencies.

6. Richard Rive, "Writing or Fighting? The Dilemma of the Black South African Writer," *Tribute* (August 1989): 50.

7. Gavin Lewis, *Between the Wire and the Wall: A History of South African 'Coloured' Politics* (Cape Town: David Philip, 1987), 13. Lewis's book provides a useful overview of the trajectory of coloured political organizations from the late nineteenth to the mid-twentieth century.

8. See James Matthews's short story, "Azikwelwa" (which translates as "we will not ride") in his collection *The Park and Other Stories* (Johannesburg: Ravan Press, 1983) about the ways the 1955 black-led bus boycott created a bond between a coloured man and his "Bantu"—to use the terms of the day—compatriots. Although coloured support for the boycott, which was centered mainly in the then-province of the Transvaal, was tepid, Matthews's protagonist was clear and unwavering in his determination not to "ride."

9. See Tom Lodge's *Black Politics in South Africa* (Johannesburg: Ravan Press, 1987) for a full account of this movement.

10. Langston Hughes, *The Big Sea* (New York: Hill and Wang, 1997), 325.

11. As complicated as the coloured condition is, it is also impacted by the urban-rural split.

Rural coloured communities are constituted differently from their urban counterparts, unevenly divided along lines of language, religion, proximity to, implication in, and dependence upon white culture. Consequently, questions of coloured identity and politics are refracted through distinct lenses, all of which are continually subject to rethinking because there is an increasing drift from, as Raymond Williams might have it, "the country to the city."

12. Samuel Delaney, *The Motion of Light in Water: Sex and Science Fiction Writing in the East Village, 1957–1965* (New York: Arbor House, 1988), 52.

13. However much Rive identifies symbolically with "Chatsworth" and "Langa," he speaks most authoritatively of "Bonteheuwel," a metaphor for the post–District Six coloured community.

14. Arthur Nortje, *Dead Roots* (London: Heinemann Educational Books, 1973), 118.

15. Rive, "Writing or Fighting," 51.

16. Ibid., 52.

17. Roland Barthes, "The Death of the Author," in *Twentieth-Century Literary Theory: A Reader* (New York: St. Martin's Press, 1997), 122.

18. Toni Morrison, *Beloved* (New York: Penguin Books USA, 1988), 118.

19. Richard Rive, *'Buckingham Palace,' District Six* (Cape Town: David Philip, 1986), 4.

20. "Klawerjas" is a card game that is especially popular in the coloured community in the Western Cape.

21. Lodge, *Black Politics*, 4. ("Reserves" is a term for homelands, the segregated, impoverished, mostly rural areas designated as living spaces for black communities.)

22. Frantz Fanon, *Wretched of the Earth*, trans. Constance Farrington (New York: Grove Press, 1968), 210.

23. Alf Wannenburgh, "Memories of Richard," *New Contrast* 71 (spring 1990): 31.

24. Evelyn John Holtzhausen, "An Interview with Richard Rive," *Upstream* 7, no. 3 (spring 1989): 5.

25. Andrew Ross, *No Respect: Intellectuals & Popular Culture* (New York: Routledge, 1989), 9.

26. Richard Rive, "Resurrection," *Advance, Retreat: Selected Short Stories* (Cape Town: David Philip, 1983), 33.

27. Jakes Gerwel, "A Tribute to Richard Rive," Programme, *Buckingham Palace, District Six, The Play*, 1989.

2

The Poetics of
Partial Affiliation:
Arthur Nortje and the
Pain of Origin

Difference is political, that is, about power, accountability and hope. Experience, like difference, is about contradictory and necessary connection.

—Donna Haraway, "Reading Buchi Emecheta"

And I Hybrid, After Arthur . . .

Poetry as a form of personal salvation in the wake of trauma, dispersion, and exile.

—Peter Balakian, *The Black Dog of Fate*

Of all the South African writers who trace their genealogical roots to the coloured community, none have grappled in so sustained or self-conscious a fashion with the historical ramifications of this condition as the poet Arthur Nortje. Within the context of this writing, where Richard Rive's commitment to transcending—and, by implication, eliminating—colouredness represents the dominant literary mode, Nortje signals a disjunctive approach to and understanding of his racial identity. However unachievable and problematic Rive's vision, it enjoys a political sanction denied Nortje, a poet who embraces his colouredness—no matter how painful, contradictory, or debilitating that condition might be. In this regard the critic Jacques Berthoud's reading of the poet assumes a special pertinence: "Arthur Nortje may be a coloured South African, but not every coloured South African is Arthur Nortje."[1] Berthoud's axiom draws out clearly Nortje's unique preoccupation with colouredness, a level of psychic investment unmatched by other coloured writers; neither his peers nor his predecessors, neither his contemporaries nor his successors share Nortje's deep-seated concern with his origins. Unlike him, their primary view of the coloured community is different: Mattera, La Guma, Matthews, and Rive regard themselves as disenfranchised black South Africans, as belonging to a community that exceeds (and in so doing negates) the hybridity of their racial roots.

Cognizant of its mixed racial heritage, "coloured fiction" (and such a school can hardly be said to exist) from the Protest School to the present consistently undermines the significance of that ambivalent "stamp of birth,"[2] to invoke Nortje's phrase from "Natural Sinner." Precisely because Nortje is the "unrepresentative" figure in Protest writing, because the "stamp of his birth" preoccupies him so, his poetry compels us to attend seriously to the designation "coloured." The product of a brief liaison between a coloured working class woman, Cecilia Potgieter, and a Jewish man, Nortje felt his colouredness with a keenness unrivaled by Rive (who also did not know his father)[3] and Jennifer Davids (the child of a fairly stable family background). A racial hybrid with access to only his mother's (coloured) culture, Nortje's family origins—or the lack of them—deeply affected his poetry. The circumstances of his birth motivated a poetic investigation into the condition of colouredness that is rare in its insistence and unexpected in its nuance. More disturbing, as this chapter will show, is the way his "bastardization" ("bastardies, abortions, sins of silence" is how he describes it in "Dogsbody half-breed") has informed his depiction of women, a representation that alternates between profound admiration and an intensely misogynistic disdain (*Dead Roots*, 105). His father, tellingly enough, features only fleetingly in his work and is then often—but by no means always—spared the vitriolic attacks his mother—and other coloured women—are routinely subjected to.

Mostly, however, Nortje's background is woven into and even obscured by a larger poetic concern: a dynamic exploration of the impact the appellation "coloured" has had on the life of a constituency that speaks from a precarious social location and of a racially ambiguous history. In the bitter and caustic, but nonetheless telling, lines of one of his seminal poems, "Dogsbody half-breed," he writes:

> *your delicate nooks and moments noble-gentle*
> *bud-open to both blond and black*
> *and I hybrid, after Mendel,*
> *growing between the wire and the wall,*
> *being dogsbody, being me, buffer you still.* (Dead Roots, 105)

Caught between these two opposing forces, the "wire" of racist white intransigence and the mounting "wall" of black anger, Nortje represents "coloureds" as reduced subjects: South Africans assigned the status of the politically insignificant "dogsbodies." Within the apartheid hierarchy, theirs is a location that demonstrates the peculiar liminality of living in the South African racial interstices; they are, in Werner Sollors's loaded run-on phrase, "neither black nor white yet both." Coloureds are precariously situated at the raw and jagged edges of that contracted and contested space between the country's disenfranchised black majority and the oppressive white minority, their bodies a reminder of the historic sexual links between European colonialists and the indigenous population. Always adept at sexual innuendo, Nortje suggests this liaison here—with a hint of disparagement—in his line "your delicate nooks and moments noble-gentle." Coloured women, possessors of those "delicate nooks," are subtly impugned for their lasciviousness and blamed for their attractiveness—they provide the "nooks" for white men, presumably, to "hide" and take sexual pleasure. These same women, however, are admired for their capacity to care, to show compassion in the face of white male sexual aggression—they are "gentle," even in moments of fear and in the face of physical attacks.

Securing an ideological space for coloureds within the ranks of the disenfranchised and crafting an artistic vocabulary that can engage the problematic of racial ambiguity and ambivalent political identification are two of the main issues in Arthur Nortje's poetry. Through a rendering of affiliation that accounts for the complications of coloured liminality, this chapter will explore the multivalent struggles at the core of Nortje's verse. His writing maps, more complexly than that of any other South African poet, the uneven, demanding, and sometimes violent (psychic) process by which coloureds attempt to accommodate themselves within black South Africa. So profound is his commitment to this project that, as he says in "Questions and Answers," "Ancestors will have to be uprooted, / uncouth will be the interrogations and bloody the reprisals" (*Dead Roots*, 141). Nortje's poetry frequently marks the failure to "uproot" those "ancestors," a process that registers itself in two contradictory ways: the determination to locate their "roots" accurately in (his) history and to articulate how he intends to free himself of his (white, male) forbears. Instead, he finds himself locked into, despite the insistence (or "uncouthness," as he might prefer it) of those "interrogations," the perpetual, irresolvable dialectic between partial affiliation and disaffiliation. Partial affiliation is that ideological instance in which coloureds see themselves as belonging only nominally, even insignificantly, to the black or the white body politic. Understanding their connections to the South African mainstream as spurious, they recognize how their links to the enfran-

chised and the disenfranchised communities are tangential, how profoundly they are disempowered in relation to both constituencies. Disaffiliation is that mode of coloured self-representation this community
takes up when it, albeit momentarily, assumes a place completely outside
the society's racial polarities, making no claim upon either the black majority or the empowered white minority; disaffiliation is the temporary
disavowing of their links with both communities.

For generations, coloureds have struggled to come to terms with an
identity that is at once a complex instance of racial doubleness—belonging marginally, in some unacknowledged historical past, to two antagonistic groupings—and racial bifurcation—of being so radically split between these two constituencies as to occupy some precarious space
between, literally in the middle of them. As "Questions and Answers"
demonstrates, Nortje is a poet intent on investigating the dissatisfactions
and the strictures of living in the "buffer" zone, the consequences of being
buffeted by contradictory pressures and "reprisals." Most important,
Dead Roots offers a unique opportunity to read how the conflicting pulls
of partial affiliation (a belonging to that is at once a belonging and not really a belonging), and disaffiliation (a sense of remove from whiteness
and blackness that is undermined by a limited affinity for both experiences) operates in—and on—the coloured community.

Disenfranchised by apartheid laws, coloureds are distanced from (in
addition to ideologically distancing themselves from) the white state and
its citizenry; in possession of an abbreviated, truncated blackness,
coloureds are too qualified in their disenfranchisement to situate themselves uncomplicatedly with the majority in crucial moments. Stamped
with the mark of a mixed birth, they have to produce a subject position by
negotiating the conflicting pulls of partial affiliation and disaffiliation, ex-
ploring the strategic or ethical advantage either (or a hybrid of the two) of
these positions might offer in a particular cultural or political moment.

In instances of disaffiliation, coloureds symbolically construct themselves either as a singular (but not homogenous) South African community or as a singularly un–South African constituency. Hybrid in origin,
molded into being by a highly sexualized colonialist desire, by a precarious but resilient sense of community, and by apartheid legislation, they
transform the "buffer zone" into a separate (and separatist) paradigm.
The South African in-between reconceptualizes itself, through the act of
disaffiliation, as the racial exterior—the interstices are transformed into
the exterior; coloureds, occupants of that precarious middle space, remove themselves to beyond the very outskirts of the nation; they stand
outside, furtively looking in, on, and at—but never away from—a nation
that cannot accommodate them. Coloureds become the Othered Other,

belonging nowhere, even while they are biologically linked to every South African community.

The title of Nortje's poem, "The Alter-Native," stands as a description of this phenomenon. (Even though coloureds do not represent an "alter-native" nation, or offer a substantively "alternative" conception of the nation, they are, in this bifurcated society, the embodiment of "alterity," the Other come to South African life.) The "native," a colonialist term for indigenees that has especially racist overtones in South African history,[4] carries a double impact for Nortje's community: Disenfranchised by whites, coloureds represent the marginalized Other in the black community. Within the disenfranchised ranks, theirs is a position of extreme alienation and psychic vulnerability. Nortje's melancholy musings in "Quiet Night, No Stars," "for who belongs nowhere, is to nothing / deeply attached," reveals the depth of this marginalization, an alienation complicated by a profound ambivalence (*Dead Roots,*). It is precisely because coloureds are so "deeply attached" and implicated in the histories of both the black and white communities that the occupation of this racial "nowhere," this indistinct political space, is so disabling. The pain of alienation is directly proportionate to the desire for unambiguous racial connection; a desire that is as unfulfillable as Rive's incorporative conception of "blackness." Colouredness becomes a coded palimpsest for the multilayered alienations imposed upon this community—socially, politically, as well as psychologically (often self-imposed) removed. This constituency stands outside the nation even as it constitutes its most palpable inside.

The final question this chapter will "interrogate" is the issue of "attachment," of racial belonging as it is amplified in Nortje's writing through the metaphor and experience of exile. Detached several times over from his several different "homes," the peripatetic poet experienced exile with regularity as he moved from South Africa to England, and on to Canada, before going back to England, where he died in 1970. Exile is, as Edward Said argues so eloquently in *Representations of the Intellectual*, a profoundly contradictory experience. It "enlivens the intellectual's vocation, without perhaps alleviating every last anxiety or feeling of bitter solitude."[5] Exile is, on the one hand, the most debilitating of deracinations: It invariably denies, to invoke Aime Cesaire, the possibility of a "return to the native's land" and produces an intense sense of loss and rootlessness, what Said calls the "feeling of bitter solitude" that is so prevalent in Nortje's poetry. On the other hand, exile offers a rare poetic license—the "enlivening of the intellectual vocation"—and the impetus to explore, free from restrictions, the nature and constitution of "home;" this liberation from the motherland is, to borrow a phrase from

the Caribbean novelist George Lamming, one of the most appreciated—
if seldom acknowledged—"pleasures of exile."[6] Although exile was
never a "pleasant" experience for the disenfranchised South African, it
allowed Nortje, by writing about his life in South Africa from cities such
as London and Toronto in ways that his residence in Cape Town was
never able to facilitate, to produce some of his most searing and cogent
reflections on the condition of colouredness. In Nortje's case, exile allowed him to reflect, ruminate, and compose with an intensity that was
largely generative, only seldom enervating. In truth, however, exile
abroad was a condition all too familiar to Nortje: His experience in
South Africa was that of the coloured outsider, the artist who wrote
from an inherently removed location. Canada and England represented
the (geographical) literalization of the exile he experienced while still a
resident in South Africa. Nortje was an exile twice over, at home and
abroad. Or, to invoke his own phrase from "Questions and answers,"
the exilic—the occupation of the outside—was the only condition natural to Nortje: *"Exile from the first / Exile was implanted / in the first
pangs of paradise"* (*Dead Roots*, 140). The poet was always already, from
the moment of his birth, an exile.

Bastardized Sexuality

*That focal point or fulcrum, that juncture where the mestiza stands, is where
phenomena tend to collide. It is where the possibility of uniting all that is separate occurs. This assembly is not one where severed or separated pieces merely
come together. Nor is it a balancing of opposing powers.*

—**Gloria Anzaldua**, *Borderlands/La Frontera*

In the opening stanza of one of his most brilliant poems, "Dogsbody
half-breed," Nortje traces coloured roots with a remarkable vividness, offering an insightful revisiting of the sexualized history of colonialism in
South Africa. Cape Town, the city to which Nortje moved to attend the
segregated, coloureds-only University College of the Western Cape and
where he remained for the rest of his time in South Africa, is home to the
majority of coloureds. (Nortje came to Cape Town after graduating high
school in Port Elizabeth, a city on the east coast of South Africa with its
own substantial coloured population.) Because of its special status in the
coloured community, Cape Town occupies a pivotal place in the poet's
work. Cape Town's prominent role in Nortje's oeuvre is fitting because
the city marks the first contact between European colonialists and the indigenous population:

> *Once this was Tormentoso, Cape of Storms,*
> *midway station for the scurvied crews,*
> *bordello for the sea-tossed Dutchman* (Dead Roots, 104)

Deploying the metaphor of in-betweenness adroitly, Nortje makes this "midway station for the scurvied crews" perform a double ideological duty. It stands simultaneously for coloureds as the "midway" point between black and white South Africans and as a geographical marker—the "Cape of Storms" (or Cape of Good Hope, as it was alternately known) represents the half-way point for European explorers on their way to South Asia. It was, as Nortje says in "Questions and Answers," a "refuge for adventurers" where English, Dutch, and Portuguese colonialists stopped to replenish themselves and their supplies before continuing their search for spices, gemstones, and other valuable natural resources in the Orient (*Dead Roots*, 140). Girding Nortje's adept and economical metaphor in "Dogsbody half-breed" is, however, a more disconcerting feature of Nortje's poetry: a tendency to implicitly, and with a certain lyrical effectiveness, absolve men (mainly, but not exclusively) of sexual accountability by shifting responsibility onto the body of the coloured woman. It is not, in "Dogsbody half-breed," the "scurvied crews" at whom Nortje aims his ire, but the women who staff the "bordello for the sea-tossed Dutchman." (The structure of the poem is such that the rhythmic emphasis falls on the harsh "b" consonant in "bordello" and the soft "s" consonant in "scurvied crews" is lost between "Tormentoso" and the "houses of pleasure" where the European sailors take comfort and "refuge," with the many valences attached to that term.)

The "storm" that rages on the Cape's seas is less meteorological than it is psychological. Unable to control the weather, and by implication, the advances and effects of colonialism, Nortje directs his anger at the lasciviousness, lewdness, and luridness of his female ancestors. Later in the poem he bristles at how these women are "bud-open to both blond and black," denigrating their sexuality by portraying it as excessive, a racially indiscriminate libido. His most stinging indictment of his maternal ancestors, "Dogsbody half-breed" goes on to displace the responsibility for a major South African historical event onto the bodies of coloured (and black) women. In a mid-nineteenth century mass exodus, called the "Great Trek," Afrikaners abandoned the Cape Colony because they did not hold with the British government's newly adopted policy to abolish slavery—which they mistook for the first step toward racial equality. Assembling in companies all over the Cape Colony, groups of ox-waggoned Afrikaners turned their backs on British rule and, as a consequence of the Trek, went on to conquer the South African interior. In rhetorical sleight of hand that is historically hyperbolic but revealing of his bias against coloured women, Nortje seems to suggest that ideological differences were not what principally motivated the Great Trek. "The magnet of exotica that draws . . . blond settlers like a hex / into the heartland, oxdrawn, ammunitioned," he argues with unreflective misogyny in "Dogsbody half-breed." Women function in this poem in those most archetypal of patriarchal roles, as witches who are also seductresses. It is not Afrikaner opposition to abolition that motivated the "Trek," but the strange, inexplicable allure of these "black" (they could be coloured or black, the poem is unclear as to their racial identity) "hexes." These women are the xenotropic "magnets," seductresses (which is frequently a metaphor for whores in patriarchal discourse), that "draws" the "blond settlers" away from the Cape Colony and into the "heartland" with the promise of sexual favors. Such is the "magnetism" of these women for Nortje, that they enable him to rewrite a crucial event in South African history.

Nortje's patriarchal ire is consistently sharp and sustained, though rarely does it achieve the intensity of "Dogsbody half-breed." Here his matriarchal line presents itself as an especial target because coloured women have offered themselves to such a weakened, reprehensible brand of European male, the "scurvied crews": these early "Afrikaner" colonialists (analogically depicted here as the "Dutchmen," seventeenth-century colonial ancestors of the apartheid regime, for whom Nortje reserves a special vituperation) are physically impaired by their Atlantic journey. They carry with(in) them disease and a weakened masculinity, their bodies ravaged by vitamin deficiencies and the rigors of life at sea. These women are despicable because, "Dogsbody half-breed," they are nothing but (servile) employees at the "bordello for the sea-tossed Dutchmen"; these women become, according to Nortje's misogynistic vision, colluders in the process of racial miscegenation, a band of subjects who, through sexual intimacy with white men, "contaminate" blackness and commit race betrayal. These women "weaken" the race through their "diseased" sexual activity with the "scurvied" European seamen.

However, his historical exaggerations apart, Nortje inadvertently shows how Afrikaner colonization operates on (at least) two levels: After the "land" and the "native" have been subdued, the indigenous women become the next objects to be penetrated—women who were not so much "bud-open to both blond and black" (though some of them were certainly culpable—or capable—of xenotropic sexual desire in moments), as they were female black subjects who were sexually assaulted and victimized by colonialism in a form that black men only rarely endured. At crucial points in "Dogsbody half-breed," Nortje, overwrought by the condition of hybridity, explicitly and implicitly absolves Afrikaner (and British, in other poems) colonialists of the violence they perpetrated against the subjugated female body through displacement: He transforms white male aggression into black and coloured sexual lasciviousness. Through his refusal to indict white men, Nortje situates himself as revisionist patriarchal historian: the poet who transcribes the coloured past as female wantonness. The patriarch(al) Nortje uses the history of colonial men, their infirmities, their reprehensibility, their sexual appetite, as a rhetorical weapon with which to misrepresent and attack coloured women. Through these various poetic devices for displacing responsibility, coloured women become, in Nortje's oeuvre, accountable for the miscegenation that so debilitates him.

Although Nortje's representation of disenfranchised females is problematic throughout *Dead Roots*, a more significant displacement and denial is taking place here, a rhetorical maneuver that further complicates the poet's relationship with women. By blaming coloured women, Nortje deflects attention from the historic impotence of the coloured male: The protagonist who threatens "bloody reprisals" cannot confront his own culpability, cannot take responsibility for being unable to resist white male colonialist aggression. However, Nortje is caught in a unique rhetorical bind, an epistemological entanglement he cannot easily free himself from. If he denounces white male colonialist aggression, he is implicitly denying the roots of his own existence; he would be denying his own selfhood, the process of his own creation. Nortje is, more than anything, the product of colonial penetration, both "benign" and violent; he is the consequence of interracial sexual desire and rape, that most offensive and penetrative of sexual encounters. Rape is a paradigm that the poet can neither engage nor articulate. Nortje is helpless on both counts, unable to speak his own disempowerment in the face of white violence, unable to protect the women he blames because he has not produced a discourse, a poetic language that can cope with the physicality written into his disenfranchisement and onto his own body. Nortje's bind is such that if he in any way countenances the actions of "my father Jew who forked wartime virgins" he is publicly siding with the European colonialists against the black majority, leaving himself open to the charge of "coloured collaboration," a tension that always already undermines black-coloured relations. Painfully aware of his physical, historical, and ideological impotence, unable to craft a position—a metaphoric middle ground—that can accommodate the complexities of his hybridity, his bodily weakness in the face of the violence that is colonial history, Nortje opts to displace his responsibility by magnifying coloured female "licentiousness."

Girding Nortje's continual return to lasciviousness is a disturbing phenomenon the coloured short story writer Zoe Wicomb labels "concupiscence . . . a pathological female sexuality."[7] From his xenotropic "magnet of exotica" to his lurid "bordello for the sea-tossed Dutchman" and "bud-open to both blond and black," Nortje continually represents coloured women as being in possession of a "pathological female sexuality." Governed by a sexuality that compels them to repeatedly offer themselves to these colonialists without any sense of loyalty to black (or, for that matter, coloured) South Africans, Nortje's coloured women continually exhibit an uncontrollable desire for white men. The persistent anger against coloured women disguises a deeper, if rarely articulated, bitterness: Nortje blames female "concupiscence" for his coloured status and the racial ambiguities and tensions attending that condition. His is a psyche rent, as the pain of the deliberately named "Dogsbody half-breed" demonstrates, by a debilitating ambivalence: "Maternal muscle of my mixed-blood life / with child you were heavy, with discontent rife" (*Dead Roots*, 104). Born out of problematic union between black and white South Africans, "Dogsbody half-breed" shows "discontent" to be inherent in— always already a by-product of—a coloured woman's pregnancy; the "heaviness" of the "discontent" is proportionate to the degree of the coloured community's unsettled psychic state. Implicit in the phrase "with child you were heavy, with discontent rife" is the disjuncture between the pregnant woman and the dissatisfied male offspring, suggesting that coloured women are complicit in white oppression and coloured men are not. In Nortje's patriarchal portrayal, it is coloured men who grapple with the historical consequences of "mixed-blood life"; they are shown to be politically conscious and aware of the ideological fallout from racial hybridity; Nortje's rationalization and denial means that the coloured male libido is never subjected to the same kind of scrutiny as that of its female counterpart. Coloured women are doubly punished: After violent penetration by the colonialists, the "maternal muscle" is psychically pounded by male offspring with a one-dimensional view of sexual and historical responsibility.

These textured lines of Nortje's poetry offer both a refutation and an affirmation of Wicomb's claim about the engagement with miscegenation in "coloured fiction" (and politics). "Miscegenation," Wicomb writes, "continues to be bound up with shame. . . . We do not speak about miscegenation; it is after all the very nature of shame to stifle its own discourse."[8] Although Nortje's poetry is imbued with a deep sense of "shame" for the sexual proclivities of his female ancestors (however misanthropic that response might be, however much it denies black and white male responsibility), the title of "Dogsbody half-breed" demonstrates how "miscegenation" is at the core of the his oeuvre. His "mixed-blood life" is the very stuff of his work, the (traumatized) psychic dynamo that propels his writing: He wants to identify the entangled racial antecedents so that he can come to grips with the conditions (and the polarized communities) that produced him. We might even say that Nortje "speaks about nothing but miscegenation." And, although Nortje's work does sometimes suggest that he is ashamed of himself, of his past, and even of the poverty he experienced, he is never "stifled" into silence by the "shame of miscegenation." Rather, only by grasping publicly—albeit patriarchally—the nettles of his "half-breed" history is he at once empowered to perform two critical ideological functions. First, he is able to write about how the miscegenated past articulates itself through (and sometimes despite the denial of) the coloured body. Secondly, Nortje uses miscegenation as, in Judith Butler's phrase, an "enabling vulnerability": by writing out of and for the racial interstices, he converts the insistent pain of miscegenated memory into a literary tool for crafting verse that recognizes the complexities of being coloured while being only momentarily debilitated, but never silenced, by (or about) it. Nortje is, in this way, not unlike other coloured writers—despite their ideological differences and the variance in their political intentions: Rive, Matthews, La Guma, and Mattera all take up colouredness in their work.

It is, in this regard, telling that Nortje's father, most often referred to unflatteringly as "the Jew," is only mentioned infrequently in his son's poetry. When the father does feature Nortje's tone of recrimination is evident in the verse, as in "Questions and Answers," where Nortje labels his father "white trash / coursing through my blood" (*Dead Roots*, 141). That Nortje's lack of recrimination for his itinerant father serves only to amplify his capacity for psychic violence against women, especially his mother and the middle class coloured woman whom he loved, Joan Cornelius, is more disturbing. Accentuating the undisguised anger of this poem "For Sylvia Plath I" is an adroit rhetorical maneuver through which Nortje seems to conflate his own father and Otto Plath, poet Sylvia Plath's father, who inflicted considerable psychic pain on his child:

> *Hate for the father. A pool of malice in my blood*
> *dribbles like yellowing water down that cliff-face of ferns.*
> *His blood confuses mine* (Dead Roots, 46)

Not only is it rare for Nortje to mention his father, but it is even more unusual for the poet to hold the father accountable for his son's racial hybridity as he does in this poem. In "For Sylvia Plath I," Nortje's father is held responsible for the poet's anger—the "pool of malice," bred out of the son's racial ambiguity—"His blood confuses mine," this brief line representing one of the few occasions Nortje comes close to outright indictment of the absent, but not forgotten, patriarch. In the Nortje oeuvre, it is the norm to blame the mother for these deeply felt psychic hurts. The un-representativeness of "For Sylvia Plath I" is especially evident when read alongside a poem such as "Casualty." Loaded though the title is, "Casu-alty" is unambiguous about the identity of the "casualty" of this struggle between the sexes: the poet himself, a victim of his mother and Joan Cor-nelius. The poem is a catalogue of assaults on both women, growing in fe-rocity until it unexpectedly climaxes in a father-son affiliation. The first half of "Casualty" is a lambasting of the poet's mother for her silence about his past and the conditions of his conception, and for the poverty of his upbringing. Cecilia Potgieter is presented as a pathetic figure, a terri-ble failure as a parent, unable either to engage her son's desperate in-quiries or to provide adequately for his material needs. Nortje recognizes how his emotionally inept mother used her domestic chores to obscure his personal history from him, a strategy that served only to remind him of the decrepitude of their home:

> *My mother always hung upon the steam*
> *of samp in soldered pots*
> *and pumped the primus stove to drown my questions*

•   •   •

> *The brown lice are buried in the old mattresses:*
> *they smothered, feeding sweetly in my highways.*
> *And the rats peeped from hiding when*
> *the scissored bag had spilled me like a wombscrape. (Dead Roots, 34)*

Intolerant of his mother's several lacks (despite her backbreaking ef-forts to sustain him physically, if not always psychically), Nortje is even more critical of Cornelius's "promiscuity." Overwrought with losing her, he turns savage in his poetic attack:

> *You haunt me with your graceful lady pains:*
> *go flirt coyly with Winnipeg's poppinjays! Or shiver among fir trees*
> *with your tan thighs,*
> *where dogs of the ice are snarling at their bitches:*
> *may blizzards blast your sterile hollows!*
> (Dead Roots, 34)

Having traveled to Canada (where Cornelius had emigrated) to be with her, Nortje found himself rejected by the middle class woman from Cape Town. Nortje's description of Cornelius's father, the affluent man so different from his impoverished mother, uses the prism of class to explain their separation. In the bitter lines of "Casualty," Nortje depicts Mr. Cornelius as a voracious slumlord:

> *your father in the gold mine of his bedrooms,*
> *the racket king of tenements. His ulcers*
> *squirmed at the Sunday peaches. I have watched*
> *him slyly stash his pockets with the black money.*
> (Dead Roots, 34)

The anger he feels for the corrupt, exploitative father pales in comparison to the venom he aims at the daughter. Unable to cope with this pain, he crafted "Casualty," a poetic response spiked with malevolence as he likens her sexual appetite to that of an exotic canine, the "tan bitch" being pursued by the "dogs of the ice" (his crude metaphor for white Canadian men). Not content with having bestialized her sexuality, he further invokes the metaphor of the harsh Canadian climate by calling upon the "blizzards" to render her resoundingly unreproductive—"sterile hollows," his bitter phrase for this condition. However, the denouement of this poem comes in the final verse, where Nortje rejects his mother and Cornelius in favor of an unlikely (and unsustainable) alliance with his father:

> *I shall be true eternally towards*
> *my father Jew, who forked the war-time virgins:*
> *I shall die at war with women.* (Dead Roots, 35)

Nortje's newfound allegiance to his father is, on at least three counts, disconcertingly expedient: First, there is no history of a relationship between the coloured son and his Jewish father, there is no reason to expect that "Casualty's" strident proclamation is anything but a strategic ploy, an opportunity to gratuitously critique the primary women in his life. Momentarily absolving his father of responsibility, Nortje commits himself to a lifelong battle: "I shall die at war with women." When the poem is read in conjunction with its title, it becomes clear that this will be not only an exacting and vicious series of exchanges, but that the poet will suffer most of all the combatants. Nortje will number among the fatalities, he will be a casualty of a war he did not start and cannot win. Second, even in his commitment to his father, the poet barely conceals anger with his father's sexual habits. (This anger is salient within the body of Nortje's verse because his attack on his father marks one of the few moments his poetry is so unbridled.) His Jewish father, a member of a people victimized in the Holocaust, becomes in "Casualty" a perpetrator of violence against coloured women, a constituency that has endured its own

historical suffering. The Jewish father becomes, in the poem's most striking double entendre, a man who "forked" coloured women (so palpable
is the violence of this line that clearly the poet intends us to hear the
echoes of the harsher expletive, "fucked," as we read it), one of whom
was Cecilia Potgieter. Finally, Jewish father and coloured son are more
bound by nothing so much as misogyny: They are both, in ways more
similar than not, violent toward women. The father "forks" then aban-
dons the mother and the son, the son is discursively, psychically, and linguistically violent toward almost every woman he has a personal relationship with—when Nortje claims that he "shall die at war with
women," he is not only accurately describing his frame of mind, he is
neatly encapsulating his approach to women. He has converted an entire
gender, in poetic (and psychological) terms, into his real and imagined
enemy; his metaphoric "forking" of women is no more subtle or less malicious than his father's. Cecilia is victimized twice over, once by the father
and then by the son; the former leaves her to care for a son he never meets
or provides for; the latter holds her almost solely accountable for his existence. Traumatized by the experience of being coloured, Nortje in his poetry (especially some of his most outstanding verse) shows how easily being overwrought by miscegenation leads to a misogyny grounded in
coloured women's "sexual infelicity." *Dead Roots* reveals a poetry all too
often populated with representations of coloured women as sirens or, as
is the case in "Hamlet reminiscence," "Ophelia," that most vulnerable of
literary women—"Ophelia," an obvious marker for Cornelius, "I think of
you, the woman, with shrill fury" (*Dead Roots*, 14). Most often, however,
coloured women are "bordello madams" or sex workers operating out of
a "gutted / warehouse at the back of pleasure streets."

Following Nortje's disparagement of women and his troubled sense of
his own racial identity, his designation of coloureds in "Pornography:
Campus" is unsurprising. They are, in his view, the "bastards of debauchery" (*Dead Roots*, 17). This is a bitingly ironic ode to his alma mater, the
University College of the Western Cape. In this poem, the lasciviousness
of "bastard" is revealed as inherently politicized and luridly sexualized
by South African ideologies of race: "Continually life / is a hunt below
the tousled surface / of pubic hair's blond shock, or jet" (*Dead Roots*, 17).
Coloureds are always searching for themselves at the most primal point
of origin, the female sexual organ, trying to determine their racial identity. Are they strands of the "blond" or the "jet?" Or are they an indecipherable blend of the two, "tousled" bastards born out of the process of
interracial commingling?

As befits the status of "bastards," especially in an apartheid society
founded upon the notion of racial purity, coloureds are not and cannot be

fully recognized by either constituency. The products of a "bastardized" past, to invoke Nortje's terms, coloureds have always been compelled to regard their history—and their very South African-ness—as a consequence of biological accident. They are derived from the "blond" European invaders and the black indigenees, partially affiliated to both but without a "natural" home with either. There are no essentialist affinities for this community (although this does not deter the poet from his tendency to essentialize all coloured women), all allegiances—to community, race, nation—are the result of historical context and ideological commitment. Coloured South Africans give voice to the challenges of affiliation that confront the hybridized body: Where do they belong, racially?

This is an investigation that Nortje maps in broad, but suggestive, historical terms, in "Native's Letter":

> *Memories apocryphal*
> *Of Tshaka, Hendrik, Witbooi, Adam Kok,*
> *Of the Xhosa nation's dream*
> *as he moonlights in another country:*
> *But he shall also have*
> *cycles of history*
> *outnumbering the guns of supremacy.* (Dead Roots, 117).

With their variegated racial background, coloureds struggle with the conflicting demands of their bifurcated black and white histories. Alone among South African communities, coloureds have affiliations with what Nortje calls, in an earlier line, the "blue strings of the blood" and the "memories apocryphal" of black struggle. The reference to "Tshaka," and the way the venerated Zulu leader is seamlessly linked to coloured leaders "Hendrik Witbooi" and "Adam Kok" is salient in this pantheon of heroes. "Native's Letter" is Nortje's attempt to situate coloureds not only as integral to the history of black resistance but also equal contributors to it. He makes an alliance between the Zulu warrior "Tshaka," the "Xhosa nation," and coloured heroes "Adam Kok" and "Hendrik Witbooi." Kok is recognized as the founder of the Griqua nation, a community many coloureds trace their roots to. In the ideological landscape of "Native's Letter," a symbolic unity between these two communities is forged and celebrated, grounded as it is in the optimism of historical inevitability. Nortje's hope for disenfranchised unity resides in that moment when the "cycles of history" will "outnumber the guns of supremacy"—when black South Africa will triumph over the violence of apartheid and the many devastations it has wrought. Unlike so many of Nortje's poems where coloureds are only partially affiliated to either blacks or whites, or, as is more often the case, where their affinities are split, "Native's Letter" is a moment of full, unqualified ideological affiliation: The issue of a separate coloured political identity is rendered both moot and mute by these historic alliances. "Native's Letter" is a poem in which the racial ambiguity that marks, or mars, the condition of being coloured is overcome, transcended by an accommodating paradigm of South African blackness.

But the difficulty of (partial) affiliation demonstrates exactly Donna Haraway's claim that "experience is about contradictory and necessary connection." Caught in that contradiction of having to choose between the proverbial "wire and the wall," coloureds are not so much unable to choose as they are confronted with the limitations of choice. Even if they choose, say, the black South African majority over the white minority, that act of affiliation does not invalidate their complicated historical links to the other community. To translate Nortje's poetry aphoristically into Haraway's terms: The need, desire, or commitment to choice cannot overcome the racial contradictions so indelibly etched into the coloured experience. Roots, even dead ones, can be traced, and they cannot be psychically truncated—in the absence of historical wholeness, the fragments of memory are sutured to produce a sense of community, no matter how disparate. Even after the act of "debauchery," this history cannot be cut off at the root.

Roots

The country he loved and left, and against himself and his own gradual divorcement from a creativity his person could not sustain.

—Richard Rive, "Arthur Nortje: A Poet of Rare Distinction"

Posthumously issued, Nortje's *Dead Roots* could not have been more aptly named. The title resonates with the kind of ambiguity so endemic to the coloured condition. *Dead Roots* suggests both the desire to and the impossibility of tracing coloured roots because they are so indistinct, so genealogically untraceable as to be "dead," so lost in the history of sexual encounter between Europe and Africa. As Nortje says of his family background in "Night ferry": "Origins—they are dim in time, colossally / locked in the terrible mountain, buried in seaslime, / or vapourized, being volatile" (*Dead Roots*, 88). It is this barely repressed "volatility," roots remotely visible or shallowly "buried in seaslime," that makes coloureds search intently for their lineage. Nortje's sense of "roots," however, differs from Rive's in that the poet is preoccupied with the biological—the (in)exactness of bloodline—while the novelist concerns himself with the cultural construction of identity—"routes," in the Stuart Hall sense of the term, where it designates the process of cultural production and a series of sociopolitical practices rather than a genealogy. These formations of "roots" and "routes" are not so much distinct as they are interdependent, delineations of the past, history, biology, and a conception of identity that complement, overwrite, and inform each other. Both these formations have sharp and jagged edges, points of engagement that sometimes come into conflict in Nortje's poetry and Rive's fiction; more often, however, they perform different rhetorical functions for these two coloured writers. Rive is simply less concerned with "roots" than he is with "routes," he is not unconcerned by the former; the same is true, in degree, for Nortje. He is a poet intensely aware of how the transAtlantic "routes" he has traveled have impacted his understanding of his "roots"; he is cognizant of how he needs a cartography of his body to help him map his place in the world.

The unattainability of coloured roots serves only to make them, in Nortje's verse, more desirable to and necessary for the coloured community. In the penultimate stanza of "Night ferry" the poet offers a playful and childlike description of this desire: "knock knock goes / the who's there night" (*Dead Roots*, 89). If Nortje is mimicking a children's game, however, it is with an assured sense of uncertainty and suspense: In response to the "knock, knock," anyone could answer, anyone could claim responsiblity for the paternity (the maternal line is firmly established) of the coloured body. The search for roots is, at the most fundamental level, a struggle for racial clarity: It marks the attempt to distinguish one set of racial antecedents from another and, in the process, recognizing the impossibility of that project. Nortje ultimately sets himself the unachievable task, ideologically engaging as it is, of disentangling black Africa from white Europe in the coloured body. Coloured South Africans, then, face an unending and inherently paradoxical struggle. In trying to discover who they are, where they come from (genealogically), they are confronted with the impossibility of that project—having been "buried" so deeply, the white and the black strands of coloured roots have melded into each other, become part of each other, demonstrating how inextricably linked and intertwined they are.

Even as Nortje adopts the Rive approach and dedicates his work, in key moments, to locating coloureds as organic to the black experience, so he finds himself facing the dilemma of racial bifurcation at every turn. As committed as Nortje is to eviscerating "colouredness"—in crucial instances—in the cause of a larger, incorporative blackness, his work reveals to him how deeply resilient, how rooted in (albeit miscegenated) history, the coloured experience is. Coloured is a substantive political category, a genuine, historically constructed set of social practices, traditions, and mores. Dennis Brutus thus only attends to half the equation (of the coloured experience) when he argues that Nortje has been "denied cultural roots in his own society."[9] Coloureds have undoubtedly been "denied" a firm cultural connection, but this crisis of identity is transformed, though only through considerable effort, into a moment for serious ideological reflection. Nortje's poetry is most salient in the canon of South African literature in those moments when he does not consistently try to overcome the condition of partial affiliation or disaffiliation. Troubled as he is by the numerous ways his roots have been deliberately obscured or hybridized, Nortje uses his poetry (as do others, though less self-consciously, such as Rive, Davids, Brutus, and Matthews) to search for, to enunciate the complexity of, to map the growth of, and, most important, to give public voice to the history (and historic) production of "coloured roots."[10] Conceived in hybridity, Nortje's verse makes a strong case for why the coloured community's experiences cannot be willed or written out of existence. Rather, theirs is testimony to the difficulties and the possibilities of living in, through, against, and with the vagaries of racial hybridity. In a society riven by polarized racial cleavages, the coloured experience marks the partial—and, some might cynically argue, Lilliputian—triumph of hybridity over racial essentialism. But what Rive, Nortje, and Davids's work offers, above all else, is instructive: an object lesson in the project of reflecting upon, constructing, and maintaining a critical notion of community. It is also, as Nortje's all too brief life demonstrates,[11] a marker of the exacting demands of that process.

For these complex reasons, Nortje's (and coloured South Africans') roots are anything but "dead." They are, to the contrary, all too vibrantly alive. The coloured community's understanding of itself in South African history and politics is, as Nortje reminds us in "Affinity (To Maggie)," incredibly sensitive to the touch of poetic memory: "Lack of belonging was the root of hurt / the quick child, he must travel" (*Dead Roots*, 62). Damaged at the "root" himself, Nortje seeks to overcome that "hurt" through putting distance between himself and his birthplace. Developing the theme sketched so elliptically in "Affinity," "Waiting" shows how the raw memory of indistinct racial roots cannot be dulled through exile, two issues closely linked in Nortje's work:

> *Origins trouble the voyager much, those roots*
> *that have sipped the waters of another continent.*
> *Africa is gigantic, one cannot begin*
> *to know even the strange behaviour furthest*
> *south in my xenophobic department.* (Dead Roots, 90)

Even from the vantage point of "another continent," of having escaped the physical degradations of apartheid, disenfranchised South Africans are still inexorably drawn not only to contemporary events there, but to the memory of their lives in that "xenophobic department" at Africa's southern tip. Coloureds are "troubled" by their "origins" because of the contradictions at the root of this community's experience; coloureds are confronted daily with the memory of bilateral exclusion; even if those forms of disenfranchisement take markedly different forms, they remain paradoxical victims of "xenophobia." Unlike black South Africans, coloureds are disliked, despised even, not because they are different but because they are insufficiently different. Their similarity, the physical resemblances between coloureds and whites, coloureds and blacks, explains the treatment they receive. Products of an earlier xenotropic desire, coloureds are now the recipients of a complicated xenophobia—a double-pronged rhetorical and ideological attack with a black edge as well as a white one.

Inextricably linked both to black and to white South Africans, the history of partial affiliation has meant, however, that during disenfranchised resistance there could be transient integration into the black struggle. In strategic political moments, such as the one "Native's Letter" celebrates, coloureds could locate themselves in the broader disenfranchised community. It is, however, precisely because these moments are so rare that they assume such a disproportionate import: Their significance is equal to their exceptionality. Yet because of apartheid's preoccupation with racial stratification, its "belief in essential racial difference,"[12] as Werner Sollors puts it, coloureds could only retrospectively situate themselves within the ranks of white South Africa. In the era of apartheid, as Nortje portrays in "Dogsbody half-breed," the links to coloureds not only were legislatively proscribed, but psychically denied:

> Yet glittering with tears I see you pass
> In armoured cars, divided from yourself
> By golden fortune (Dead Roots, 104)

In the process of whites being divided from themselves, they are of course also denying coloureds access to a community they in part derive from. Moreover, whites are doing so violently and with a deliberately impaired historical vision—the "armoured cars" offer only a myopic, narrow view of the world. If the "armoured car" is a symbol of violence, then it is also by that same token a sign of power—it separates the enfranchised from the disenfranchised, white from coloured, indian, and black.

Nortje's community is, to invoke the title of Sarah Gertrude Millin's work on a coloured protagonist struggling to make his way in colonialist South Africa, "god's stepchildren." Evoking this phrase in the evocatively entitled "Autopsy," Nortje animates it with a painful sense of the rejection endured by coloureds:

> *knowing only the blond*
> *colossus vomits its indigestible*
> *black stepchildren like autotoxins.* (Dead Roots, *52)*

A progeny unclaimed both by its (presumably black) mother, for whom it is a "toxic" "stepchild," and by its "blond colossus" father, who rudely dispels it as an "indigestible," "Autopsy" demonstrates more than the extreme liminality of the coloured community. Coloureds are incidental to the functioning of the South African body politic, a minority within the disenfranchised black majority they generally, albeit with certain reservations, identify with.

Moreover, in the terms of "Autopsy," coloureds contain, if not a potent means of self-destruction, then a powerfully unsettling psychic capacity. They function as "autotoxins," a poisonous substance originating within the organism (the coloured body politic) itself. (The metaphor of the chemically self-destructive is made all the more resonant by the poem's title. Within the framework Nortje has constructed, the "autopsy" he is conducting is an ominous one: He is dissecting the body of the "deceased" and "dis-eased" coloured community; this poem is Nortje's study of the how ill at ease coloureds are in the South African body politic, a measure of how "rife" coloured "malcontent" is.) The Nortje oeuvre identifies these "autotoxins" variously as the racial ambivalence, the genetic and cultural hybridity, the doubt about its proper ideological location, and the uncertain, shifting political affiliations that have historically characterized the coloured experience. In his two collections of poetry, of which the acclaimed *Dead Roots* is decidedly more important than the slight *Lonely Against the Light* (which contains many of the same poems published in the more widely acknowledged work), Nortje returns time and again to the project of engaging the coloured psyche and then ridding it of these toxic instabilities.

Most striking about the language of narrative autopsy, which wends its way through the paradigm of apartheid-induced migration ("The world receives them, Canada, England now that the laager / masters recline in a gold inertia / behind the arsenal of Sten guns") that forced disenfranchised South Africans to seek refuge in the old world and the new, are the metaphors of silence the poem opens and closes with (*Dead Roots*, 52). Compelling as "Autopsy's" introductory ("My teachers are dead men. I was too young / to grasp their anxieties") and culminating lines ("The luminous tongues in the black world / has infinite possibilities no longer") are individually, it is the conceptual connections between them that give the poem its rhetorical strength (*Dead Roots* 52). Often read as a tribute to Dennis Brutus, a politically committed writer who was Nortje's high school English teacher in Port Elizabeth, "Autopsy" records the young poet's high regard for the tribulations that his mentor endured. Brutus was a model of intellectual resistance before and after he was captured by the authorities and imprisoned with Nelson Mandela and other ANC leaders on Robben Island—described in the poem as "a little-known island prison which used to be / a guano rock in a sea of diamond blue" (*Dead Roots*, 53). On escaping South Africa, Brutus made his way to the North American metropolis where the fiery poet quickly became politically active but never quite settled. Brutus, like Nortje, was seldom without vibrant memories of home—"Origins," in his poem "Waiting's" memorable phrase, "trouble the voyager much" (*Dead Roots*, 90).

The 1966 poem "Autopsy" takes ideological aim at a slightly different, but not unrelated, target. The poem issues a death certificate that is hubristic but not premature in political and literary terms—although the voice of coloured opposition, and indeed disenfranchised resistance in general, was more variegated than Dennis Brutus and more resilient than Nortje suggests here. 1966 proved a year fraught with difficulty. "Autopsy" articulates more than a personal tribute, it functions as a requiem for another cultural movement. Politically, 1966 was an especially draconian year in terms of apartheid legislation, particularly with the full-scale implementation of the Group Areas Act, which saw countless disenfranchised communities deracinated, and the sustained crackdown on the resistance movement. It was also a culturally significant year because it marked the moment in which, as Richard Rive put it with a gravitas not in the least unwarranted, "South African literature became white by law." Having produced the first expression of urban black South African fiction, a dynamic articulation of the turbulence and excitement characterizing life during the opening twenty years of the apartheid regime, the country's disenfranchised suddenly found themselves without a voice of public resistance. In place of the short stories, published in such journals as *Drum*, *New Age*, and *Fighting Talk*, which had protested forced removals, captured the spirit of the Defiance Campaign, followed the Rivonia Trial, and cast a simultaneously celebratory and critical eye on cultural developments in the black (and, to a lesser extent, the coloured) ghettos, there was an ominous silence. 1966 saw the proscription of the works of Brutus, Ezekiel Mphahlele, Peter Abrahams, and the entire *Drum* magazine school; frustrated by and powerless at their banning, most of the writers—Rive and James Matthews were among the few who remained in South Africa—went into an exile from which none of them, Brutus and Mphahlele excepted, returned. The narrative, if not the literal, bodies of Nat Nakasa, Can Themba, and Arthur Nortje would feature prominently on the table of the coroner who conducted South Africa's "cultural autopsy." In 1966, the "luminous tongues" of the "black world" Nortje so admired were now legally restrained, the "possibilities" for disenfranchised articulation, to say nothing of resistance, were "infinite . . . no longer" (*Dead Roots*, 54).

Exile and Denial

> *Every voyage is the unfolding of a poetic. The departure, the cross-over, the fall, the wandering, the discovery, the return, the transformation. If traveling perpetuates a discontinuous state of being, it also satisfies, despite the existential difficulties it often entails, one's insatiable need for detours and displacements.*
>
> **—Trinh T. Minh-ha, "Other than myself / my other self"**

The opening lines of "Native's letter," arguably Nortje's most brilliant poem, show how he can only deal with the pain of exile through denial:

> *Habitable planets are unknown or too*
> *far away from us to be*
> *of consequence. To be of*
> *value to his homeland must the wanderer*
> *not weep by northern waters, but love*
> *his own bitter clay*
> *roaming through the hard cities, tough*
> *himself as coffin nails.* (Dead Roots, 117)

Struggling to cope with his remove from his "habitable planet," the poet attempts to undermine his ability either to connect with or influence events in South Africa. (Nortje ends "Native's letter" on a different note, claiming a rare artistic agency for himself. In the memorable final couplet that Rive so admired he writes, "for some of us must storm the castles / some define the happening." Here Nortje ascribes a signal importance to the poet's role in writing and interpreting history.) Clearly, however, the memories of those "uninhabitable planets" are too immediate, poignant, and raw to be forgotten. Home is of pressing and continuing "consequence." As much as exile is about the impossibility of home, it is simultaneously (and inversely) about the ways the psychic links, images, and memories of home impress themselves into and onto the exile's daily life. Home can be temporarily denied, but it can never be permanently forgotten—home is portable because the exile carries with(in) him or her the all too pressing memory of that once "habitable planet." Remembering even as he (unsuccessfully) tries to forget, Nortje writes himself back into

South Africa at the end of "Native's letter." One of the possibilities exile affords is reinscription; the poet can "define" not only the political "happenings," but his relationship to those events—he is "storming the castle" of his own strong tendency to symbolically disenfranchise himself.

Complex and as full of unexpected responses as Nortje's description of exile is, there can be no gainsaying the tremendous sense of loss and longing that girds it. His verse is replete with images of loneliness: "What journals of the exile yesterdays / will be carboned in that grate" ("Poem"); "my nomad loyalties, regardant, / find nothing to remember or prepare" ("September poem"); and, perhaps most searingly, "The soul decays in exile" ("In Exile"). Although there is no disputing that Nortje's "soul decayed in exile" (his poetry testifies amply to that), the experience of external exile has an a priori and internal dimension that should be neither forgotten nor obscured by his writings from London and Toronto. Many elements of his exile abroad, alienation, the loss of love (and a loved one), the sense of not having a place in a society, the futility of life, the drinking and the drugs, and the all too evident self-loathing, were already manifest before he left South Africa's shores. Nortje had already suffered significant psychological damage by the time he went to Europe and North America. Much of his early poetry, such as "Soliloquy: South Africa," "At Lansdowne Bridge," "Song for a passport," and "Pornography: Campus," reveal his deeply troubled relationship to South African society. Nowhere, however, does he bring together all the elements that characterize his exile more poignantly nor reveal his despair so insistently as in his 1963 poem "Hangover":

> *In case of foul play, imprisonment, death*
> *by drinking (identity is*
> *268430: KLEURLING*
> *Pretoria register, male 1960)*
> *inform Mrs Halford, Kromboom Road, Crawford*
> *House without garden. No reward.* (Dead Roots, 10)

Nortje was, tragically enough, all too prescient about his own demise, dying as he did seven years later in Oxford from a reputed drug overdose (though the coroner returned an open verdict). A poem overburdened with self-indictment, "Hangover" captures succinctly the anonymity (reducing himself to an identity number), the hopelessness, the nondescriptness ("House without garden"), and the worthlessness of his life ("No reward") that he so frequently felt. All, of course, emanating from his perception of himself as a coloured—or "KLEURLING," in the poem's terms, as Nortje lapses into the harsher-sounding Afrikaans designation. As Berthoud observes, this sense of racially induced alienation gives

Nortje's exile a sharply materialist edge, an implicit connection between psychic debilitation and the context that produces that condition: In Nortje's expression of the "chronic mutilations of exile—the endless processions of departures, depressions, dissipations and disgusts that drives through his verse—what we will discern if we are able to look beyond the neuroses is nothing less than the pressure of history."[13]

The "pressure of history" affected Nortje's exile in a variety of ways, compelling him to think critically about his disaffiliation. If "Hangover" marks the origins of his exile and "Native's letter" charts his symbolic reattachment to South African society, then it is "Autopsy" that demonstrates the complicated links between the two processes. This poem shows how the experience of being coloured is integral to Nortje's exile, revealing the deep connection between internal dislocation and external alienation; "autopsy" becomes the ideal opportunity for self-reflection, for an in-depth self-analysis. He writes in "Autopsy" (with a sentiment approaching an indifferent self-pity), "too nominal an exile / to mount such intensities of song"; here Nortje not only belittles his status as a political "exile," an experience that is significantly different from his conception of himself as a psychic alien from and within the land of his birth, so debilitated is his sense of unbelonging that he almost renders the disenfranchisements of apartheid redundant (*Dead Roots*, 52). As much as anything, Nortje is mocking the incommensurability between the legitimacy of his claims to exile and the disproportionate "intensity" of his protest songs. By undermining the political authority and ideological validity of his own "exile" ("I am no guerilla," he insists in "Questions and answers," distinguishing himself from the political activists who left South Africa to fight the apartheid regime), Nortje implicitly draws into question coloureds' right even to "mount" "protest songs," let alone to sing them with any degree of "intensity." As coloureds, what is the maximum pitch and volume their "intensity" is allowed? Should their "intensity" strike a different tone, be sung in a different register? Salient again in these brief lines from "Autopsy" is coloured marginalization within the ranks of disenfranchised South Africans. For this community, exile is a double-edged sword, the domestic and diasporic blades cutting equally with the sharpness of disempowerment.

The "Kleurling" in "Crawford," Cape Town easily became the "dispersed Hotnot" abroad. A contraction of the derogative "Hottentot," a name given to the indigenous Khoi community by early European colonialists and freely used by white South Africans to describe coloureds in the apartheid era, Nortje's international deracination served only to amplify the domestic dislocation of his community. "Question and Answers," his critique of the homeland system that disenfranchised and uprooted blacks in the land of their birth ("Cape Town to Transkei on the

night train: / Matanzima ruled there a land / of eroded paupers"), translates easily into an analogy for Nortje's experience of exile and his struggle to achieve some of kind of psychic rootedness: "I will not to salvation
move / being transplanted from here to there / endorsed out to some
alien native land" (*Dead Roots*, 139). (Kaiser Matanzima was appointed as
"homeland" leader of the impoverished Transkei, the metaphoric "home"
of the Xhosa people, by the apartheid government; his status was rejected
by most disenfranchised South Africans, especially those in the antiapartheid movement who labeled him a "puppet" of the regime.) "Salvation," the process of securing a home, is clearly revealed here to involve
much more than geographical relocation. The act of being "transplanted,"
whether through enforced removal or through an (in)voluntary trans-
plantation from one place to another, does not guarantee a safe psychic
space—Nortje remained, at home and abroad, an "alien," a subject denied
the status of a "native" in the land of his birth. To be coloured was, for
Nortje, not so much to be displaced (as black people were from the "white
cities" to the devastated "Matanzima" homelands) as it was to be permanently without a settled sense of place in South Africa. *Dead Roots* marks
the struggle to anchor, however precariously or tentatively, the coloured
community in the South African landscape.

Notes

1. Jacques Berthoud, "Poetry and Exile: The Case of Arthur Nortje," *English in Africa* 2, no. 1 (May 1984), 8.

2. Arthur Nortje, "Natural Sinner," *Dead Roots* (London: Heinemann, 1973), 137.

3. The issue of patriarchal lineage is present in Rive's work through (a reluctant) suggestion. Rive created a couple of fictions to deal with his absent and unknown father: He suggests, in *Writing Black*, that his father was either white or an
African-American seaman who had a liason with his coloured mother. Although
the merit of either of these explanations is especially plausible, it evinces—in
muted terms—the same kind of desire that Nortje has for "naming" the "lost" father.

4. "Native" has, historically, been a pejorative term used to demean, infantalize,
undermine, and discredit the indigenous population, a designation that had currency as recently as the late 1960s in apartheid discourse. When Nortje employs
the term in this poem, he is signaling its peculiarly South African—not colonialist—usage.

5. Edward Said, "Intellectual Exile: Expatriates and Marginals," *Representations
of the Intellectual* (New York: Pantheon Books, 1994), 59.

6. Earlier in "Intellectual Exile," Said also invokes Lamming, briefly discussing
the "pleasures of intellectual exile."

7. Zoe Wicomb, "Shame and Identity: The Case of the Coloured in South
Africa," *Writing South Africa: Literature, Apartheid, and Democracy 1970–1995*, ed.

Derek Attridge and Rosemary Jolly (Cambridge: Cambridge University Press, 1998), 92.

8. Ibid., 92.

9. Dennis Brutus, "In Memoriam: Arthur Nortje, 1942–1970," *Research in African Literatures* 2, no. 1.

10. Similarly, Hedy Davis argues in her reevaluation of his work that "Native's letter" marks the moment when "at last Nortje comes to realise that he can not deny his roots, that he must come to terms with his 'own bitter clay'" (Davis, "The Poetry of Arthur Nortje: Towards a New Appraisal," *UNISA English Studies* 18, no. 2 (1980): 29.

11. Richard Rive recognizes the costs of this process when he writes, "But running parallel to his creative development was a personal disintegration caused by a sense of rootlessness with which he was unable to come to terms" (Rive, "Arthur Nortje: A Poet of Rare Distinction," *Weekend Argus* (Cape Town), 15 December 1973).

Although one could take minor issue with Rive about his understanding of Nortje's "rootlessness," his larger point about the psychic havoc exile played with the poet's life is beyond dispute.

12. Werner Sollors, *Neither Black Nor White Yet Both: Thematic Explorations of Interracial Literature* (New York: Oxford University Press, 1997), 35.

13. Jacques Berthoud, "The Case of Arthur Nortje," *English in Africa* 2, no. 1 (May 1985), 5.

3

Searching for Colouredness: Reading the Poetry of Jennifer Davids

By "reading" I mean our exposure to the singularity of a text, something that cannot be organized in advance, whose complexities cannot be settled or decided by "theories" or the application of more or less mechanical programs. Reading, in this sense, is what happens when we cannot apply the rules. This means that reading is an experience of responsibility, but that responsibility is not a moment of security or of cognitive certainty. Quite the contrary: the only responsibility worthy of the name comes with the removal of grounds, the withdrawal of rules or the knowledge on which we might rely to make our decisions for us.

—**Thomas Keenan,** *Fables of Responsibility*

In a conception of "reading" that recalls Nietzche's critique of "epistemologies" and "knowledge," Thomas Keenan throws into question the process of literary or political interpretation by evacuating the very "grounds" on which we make decisions about the "meaning" of a text or a historical situation.[1] Keenan invalidates the "rules," the "mechanical programs," and the "theories" that guide us as we interpret narratives. His provocative understanding of "reading" is, however, indivisible from another issue: declaring insolvent the commonly held notion of "responsibility." Keenan implicitly rejects "responsibility" as a set of philosophical precepts and ideological commitments according to which we act with a sense of expectancy; "responsibility" cannot be conceived as a series of actions that produce consequences or scenarios (affirmative or negative) that can be anticipated in advance. "Reading responsibly" is, rather, an act of ideological courage: interpretation without guarantees, but not without the commitment to producing meaning through serious critical engagement.

Keenan, whose "argument is situated, somewhat tenuously, between literature and politics,"[2] unmoors us as readers because there is no longer a fixed set of principles to chart our course by. *Fables of Responsibility*'s paradigm privileges hermeneutic "unpredictability," the "singularity of a text," above rote interpretations—knowledge that can be "organized in advance." We can no longer be, to borrow a line from T.S. Eliot's "Preludes," "Assured of certain certainties." Only with the liquidation of "certainty" can "responsibility" exceed itself as merely a colloquial practice (we behave "responsibly"), a metaphor, or a "fable"—a (more or less fantastical) story that contains within it a valuable lesson. Only when there is the "certainty of uncertainty" can we extract from our reading of the narrative a "moral," or a meaning, that has interpretive substance.

If, however, reading is "what happens when we cannot apply the rules," then how do we read without being, in Keenan's sense of the term, "irresponsible?" How do we discover the "singularity of a text" when we have "organized in advance," if not a set of rules, then certainly a discursive framework? What happens to a philosophical context in which texts are taken to be in dialogue with each other because they share a number of ideological premises? How do we read for "singularity" when a group of issues are presumed to be at stake?

Because of the highly mediated relationship of Jennifer Davids's poetry to the issue of "colouredness," Keenan's provocative inquiries assume an especial pertinence in this chapter of *Midfielder's Moment*. Unlike Richard Rive, whose work is committed to transcending "coloured" identity, and Arthur Nortje, whose poetry is fully immersed in the painful vagaries of that experience, Davids's writing on the subject is of a more elusive quality. In her slim volume, *Searching for words*, "colouredness" is a political condition for which we have to "read" not only with assiduousness but with "uncertainty." Davids's poetry displays no obvious preoccupation with "racial hybridity," the founding tenet of Rive and Nortje's writing; her poetry has none of their a priori ideological fixations, nor their literary fixities. In the place of Rive's tableaus of coloured life in District Six and the scarred psyche of a deracinated and miscegenated protagonist in Nortje's *Dead Roots*, is a more lyrical, contextually ambivalent landscape. *Searching for words* is full of wry verse and cryptic metaphor, vacillating between a grounding in and a disconnection from a locale identifiably South African.

Adept wordplay and amorphous settings are, as this stanza from "In a King-Coloured Garden" shows, integral to her poetry:

> *And I at this point*
> *on this planet*
> *on a bit of earth*
> *no bigger than my two feet*
> *placed together*
> *hold this moment*
> *of the universe*
> *contracted within me*[3]

The image of a "bit of earth / no bigger than my two feet" is a particularly apt metaphor for Davids's poetry. Her verse is characterized by circumscription, a politically modest and deeply personalized—"no bigger than my two feet"—tilling of her "bit of (literary) earth." The self-imposed restrictions on her poetic scope stand in contradistinction to the "grand narratives" of disenfranchised unity, antiapartheid opposition, deracination, and the psychic costs of coloured identity at the core of Rive and Nortje's work; while they write about matters of "planetary" significance (in so far as South Africa can be construed of as a "planet"), Davids tends only to the affairs of her "garden."[4] Although her verse is frequently not embedded in the South African soil in the ways that Rive and Nortje's work is culturally and biologically grounded, respectively, her ability to affect her surroundings is seldom in question. In the telling "moment," she is able to reduce and control the world. The "universe," she claims with a boldness that is at once surprising and disarming, "contracted within me"—the world can be made to fit the scale of her "garden." In a telling moment of agency for a disenfranchised South African woman, Davids is able to shrink the "universe" to a manageable size.

Davids's poetry is not distinguished primarily from Nortje's, however, because her vistas are "contracted" and his horizons are expansive. (Her sense of the universe is, in other poems, often as extensive as his.) Nortje and Rive's work is marked less by the breadth of subject matter than by the singularity of ideological focus: the condition of "colouredness," a preoccupation not shared by Davids. Her poetry, even more than Rive's fiction, attempts to transcend (however unsuccessfully) not only colouredness but South African-ness; whereas Rive's aim is to achieve an unqualified blackness, her verse strives, in its best moments, for a kind of late-modernist, post–World War II, Western feminist universality. As this chapter will demonstrate in our reading of *Searching for words*, the key concern is whether or not we can "apply the rules" of reading for "colouredness." In engaging Davids's verse, do the "rules" that lend themselves so readily to Rive and Nortje's writing apply to her at all? An investigation which, of course, begs a further series of crucial questions: Can Jennifer Davids be categorized as a "coloured" writer? How does gender effect her status as poet? Do we read female (coloured) writers differently? Indeed, what happens to her poetry if we examine *Searching for words* through an ideological lens that is potentially inappropriate? Is this a misreading? What happens to her work when it is misread? Or worse, as has been the case with her poetry, what are the consequences of critical neglect? In place of Rive's sense of political responsibility, commitment to the preservation of community (or the memory of a community) in the face of apartheid violence, what are we to make of *Searching for words'* "irresponsibility?" How do we explain Davids's inability, or refusal, to declare her "colouredness?" (Davids is, in this regard, not unlike Bessie Head, another coloured woman writer who refused her racial categorization.) Is this an implicit commentary on the added marginalization women experience within the coloured community?

A Different Kind of
South African Poet

There is always a price of incorporation to be paid when the cutting edge of difference and transgression is blunted . . .
Stuart Hall, "What Is This 'Black' in Black Popular Culture?"

In reading read *Searching for words*, we must properly locate Davids on the map of disenfranchised South African literature. Her status as "anomalous" coloured artist (when set alongside her male counterparts) can only be comprehended when she is critically engaged in her proper literary persona: a woman producing a distinct brand of poetry at a particular moment in disenfranchised South African writing. Davids's verse complicated (some might even say contradicted) the prevailing ethos of 1960s and early 1970s "black" fiction (in Rive's inclusive understanding of the term) on three crucial counts: She was writing poetry in an overwhelmingly prose-centered era; she was a woman producing verse in an unreflectively patriarchal moment; and she was influenced (mainly, but not exclusively) by European modernists at a historical conjuncture when disenfranchised South African writers were trying to forge an independent literary tradition. Although Protest figures such as Rive, Ezekiel Mphahlele, and Bloke Modisane were deeply versed in and drew on this same Western canon, their own work spoke of a commitment to produce a black literature that spoke of, for, and in a language derived from the particularity of their local experience of disenfranchisement. (Davids's other influences included the American Sylvia Plath and white South

African poets such as the Afrikaner Ingrid Jonker and the English-speaking Sydney Clouts, all of whom accentuated, in different ways, her distance from other "black" writers.)

In the company of the Black Consciousness School, which succeeded the Protest Writers in the late 1960s and early 1970s, Davids cuts an alienated figure. Although she belonged chronologically to this generation of disenfranchised writers, Davids did not share their primary ideological influence: the black nationalist philosophy articulated by Steve Biko (the political activist who advocated an ideology of black cultural pride that was shaped by the anticolonialist movements in sub–Saharan Africa—and, not so apparently, impacted by black political developments as they were unfolding in the United States in the 1960s). As a literary movement in South Africa, the Black Consciousness School comprised a grouping of poets centered around Mafika Pascal Gwala, Wally Serote, and Oswald Mtshali, all of whom who were Davids's historical contemporaries. Aesthetically, however, she shared little in common with these poets. Although they all wrote in the same genre, Davids's verse lacked their ideology, anger, and the recognizably South African images and metaphors that so forcefully propelled their work.

Most important, it was her being a woman producing verse in an unreflectively patriarchal moment in South African literature that distinguished her from the Black Consciousness movement. The alienation of the female poet is relayed by a critique of patriarchy moving in its poignancy. In the poignantly, and ironically, titled "Poem For My Mother," she writes:

> *That isn't everything, you said*
> *on the afternoon I brought a pome*
> *to you hunched over the washtub*
> *with your hands*
> *the shrivelled*
> *burnt granadilla*
> *skin of your hands*
> *covered by foam.* (Searching for words, 3)

The distance between the two women, mother and daughter, is revealed most obviously in the mother's distrust of (and disregard for) poetry: an alienation in which generational difference is overwritten by the pathos of an implied class distinction—the working (class) mother who cannot relate to her daughter's newfound interest in the world of literature, a privileged environ where the mother has no place. (Despite the several difficulties that riddle the relationship between Davids and her

parent, "Poem For My Mother," her verse is remarkably free of the recrimination that marks Nortje's writing. Davids, unlike Nortje, is not so
much angry with her mother—though she is that in moments—as she is
rendered emotionally and linguistically distant from her mother by her
poetry; the mother is psychically removed, but never indicted. Paradoxically, the "poem" Davids writes "for" her "mother" exacerbates the divide between child and parent instead of closing it. This gesture, however, regardless of its apparent futility, nevertheless distinguishes the
female coloured poet from the male: Nortje always writes poems against
his mother, either implicitly or explicitly.)

For the hardworking older woman, "hunched over the washtub," poetry represents an indulgence—the very opposite of the intensely physical labor in which she is currently engaged. Writing a poem has little—if
any—material or utilitarian value to "hands/covered by foam." To the
woman who labors so intensively with her hands, the poem her daughter has just given to her—in attempting to honor her—represents nothing so much as the luxury of the intellect; for someone who has worked
so hard that her skin has "shrivelled" to the color of "burnt granadilla," a
poem certainly "isn't everything." These two women are related by
blood but removed from each other by the very different uses of their
"hands": The value the mother places on domestic labor makes her
daughter's poetic labor indecipherable and inaccessible. Thus the
daughter's language, her most honest form of expression and love (dare
one say?), is precisely what makes her efforts to communicate with her
mother so unsuccessful—her "words," she finds, are "being
clenched/smaller and smaller," reduced to a bitter nothingness. The un-
satisfactory mother-daughter relationship, the mutual incomprehensibil-
ity, in this poem stands as a metaphor for Davids's place within disenfranchised South African literature: Her "words" have been "clenched"
to the point where they are no longer "small": they have been completely
washed away by the "foam" of critical neglect, a condition this chapter
will, in part, seek to redress.

Because of genre, gender, and a debt to (colonial-ist) European art,
Searching for words compels an engagement with the issue of coloured
identity against a societal canvas that bears only a passing resemblance to
the landscape in which Rive and Nortje produced their work. Confronting
us as she does with issues her male counterparts do not consider, writing
about South Africa and metropolitan England from an unusual creative
angle, Davids has "removed" our customary "grounds" of "reading" for
colouredness. At the very least, she significantly alters our understanding
of the aesthetic and ideological terrain inhabited by Rive, her fellow Cape
Town writer, and Nortje, her fellow (sometime) London exile.

Where Poetic "Value" and Politics
Are Both Presumed Missing

once breath-blown like spores
now platooning on quadrangles of soil
small green
poems.
—Geoffrey Haresnape, "At the Nurseryman's"

As much as Jennifer Davids's writing demonstrates the lack of an os-tensible engagement with "colouredness," so politics of the Protest and the Black Consciousness literary variety is also noticeably absent from *Searching for words*. Apart from "Location Fires" and "For Albert Luthuli" (and even these are politically subdued texts), her poetry is in many in-stances (but by no means always) remarkably free of the kind of strident protest songs that marked black literature of that period. The judgment of her work, scant as it is, can be characterized as idiosyncratically "depoliti-cized"—to coin a phrase that describes how surprising it was for mid-1970s reviewers, all of whom were white and male, to encounter a disen-franchised poet whose writing did not conform to the paradigm of Protest or Black Consciousness literature. The view of Davids as poet sans politics reveals itself most saliently in the reviews *Searching for words* re-ceived on publication in 1974. Most of the reviews were unflattering, and were marked by a commentary that ignored the political impact (and im-port) of her work.

The mode, the quantity, and the content of criticism to which Davids has been subjected have conferred upon her an anomalous status as dis-enfranchised poet. Not only has her writing been critically disregarded, but it has been restricted mainly to a batch of newspaper reviews—a genre that is valuable, to be sure, but one that is seldom able to substitute for a more reflective engagement. All the reviews attend to her failings as a wordsmith rather than focusing on how her work represents the experi-ences of her oppressed community. (In adopting this approach, Davids's reviewers missed the point of her work entirely: Her originality resides not in her refusal to be representative of a particular racial experience, but in her ability to do so elliptically.) Other black and coloured writers, re-gardless of their creative talents, were read by critics first as "political spokespersons," and evaluated only secondarily as literary craftspersons. For the journalists who reviewed *Searching for words*, however, this critical order was not so much reversed as halved. She was measured, unlike Nortje or even Dennis Brutus (an intensely political poet gifted in his command of the language), strictly by her ability to turn a phrase and to mold metaphors. On this count, in the view of the mainstream press, *Searching for words* was thought to have some potential, but was ultimately judged a poetic failure. Robert Greig blames Davids's obtuseness for her inability to fulfill her literary promise. Her "poems," he suggests, "are leading up to saying something but Jennifer Davids—is it self-consciousness?—won't let it through."[5] (The only dissenting evaluation came from *The Cape Times'* John Bowers, who thought that Davids wrote with a "lyrical clarity, and a delicacy of observation which shape her poems to a satisfying coherence."[6] It was precisely these qualities the other reviewers found lacking.)

The most scathing of the reviews of *Searching for words* appeared in the Johannesburg *Star* and the *Rand Daily Mail*. Damning with faint praise, the *Star*'s reviewer finds the "verse . . . rich with ideas, few of which have been nailed into the page for the reader, it is a poetry still in embryo, in need of considerable reworking before it can succeed."[7] Davids's lack of craft is an appraisal shared by Brian Ros of the *Rand Daily Mail*, except that he absolves the editor implicitly admonished by the *Star* with a clever pun: "One can only regret that Jennifer Davids's *Searching for words*, despite editing by veteran Jack Cope," Ros argues, "is too well named at times."[8] Not even the "veteran Jack Cope" could compensate for Davids's inability to find the right words. For that failure of craft, the poet herself—and only she—is accountable.

The overwhelmingly negative response to *Searching for words*, however, is in and of itself an insufficient explanation for why, in the twenty-five years since her volume was published, Davids's work has only twice been the subject of academic scrutiny. On both occasions the critic is a fellow poet (and university-based scholar), the admiring Geoffrey Haresnape. Although neither of his essays on Davids focuses on her individually or deals with her work in any depth, he is appreciative of the "paradoxes, ambiguities, ironies, antinomies"[9] so integral to her poetry. These very poetic qualities that Haresnape praises serve only to reinforce the prevailing view that Davids's writing is deliberately muted on matters of politics— the political is adeptly obscured, rendered idiosyncratic, a disguised but not sufficiently sharp presence in her verse. *Searching for words* belongs, in Haresnape's mind, to a rare school of South African poetry and prose composed of artists who "may well make comments upon the political scene, but will not be subservient to it. They steer away from the easy sentiment, the easy answer, and the easy anger."[10] Instead of the "easy sentiments" and "anger" so (understandably) widespread amongst South African authors, Davids sketches nuanced portraits of "individual experience"; in place of the "easy answers" she waxes existential, asking the "big, difficult questions: What is society? What is love? What is hatred? Who am I?"[11]

Haresnape's refusal to distinguish between the social significance of these questions, to not ascribe to "What is society?" a greater urgency than "What is love?," offers a critical perspective alert to how these complexities—or what some might view as a contradiction—inform and affect Davids's verse. For her, "Who am I" is frequently an inquiry refracted through the prism of "What is hatred?," thereby adroitly transforming the singular "I" into a collective experience[12] that addresses the consequences of oppression and the impact it has on subjugated communities. These are both important questions, with Davids assigning the former a poetic weight rare within the body of disenfranchised writing. *Searching for words*, we might suggest, has a preference for engaging larger social issues in the guise of narrowly "poetic" ones. So much so that Davids (and here she diverges from Haresnape's theory) seldom, if ever, interrogates as "big questions" how apartheid's injustice impairs the lives of millions of blacks or how the government's "hatred" of blacks has resulted in disenfranchisement, deracination, and poverty. But Davids and Haresnape are both, obviously, deeply interested in how "committed poetry" can be "more diverse, will pick on unexpected themes, will probably be less clamant, sometimes amusing or shocking, sometimes introspectively lyrical."[13]

In the brief lines from "In a King-Coloured Garden" and as the reading of "Departure at Dawn" demonstrates, Davids has already shown herself to be amongst the least "clamant" and most "introspectively lyrical" of South African poets, both of the enfranchised and the disenfranchised variety. But "who" she is as a disenfranchised artist, and why her work has received such anomalous critical attention, is only nominally explicated by the "unexpected themes" of her poetry. Indeed, sometimes her unusual treatment of "expected themes," such as the condition of exile that percolates so uneasily beneath the surface of "Departure at Dawn," lends her poetry—in its finer moments—a spare, Hopkins-esque strength. (Gerard Manley Hopkins was one of her main influences.) Reading Davids on her terms depends, without the benefit of ideological certainties, on a critical recuperation of *Searching for words*. It implies less a wholesale rebuttal of her detractors than it does a more demanding engagement: reading, in Keenan's sense, against the hardened grain of South African literary, political, and gender expectation. It is, in the narrowest sense of this project, to deliberately read her against the profiles of her coloured male counterparts; such a reading can only obtain if we map the differences between Rive (or Nortje) and Davids, are alert to the ways these writers are in dialogue (that is, we deploy Keenan's concept of "singularity" in an expansive, dialectical sense without sacrificing the "individualism" that girds his thinking), and attend to the tropes that dominate her verse.

Davids's poetry relies, more than Nortje's, upon tension, the creative energy released through her use of "antinomies." This tendency is evident in the pithy opening stanza of "Departure at Dawn:"

> *Even the cranes*
> *On this quay*
> *Have a kind of strength*
> *(like grief)*
> *their iron framework*
> *etched against the lightening sky* (*Searching for words,* 11)

Here Davids's central image, the imposing "cranes," is alternately representative of "strength" and symbolic of weakness. "Grief" itself functions dialectically, coming to stand for resilience—the capacity to acknowledge, absorb, and transcend loss—and frailty. By transforming "grief" into a cryptic metaphor for strength, Davids subtly undermines the almost cinematic resonance of the "cranes." As much as the "cranes" dominate the skyline, so they are rendered vague, almost fragile, outlines against the "lightening sky." In this poem the cranes, symbols of a phallic and muscular power visible for miles around, are imbued with an ironic authority. They derive their "strength" not from their vertical (and visual) salience, but from their capacity to hunker down and perform their utilitarian, almost domestic function: "When ships depart / they do their work / silently and well," the second stanza goes, recalling the stolid, unmoving "silence," if not the unspeakable anger, of the maternal parent in "Poem for My Mother": The mother is the stationary "crane" to the daughter's "departing" ship. In an incongruous, difficult to imagine visual inversion, the anonymous cranes (tall as "they" are), are "hidden" by the shorter ships—these "departing" vessels dominate the poet's view of the harbor. The "cranes" become, through Davids's juxtaposition, reliable, faceless workers who execute their tasks "well." Because of their discrepant smallness, Davids cannot celebrate the "cranes" for their spectacularity. Not only do the "ships" inexplicably dwarf them, but their steely beauty pales in the face of the "lightening sky:"

> *not silent like the cranes*
> *on the grim line of the quay*
> *is this tautening of the sky*
> *for the birth of brightness* (*Searching for words,* 11)

Instead, she is impressed by their rootedness—they remain when the "ships depart"—because it is in tension with her own tendency toward transience. In contrast to the poet's peripatetic inclinations, the symbolic "fragility" of the cranes reveals itself to be, almost contrary to the poet's expectation, a strength that she cannot match—a fortitude, borne out of the simple capacity to remain in one place, that assumes a near-heroic (though understatedly so) status in "Departure at Dawn."

In this regard, the title of the poem is telling because the steadfastness of the "cranes" can be read as an implicit rebuke of the writer herself. After all, she is one of those disenfranchised "ships" fortunate enough to be able to "depart," at the height of state repression, from apartheid South Africa for some three years in metropolitan London. Between 1969 and 1972, she spent time in the British capital, first as a dishwasher in Chelsea and then as a member of the staff at a Southwark school. Although Davids's poetry is remarkably free of the angst that both (occasionally) debilitates and (more often) enriches much of the poetry Nortje composed while in Canada and England, it is not without psychic perturbation. As is customary with Davids, "Departure at Dawn" uses the unlikely tension between the "cranes" and the "ships" for its visceral impact and, more important, as metaphor for authorial displacement. The narrative motor of this poem, the psychological tumult, is displaced from the metaphoric "ships" onto the forces of nature:

> *But at a point*
> *on the horizon*
> *the tension tightens*
> *and grows until all*
> *of the towering sky*
> *has a turbulence (Searching for words, 11)*

Unlike the anonymous "cranes" that continue to "do their work," "silently" endorsing the value of permanence and of remaining in South Africa (regardless of what one does, politically or otherwise), the "departed ships" are soon confronted by the "turbulence" brewing in an ominously "towering sky." There is clearly too much foreboding for this to be an ordinary leaving—it is not so much a "departure" as a psychic break of substantial proportions. The "ships" that "depart," these lines suggest, are being indicted for leaving the troubled shores of (the port of, presumably) Cape Town and so they are, consequently, met with a "dawn" devoid of romance. This "dawn" promises neither the newness of day nor hope; it offers nothing but a portentous and stern judgment from on high.

With nature enthroned as a powerful moral authority, Davids is able to encode the unspeakable guilt about the privilege of (temporary) exile as a series of natural phenomena—the "tense horizon," the "turbulent sky." "Departure at Dawn" culminates, not surprisingly, in an apocalyptic upheaval. This disaster follows, ominously enough, the "birth of brightness":

> *dispelling in one groaning*
> *upward movement*
> *all the rigidity*
> *of the horizontal (Searching for words, 11)*

Even if the "sky" is the arbiter and dispenser of cosmic justice, the final destruction here emanates from within. In contrast to the vertical strength of the "cranes" there is, in the telling moment, an implosion of the "horizontal": the earth-shattering violence of being destroyed from inside while the surface remains ostensibly intact, a devastation made all the more painful because it remains invisible, undetectable because of its interiority. Not as spectacular as a natural disaster originating from above, the implosion is no less cataclysmic; it is an internal force so disruptive that in a single "groaning / upward movement" everything above it is laid waste. The "rigid" terrain, on which the "cranes" and the poem itself stand, has been eviscerated. In the act of destruction, the poem demands a plumbing of the depth, a reading that will grasp the tensions emanating from beneath the surface. It is as though the deeper psychic (or political) forces that gird "Departure at Dawn" have, despite attempts to repress them, rudely forced themselves to the surface. In place of the silences that hover around the "cranes" and the "departing ships," there are now gaping aporias, psychic holes that cannot go unremarked upon. Like the remarkably textured "grief" that opens the poem (a concept so much of the lyrical richness in "Departure at Dawn" is founded upon), so Davids's poetry can only be understood by unusual means: It has to be critically imploded, read from within so as to render it visible, read from beneath the harsh grains of (coloured, as an apartheid) racial designation, gender discrimination, and a propensity for deracination.

"Departure at Dawn" demonstrates how Davids's poetry does not directly pose the "big, difficult questions," those interrogations that Harensnape finds so rare in South African literature. Rather, those "questions" (and they are integral to her writing) are embedded deep in her verse, concealed by redolent scenes and unlikely "antinomies." (These "big questions" have a canvas broad and panoramic in natural and industrial scope, yet poems such as "Departure at Dawn" are utterly devoid of human occupation—if not profoundly human concerns. It is a telling absence, one that draws attention to itself because the metaphor of loss and internal devastation is so resonant that it dwarfs even the "cranes" and the "horizon.") The issue of Davids's exile is submerged, in this instance, beneath layers of richly embroidered natural phenomena and arresting industrial images, always already metaphors for a profound set of psychic and political "turbulences." Because this poem is so stripped of human life, "Departure at Dawn" presents itself as a reluctant political interlocutor. The questions it raises, however, nevertheless demand answers that have a real pertinence for the lives disenfranchised South Africans. From beneath the taut metaphors, "Departure at Dawn" calls the poet to account for the breaking of ties, the choice of exile, the costs it exacts from an individual (and the unmentionable community of stationary "cranes"), and all the attendant psychological debris strewn on this deeply punctured landscape.

As much as any of her poems, "Departure at Dawn" simultaneously confirms and exceeds Haresnape's estimation of Davids's work. She only intimates "big questions," never explicitly asking "What are the consequences of exile?," registering them instead, as Ralph Ellison's Invisible Man would have it, on the "lower frequencies," in a voice barely audible but tellingly incisive. Davids's questions are poignant (almost always tinged with a sense of loss, or the potential for loss), self-reflective in tone, reduced to a crucible of simplicity: "Am I an exile?" She poses her inquiries in so furtive and adept a literary way as to almost obscure its presence. But it is, more important, a profoundly personal and ideological question. It concerns an issue that goes to the core of her identity as a disenfranchised South African: She went to England not as a political exile, as several members of the resistance movements (and Protest School) did, but as an educated middle-class coloured woman who was in a position that enabled her (both economically and politically) to do so. She went abroad not out of political "necessity" but out of an interest in and a cultural familiarity with metropolitan life, a different but not comparable kind of necessity.

The narrative reticence about exile, the condition that cannot speak its name (except as metaphor), is well founded. Davids, ever astute in her comprehension of politics, recognizes that she (much like Nortje's conception of himself) has no legitimate claim to the status of "exile" as it applies to disenfranchised South Africans. Instead, she crafted "Departure at Dawn" as a muted contemplation on the experience. Even so, this poem grasps—despite its author's reluctance—the pain of that "one groaning / upward movement" experienced by all disenfranchised South Africans, regardless of their motivation for leaving. In Davids's case, "upward" performs two contradictory narrative functions: It is a marker of Davids's class position, the mobility she enjoyed because of her material conditions (her ability to move "up" in the world); and it suggests a kind of involuntary expulsion, the experience of having been rejected from a body to which she wanted to belong. So powerful is the image that it is as though Davids is being birthed, thrown against her will in "one groaning movement" from one physical body (South Africa) to another (England). Her class status may have improved, her experience of the world may have expanded, but the psychic damage seems to be more difficult to calculate, so strong is her sense of having been evicted. "Departure at Dawn" succeeds in this, and several other ways, as a contemplation on exile because of a rare admixture of empathy, political modesty (because the poet has an acute sense of her relation to the political struggle and so ensures that it does not deteriorate into confession of guilt), and a faith in metaphor to simultaneously conceal and reveal.

The Impossibility of Disguise

A space that is internally marked by cultural difference and the heterogeneous histories of contending peoples, antagonistic authorities, and tense cultural locations (original emphasis).

—**Homi Bhabha, "DissemiNation"**

Immanuel Wallerstein describes the designation "coloured" as the most "nettlesome"[14] of South Africa's four racial categories. It is an estimation that Davids, whose engagement with her community's identity is so tentative, circuitous, and hesitant, might well agree with. Her poems, more than anything, appear reluctant to grasp and grapple with the "nettle" of colouredness. Davids's reticence on the subject is so pronounced that she never once mentions the word "coloured" in *Searching for words*. But "colouredness" is by no means absent from her work. Instead, coloured identity is present mainly through implication, a salient absence, and by unspoken comparisons (and links) to the black community.

Engaging her primary community represents a struggle of immense proportions for Davids, an explicit recognition, naming an implicit association she studiously seeks to avoid. The abundant metaphors, so central to her poetry, enable her to achieve a deliberate distance from the question of colouredness; it is a technical device that secures for her a lyrical alienation and a problematic (even prelapsarian) innocence. "We acknowledge / the meeting point to be / ignorance," she claims in the opening lines of "A Possibility of Speaking." The extent of Davids's efforts to remove herself directly from the experience of assuming a coloured identity is mapped with a singular vagueness in this poem:

> *we are locked*
> *by particular associations*
> *of ages in us*
> *to the symbol*
> *the word*
> *and cannot reach*
> *beyond the limits*
> *of this cycle* (*Searching for words*, 8)

How "particular associations" are restricted, who defines the "limits," what the "symbol" and the "word" might be, are all momentarily unclear. Unerringly evident, by contrast, is Davids's commitment to "reach beyond" those proscriptions, to write herself out (and outside) of that narrowly circumscribed "cycle." Her determination to "reach beyond" offers itself as a subtle, but stubborn, refusal to be racially categorized as a coloured woman; her anomalous positioning challenges the rigid fixities of apartheid's classifications. Davids is always working against the dominant terms, searching for definitions that are more politically and poetically supple—she is always pruning her verse, tending her plot in the garden of South African literature and politics so that it bears the imprint of her restrained, provocative ambivalence.

In the very next verse of this poem, however, Davids undermines her own tendency for ambiguity by making a key identification: She alludes to the place, and therefore the people, she is writing about (and from):

> *We*
> *I*
> *perched precariously*
> *for one moment*
> *at the tip of a continent* (*Searching for words*, 8)

Through geography (the "tip of a continent" is an obvious reference to Cape Town's location at the southern edge of Africa), Davids identifies the poem's community as coloured. Within the city, and the Western Cape region in general, coloureds constitute the dominant oppressed constituency. Coloureds are represented by the "We" that so swiftly transforms into the "I," which so problematically establishes the speaker in relation to the (if not her) community who inhabit that space at the fringe of the African continent. A community and a point of origin that, it should be said, Davids steadfastly refuses to claim in "Star," the collection's opening poem: "lost in the darkness / the silence / of my birthplace." Paradoxically, her "birthplace" (and by implication the "we" who share it), is brought sharply into focus rather than denied through its articulation as a "silence." A "silence" announced is a complex of events disclosed: Silences draw attention to themselves, provoking interrogations (however surreptitiously) and questions about the process(es) that it is meant to obscure; even "silences" forcefully imposed are more likely to produce than to effectively shut down discourse; even when "silences" are maintained they are, in the Derridian sense of "erasure" (for everything we say we leave several things unspoken), finding a distinct kind of public articulation. Because of the multivalent quality of a "silence," once it is voiced (or even probed), entire (or partial) histories become public, trajectories are mapped, and metaphors are transformed into recognizable moments, communities, and places. In this instance, Davids's place of origin and her apartheid-imposed racial identity are, despite her efforts to disguise them, revealed. The "silence" in "Star" can no longer be concealed, partly because it provokes questions about itself. Why is she "silent" about her "birthplace?" What is she hiding? (Or why is she hiding her coloured origins?) What political or ideological vulnerabilities does "Star" disguise? Since she will not name (let alone embrace) her colouredness, what kind of identity does she desire?

In a tellingly self-reflexive moment in "Camp Site," one tinged with self-recrimination, with the promise of narrative development, and with confusion, Davids begins to explicate why she will not own her coloured identity. At the beginning of the poem, she suggests that coloureds are both morally reprehensible—"Coward / you lurk nameless / in the shadows"—and insubstantial—"you are lost on the air / like smoke." Unlike their black counterparts, coloured South Africans have always found themselves, if not as inconsequential as the "smoke" of a "camp" fire, then certainly "precariously perched" on the nation's landscape. They are, in Nortje's memorable but disturbing phrase, "caught between the wire and the wall"—a precipitous condition emphasized in "A Possibility of Speaking" by the irrefutability of geography. As the poem progresses, however, she challenges this community (and, by implication, herself) that she will neither name nor claim, to "un-lock" the complications of their "particular (racial) associations." To develop the "possibility of speech" that exceeds the "symbolic" and the empty, vacuous "word," she suggests that coloureds have to disentangle one set of historical "associations" from another; this requires undertaking the demanding task of understanding how the layers of "associations"—perceptions of their identity—have impacted and shaped who they are, how they are seen, and how they see themselves.

Coloureds have to, Davids says as "Camp Site" progresses from outright repudiation to subtle probing, "crack the letters" of their name. This community has to decipher its genetic, cultural, and ideological code, grapple with itself seriously, and wrest some meaning—some sense of place, some understanding of its complicated racial location—for itself from this protracted, tortuous experience. Coloureds have to learn how speaking will enable them to overcome the "ignorance" (feigned on the part of the author, in this case) of the meeting between the white colonizer and the black colonized that first occurred on the shores of Cape Town. There is, as Davids so crisply recognizes in "As if This Were Brightness,"

> *A need to break*
> *what is tangled*
> *and useless (Searching for words, 7)*

But the "break" with the entanglements, incomprehension, and "associations" of the past can only take place if it is properly understood why coloured history is "tangled" (or "mangled" as she says a couple of lines earlier). "As if This Were Brightness" demands that coloureds determine which aspects of their culture, traditions, and past are "useless." Mainly, however, coloureds have to learn to how to make the "word" coloured politically usable, to ensure that it is not "mangled" because of misuse or denial—coloured has to be made critically applicable. Coloureds must fashion an identity that is communally and personally efficacious and not, in and of itself, disabling. If it is not, this community will not be able to break the "tangled cycle" of silence—they may even become victims of their own silence, unable to speak for themselves, disenfranchised by their own recalcitrant engagement with how they are "publicly" and "privately" perceived. The very word "coloured," with its multihued, heavily impacted "associations," is at the core of this community's "tangled" history and its complicated relations to other disenfranchised communities. Omnipresent but never once mentioned in this poem, "coloured" stands as the dominant text that will not tolerate its status as (unspoken, barely recognized) subtext. At this crucial juncture, where metaphoric elusiveness (and allusiveness) intersects with an unarticulated political urgency, Davids's verse calls for a reinscription of Keenan's injunction: the need to produce a ground for reading, however tentative or shifting, because the costs of not speaking are so potentially debilitating for the coloured community. The possibility of speaking to, for, and about coloured history, culture, gender, or sexual orientation (so key for reading Rive at certain points) with any measure of "responsibility" seems unlikely. The recognition, however, of a permanent uncertainty, an intellectual terrain that is constantly in danger of being "removed" is what makes the project of "reading responsibly" more, not less, crucial. Because coloureds have seen the "rules" and systems of "knowledge" as applied to them change so often, they are eminently well suited to situating, understanding, and explicating themselves "responsibly"—their sense of political, aesthetic, intellectual, ideological "responsibility" has always, of necessity, been malleable and mobile.

If there is to be any "possibility" of meaningful "speaking" in South Africa, about race, nation, ethnicity, and gender, it should begin at that original "meeting point": "the tip of a continent." That dialogue, the need "To learn how to speak / With the voices of this land"[15] (the title of a Jeremy Cronin poem that clearly echoes Davids's work), has to incorporate all the "voices." Davids's silence about the community that emerged from the sexual desires and ideological conflicts of that historic "meeting point" is deliberate and stubborn (albeit eloquent); this obdurate silence signals the symbolic, and double, disenfranchisement of a region, and thereby its constituents. Coloureds are disenfranchised first by the apartheid regime and second by a poetic silence that will not acknowledge its political or social presence. By refusing to speak the name of colouredness, Davids modulates voicelessness. Colouredness is a name she can problematize, reject, dissociate herself from, but whose existence, affect, effect, and impact she cannot ignore. Nonetheless, interrogating colouredness is a project she conscientiously attempts to undertake in *Searching for words*. A denial as stringent as hers is counterproductive. If Davids is attempting to find a distinct voice through her "search for words," what she calls a "groping / striving through darkness" in "A Possibility of Speaking," a significant aspect of that "search" is borne out of a willful "ignorance." *Searching for words* is a determined, if ultimately unsuccessful, rejection of colouredness as a political identity that has relevance in the struggle for a democratic South Africa.

By deliberately excluding the coloured voice from that conversation, as Davids does, she serves only to draw attention to its absence. The term becomes, in *Searching for words*, a political unspeakable rather than an ideological label that has an uneven purchase on a particular disenfranchised community's sense of (it)self. Unless coloured is engaged, critically, self-consciously, and with a complex sense of its attendant history, it will become one of the most cutting—and disruptive—terms in the linguistic "garden / overgrown with words / sharp as blades" Davids is tending in *Searching for words*. In some senses, as "As If This Were Brightness" suggests, Davids's is a futile, anti-Sisyphean "search":

> the inch by inch
> struggle for a clearing
> where I'll find
> the voice I clearly hear
> the only voice I want
> of an up-moving sun
> breaking my horizon. (*Searching for words*, 7)

Unlike the genuine courage of the mythical Sisyphus who repeatedly endeavors, unsuccessfully, to roll the huge boulder to the top of the mountain, Davids's "struggle" self-consciously averts the very object she should be attempting to move. For every time Sisyphus courageously turns back for yet another (futile) effort to push the rock up the mountain, Davids momentarily (and willfully) shifts her gaze from colouredness. It is a "rock" that her poetry dissociates itself from and circumvents when it should constitute, paradoxically, the internal logic of her verse, the very epistemological ground she literally, not metaphorically, stands upon: her own unacknowledged colouredness and the sociopolitical conditions out of which she produced her poetry. There is, throughout *Searching for words*, a desire to exceed boundaries that is ultimately unfulfillable: the commitment to "breaking my horizon," a distant, fixed point that is neither defined nor transcendable. (A desire repeated in *Searching for words* as the poet strives, with no greater success, to see "beyond the line of trees.")[16]

Much as the damned Sisyphus (the perpetual futility of his effort was a punishment for his greed) is not deluded in his endeavor, so the title of this poem suggests that Davids understands the contingencies of her struggle. Her insights are a conditional "as if" rather than an indisputable "brightness." But other moments contradict these ambivalent perceptions; in "As If This Were Brightness," Davids is not so much blind to her struggle as she is stubbornly obtuse about interrogating why it is limited. She will not account for why her struggle is (permanently) compromised: "I'll work in this half-light," she says in a line full of hybrid resonances, "as if it were brightness" (*Searching for words*). This is a "half-light" replete with implications about impaired vision, racial ambiguity, and, read alongside Nortje's "Dogsbody half-breed" or Don Mattera's *Sophiatown*, miscegenation. As Mattera says, he lives in a twilight zone, the "fruit of miscegenation and an in-between existence; the appendage of black and white."[17] Unlike Mattera and Nortje, Davids is determined not to account for why she finds herself in this "half-light"—this poetic twilight that is so resistant to the production of her "voice." She does not ask why her struggle is contingent, what it depends upon: Why is only the "half-light" available to her? Because, one is tempted to offer, she is a woman struggling to affirm her voice within (and against) a patriarchal tradition of South African writing? Because she ignores where she comes from? Her origins are, in an ideological sense, different from (but not always independent of) who she is as a political subject: a disenfranchised woman mapping a literary trajectory that will enable her to escape the double historical bind of racialized and gendered Otherness.

Because the poet takes up these issues in so elusive and muted a fashion, or sometimes does not take up them up at all, her "brightness" retains an illusory edge. She does not recognize that to "break" the "horizon" of colouredness (to "crack the letters" of its "name"), to move beyond it (from the "half-light" to uncontingent insights), the racial paradigm has to be engaged. So skilled at disguising the grounds she is operating on, Davids has to—as Keenan says—"remove the grounds" to produce a representation of colouredness, and her own fraught relationship to the identity, that is responsible to "her" community's complicated history. It is unlikely that colouredness can be transcended, but this project can only be imagined—if not attained—by working through what it means, what social and ideological purchase it has, how it influences a constituency's view of itself, and, of course, why colouredness resonates in particularly potent ways in certain moments, in certain contexts, for some members of this community rather than others. Much like Sisyphus's quest to move the rock demands great effort, so colouredness is an exacting, exhausting condition—a boulder that can only ascend to the mountain top of nonracial democracy by acknowledging it as a political and cultural identity.

Notes

1. As Gayatri Spivak points out, Nietzsche was a "philosopher who cut away the grounds of knowing" (Gayatri Chakravorty Spivak, "The Translator's Preface," *Of Grammatology* (Baltimore: The Johns Hopkins University Press), L. Corrected edition, 1998.

2. Thomas Keenan, *Fables of Responsibility: Aberrations and Predicaments in Ethics and Politics* (Stanford: Stanford University Press, 1997), 1.

3. Jennifer Davids, *Searching for words* (Cape Town: David Philip, 1974).

4. The "garden," as Illena Rodriguez in her work *Home, Garden, Nation*, is a powerful metaphor in Third World's women's writing. Rodriguez argues that the "garden" is both a personalized and a domesticized signifier for a larger, but difficult to articulate in a patriarchal world, feminist concern with the issues of nation and female citizenship in that political construct. Davids's relationship to the South African "nation" is problematic, one of the richnesses of her verse, but her poetry is certainly cognizant of the ways society restricts the spaces available to women.

5. Robert Greig, "Best and Worst of Current South African Poetry," *To the Point* (April 1974).

6. John Bowers, "Poets' Voices," *Cape Times* (Cape Town), March 1974.

7. "Elusive Verse," *Star* (Johannesburg), 11 April 1974.

8. Brian Ros, *Rand Daily Mail* (Johannesburg), 29 April 1974.

9. Geoffrey Haresnape, "The Creative Artist in Contemporary South Africa," *English in Africa* 8, no. 1 (March 1981): 49.

10. Ibid.

11. Ibid.

12. The notion that the "I" can stand as a metaphor for the community has a certain resonance and history in feminist writing. In her "biomythography," *Zami: A New Spelling of My Name*, Audre Lorde develops this concept by suggesting that the autobiography is a communal document, a genre where the individual "I" is a composite figure, a representative of the larger social construct and not the singular protagonist.

13. Haresnape, "The Creative Artist," 46.

14. Immanuel Wallerstein, "The Construction of Peoplehood: Racism, Nationalism, Ethnicity," in Etienne Balibar and Immanuel Wallerstein, *Race, Nation, Class: Ambiguous Identities*, trans. Chris Turner (New York: Routledge, 1991), 72.

15. Jeremy Cronin, *Inside* (Johannesburg: Ravan Press, 1987). One of the most important poems in this collection is called "To learn how to speak," a work that clearly recalls Davids's writing.

16. Davids is "searching" for a "clear voice," one without dissonance, a disenfranchised community that resembles Rive's, but exceeds his poetic scope. It is also, however, a political vision that is unusual—and deeply buried—in her verse; it represents a lyrically disjunctive impulse, but one that sheds yet another light—from a different viewpoint—on her poetry. "I ache," she writes longingly in "Clear," "for words to pinpoint / and coalesce." In a society so fraught with racial conflict, historic inequities, and full of "fury / at the centre," Davids's is a quest for univocality—a form of articulation, a poetics, and a politics that seem difficult to attain in a divided South Africa. This poem marks one of the rare points where Davids's work seems to even gesture toward the influence of the Protest School. Motivating the desire for a single "voice" is the "search" for a singular political identity—one not available within the ambit of colouredness and that lies just beyond the "horizon" of colouredness. Davids is a poet reaching beyond herself, beyond the immediate and familiar, for "blackness," the only disenfranchised experience her work validates. Blackness appears to be the only political heritage she claims, albeit through allusive metaphor and a strangely unportentous imagery. In place of Rive's problematic, fractured, achieved, and intensely political sense of "blackness," Davids offers a understanding of the concept that is largely confined to natural tropes; these tropes, however, function as loaded—but inefficacious—political signifiers. Poems such as "Star," "Dead Tree," and "Location Fires" pivot upon a "blackness" that is as remarkable for its alignment with natural imagery as it is for the portent those tropes are intended to convey. "Location Fires" makes this point amply: "The stars tonight / are blue backyard fires / studding the black / location of the sky." The most obviously political of the poems, a "location" is the colloquial (and derogatory) name given to the sparse, structurally underdeveloped, and impoverished urban living areas to which blacks were restricted (as opposed to the coloured "township"), "Location Fires" is richly textured and bristling with ambivalence.

The "blue backyard fires" that burn so brightly "tonight" are not, of course, a substitute for a dark, starless night. They constitute a constant feature of "location" life. The dominant experience of the "location" is a grimness that Nature cannot counter. In the "location" the "fires" have not only replaced the "stars," they have become the "stars"—the "stars tonight," as Davids so succinctly reasons, "are blue backyard fires." The metaphor has been literalized by poverty and disenfranchisement, the "location" is so circumscribed that it has become a galaxy unto itself. The unnatural absence of the "stars" thus come to stands less as a metaphor than an indictment of the structural and material lacks endured by the "location's" inhabitants. There is no electricity to black homes and so the "fires" provide the only heat and light on which the residents can rely.

So effective has this structural deprivation been that the poet's effort to implicitly invest "blackness" with the capacity to threaten, although it is unclear who or what is susceptible to attack, emerges as impotent. "Burning / From Langa to Nyanga / the fires are hidden / the landscape is flattened / frightened and silenced."

The "fires" that "stud the sky," punctuating the black presence at the edge of this white and, more important, coloured city, ultimately reveal themselves as "frightened silences" ("silences" that are aware of their inefficacy rather than "silences" that provoke interrogation), "flattened" voices that have no public resonance. The "fires," that most incendiary symbol of political upheaval, are so obscured by geographical remove that they are "hidden" from view, signifying nothing so much as black disenfranchisement; these "fires" represent sustenance and survival, not resistance.

17. Don Mattera, *Sophiatown: Coming of Age in South Africa* (Boston: Beacon Press, 1989), 21.

4

"Theatre of Dreams": Mimicry and Difference in Cape Flats Township Football

Football is not a matter of life or death, it's much more important than that.

—Bill Shankley, Former Manager of Liverpool Football Club

The "most damaging blow against apartheid,"[1] the English editor and author Anthony Sampson suggests, was the "sports boycott."[2] In view of the pivotal role that decades of sustained internal opposition, economic sanctions, and diplomatic pressure played in securing a democratic South Africa, it is difficult to regard Sampson's claims as anything other than an exaggeration. Culturally, some might validly argue, the boycott by artists, actors, writers, and musicians was more important than the sports one. The refusal to "play Sun City," as guitarist Stevie van Zandt described the musicians' prohibition on performing at the homeland venue, was hugely influential in alerting audiences about the conditions of life in South Africa—in some cases, artists educated their audiences about apartheid. There can be little doubt that the "Sun City" boycott impacted a more numerous and international audience than those affected by or interested in the cancellation of a rugby or cricket tour to the country.

However, the argument advanced by Sampson, an anti-apartheid white liberal with a longstanding interest in black culture (he was the editor of *Drum* magazine, a major mouthpiece for the first generation of urban black South African writers), cannot be summarily dismissed. South Africa is, as current Trade and Industry Minister Alec Erwin might argue, too "sports mad" a society for an easy rebuttal. In an earlier incarnation Erwin was a trade unionist, so he was well placed to evaluate the role of sport from a position quite unlike that of Sampson: "Not all societies that have gone through liberation struggles have had in sport such a central political place as we had in South Africa."[3] Allowing for the awkwardness of Erwin's phrasing and the predictable difference in emphasis, with the ex-trade unionist clearly in favor of the sports boycott and the *Drum* editor more taciturn about his position on the subject, the minister and Sampson both acknowledge its centrality in the anti-apartheid struggle. It is not surprising, then, given the substance of Sampson's and Erwin's arguments, that barely had Nelson Mandela been released from prison in February 1990 than white athletics administrators began to (successfully) clamor for the termination of the sports boycott. Plans were made, almost immediately, for a South African cricket team to visit India, for an Olympic squad to participate in the 1992 Barcelona Games, and for rugby tours to and from the country to commence. It is also no coincidence that all of these teams were dominated by white personnel. White South Africans were especially, but by no means exclusively, all too eager to take the sting out and slightly amend Sampson's phrase, that "most damaging of anti-apartheid blows."

Much as during the apartheid era, however, some sports were treated more equally than others. Certain codes of sport were better positioned for the admission (or readmission) to the international arena; these sports were better organized because they had greater financial resources—better facilities, ready access to the media, and stronger links to international bodies, despite the boycott. Like every other feature of apartheid society, sport bore the imprint of segregated life—often in politically salient ways. Sport, and sports journalism, was not only raced but classed and ethnicized. The main codes, rugby, cricket, and football, were all assigned places overdetermined by the cultural stratifications apartheid was based upon—football formed the broad base of the cultural pyramid and rugby and cricket combined to make up the apex.

The most popular sport in the world, football occupies a politically loaded place within the South African cultural psyche. Historically the sport of the nineteenth century British working class (adopted soon after by the French and then the other European proletariats),[4] local football was considered a second-rate code by the apartheid regime and the white press. The Afrikaner government's dismissive attitude toward football served simultaneously as measure of its anti-British sentiments and as a marker of the ambivalent cultural and political relationship it has with its own white, English-speaking population. Historically opposed to the local "English" since the early moments of European colonialism, Afrikaners nevertheless favored rugby and cricket, those gentlemanly codes so beloved on the playing fields of Eton and Harrow;

although they had a long tradition of espousing a Manichean white South African politics (Afrikaners versus English speakers), from the early 1960s the National Party (NP) government increasingly (though not without considerable reservations and misgivings) began to court the "English" vote. Most important, however, football largely was shunned by white South Africans because it was *the* sport of the disenfranchised black masses. In the coloured, black, and indian communities, rugby and cricket constituted minority cultural practices: Football was the code most practiced and revered. Football represented disenfranchised South Africa's cultural "theatre of dreams," to borrow the endearing nickname Manchester United Football Club (F.C.) fans have given their team's Old Trafford stadium.

Football was a marker of the ethnic, historical, and ideological distinctions within the white South African community. Afrikaners read football's preeminence amongst the oppressed as the most culturally explicit evidence of black, coloured, and indian "anglicization." Because of its popularity amongst the disenfranchised, football gave public voice to these communities' propensity to value English cultural practices and artifacts above those the regime held dear—in a word, football was favored, not rugby. (The "anglicization" of South African society was manifested, of course, only secondarily in the disenfranchised communities. It was a process that spoke more volubly of a British colonial heritage that had deep roots amongst the country's white English speakers.) The investment in metropolitan football, both in the disenfranchised and the enfranchised ranks, was helped by the extent of media coverage it received in local English-language newspapers such as *The Cape Times* and *The Cape Argus*. England's professional leagues constituted a staple interest for white, English-speaking South African sports journalism, a practice that impacted the cultural outlook of the disenfranchised. The widespread circulation of English-language newspapers in the disenfranchised communities facilitated (we might even say encouraged, in the Althusserian sense) the interpellation of oppressed South Africans into metropolitan culture. Because local football (of both the professional and the amateur variety) was implicitly denigrated through the media's determined underreporting of it, metropolitan football assumed a disproportionate public import.

The regular, if not extensive, reports about the exploits of Liverpool, Manchester United, Leeds, Chelsea, Tottenham Hotspur, Arsenal, and Nottingham Forest Football Clubs made them, in the absence of a local equivalent, hugely significant. These English clubs became double-edged symbols of sporting accomplishment for coloured South Africans: These metropolitan institutions became football clubs that could be adored but never emulated, creating a cultural desire that was palpable but unfulfillable. Players in the townships of Hanover Park or Mannenberg could admire a goalscorer such as Liverpool's Kenny Dalglish or a goalkeeper such as Spurs's Pat Jennings, little boys could tackle like Leeds's Billy Brenmer or dribble like Forest's John Robertson, but apartheid ghettoized their cultural horizon. They could pretend, not unlike countless thousands of youths in England, Scotland, and Ireland, to be performing for Liverpool in their after-school pick-up games, but they could never hope (unlike their metropolitan counterparts) to actually play for an English League club. "Liverpool" was both a priori and always already a dream, not so much a sign of the distance between metropole and periphery but an indicator of the deliberate circumscription of apartheid society.

Although apartheid reduced the "theatre of dreams" of the disenfranchised to the microcosmic ghetto, the relationship between English and South African township football frequently exceeded and complicated those boundaries. Restricting itself to the final two decades of the apartheid era, this chapter will examine the unique cultural links between the working-class coloured community of the Western Cape and English football clubs. Through a discussion of the mimicry, both of the possibilities it offers and the complex ways it is "surpassed," this chapter will engage the significance of the singular support for metropolitan cultural institutions by the coloured working class. This coloured constituency is different from not only white South Africans but also from its black and indian counterparts, and from its own middle class. The coloured township–English metropolis link is a cultural affiliation that has a long history, one that has endured into the postapartheid moment. This relationship has even thrived during the past ten years because satellite link-ups have made several English games available every week on MNET, the lone South African "cable" station.

This chapter, however, has been circumscribed to the years between 1970 and 1990 because of the era's cultural and historical significance. After some fifteen years of almost relentless struggle against the NP government (beginning with the Soweto uprising of 1976), the end of this era marks apartheid's terminal point—perhaps best remembered simply as "February 1990," the historic moment when Nelson Mandela was released and the black liberation movements were unbanned. As an inaugural moment, 1970 stands less as an absolute historical marker than as a metonym: a sign of deracination, the uneven and lengthy process by which the Group Areas Act had uprooted several disenfranchised communities. One consequence of the Group Areas Act was that it inadvertently facilitated (some might even suggest initiated) the process of community (re)construction for the coloured working class through the cultural appropriation of metropolitan football clubs. Forcibly relocated from urban (and suburban) areas they had occupied for generations to the outlying Cape Flats, the new residents of the coloured townships formed football clubs that borrowed the names of English professional clubs.

Teams from the Cape Flats townships, which from "1970" became the new home of the coloured working class, used their metropolitan counterparts as a template to produce their own football identity. In the process, township teams displayed both familiarity with the metropolitan club and a complicated cultural agency—one where the tendency to replicate the English club coexisted with the latent (or not-so-latent) desire for an independent football identity. Township clubs adopted not only the name but imitated the style of the metropolitan institution—the several Cape Flats teams called "Chelsea" or "Leeds" acknowledged their debt to Chelsea of London or Leeds of Yorkshire by playing the game the way the English clubs did in that faraway league. For all the similarities between the township and the professional clubs, they are, however, misleading in one crucial way: The superficial mimicry, significant as it is, (appears to) undermine the agency of the local football community. However, the choice of names and football aesthetics (to call a club Chelsea rather than Spurs, to play like Leeds rather than West Bromwich Albion), the adaptation of the metropolis to the township, articulates a complex and often disguised agency; it marks a negotiation between idealizing the metropolis and appropriating the cultural values that speak most directly to and of conditions in the townships (and the football aspirations of its inhabitants).

Township football mimicry, the process by which township clubs produce a cultural identity that self-consciously idealizes, imitates, and appropriates the metropolitan original, is remarkable for at least two reasons. First, in an era when the print media dominated sports reporting (an informational monopoly only effectively challenged in the last few years by the advent of satellite television), working-class coloured teams constructed themselves as "Leeds" or "Chelsea" out of a largely "imagined" and truly imaginative sense of who and what the "original" was. They read about "their" teams (English clubs with whom they experienced a real affinity and whose wins and losses were of great consequence to them) in the *Cape Times* and the *Cape Argus*, and then "read" themselves off of those metropolitan clubs. The township residents translated imaginatively from the English city of Manchester to the Cape Flats township of Mannenberg, creating a vibrant, mobile football imaginary out of the "stationary" words (and the few accompanying pictures) on the page. The *Cape Times* did not only transport the township residents to

England, but the Cape Flats fans transported metropolitan football matches back to Mannenberg and Hanover Park—they "replayed" those matches, domestically, in their collective and individual imaginaries, and in their animated conversations about the latest performances of Liverpool, Arsenal, and Spurs.

Second, as Homi Bhabha has so convincingly argued, mimicry is also invariably about difference—"in order to be effective, mimicry must continually produce its slippage, its excess, its difference."[5] The condition of apartheid, the remove of geography, the distinction between metropolitan professional institutions and those of amateur township, questions of race, and even the very process of cultural translation, are all not only obvious but crucial (and even problematic) markers of the "difference" between London and Heideveld's "Chelseas." Mimicry is also, as Bhabha makes clear, about the potential of the imitator to "exceed" the original object or identity. Therefore, as much as township clubs sought to become like their metropolitan templates, some Cape Flats teams "exceeded" imitation. Mostly, however, mimicry is an uneven, hybrid process that comprises different modes (and degrees) of imitation and innovation. Negotiating between their own sense of footballing style and that of their metropolitan models, clubs such as Leeds of Hanover Park and Heideveld sometimes struggled (with greater or lesser commitment) to overcome their status as "cultural derivatives"; for some township clubs, the English model sufficed and they amended their identities only minimally; others, however, attempted to transform themselves, with varying degrees of success, into local "originals."

Although this chapter focuses extensively on the ways amateur township clubs imitated professional English clubs, it concludes with an all too cursory reflection on a working-class Cape Flats institution that throws into question the very process of cultural imitation. Everton Amateur Football Club (A.F.C.) of Heideveld, a highly successful team from a township on the eastern fringes of the Cape Flats, represents an instructive instance of an "original." Everton A.F.C. is a local club that did considerably more than distance itself from Everton F.C. of Liverpool, England: Unlike township clubs such as Leeds and Chelsea, who successfully mimic (in the superficial sense of the term) and achieve an aesthetic symmetry with their metropolitan counterparts, Everton A.F.C. marks the unmooring of the township from the metropolis. The Heideveld club articulates both a distinct agency and a cultural reinscription of Cape Flats football. Everton A.F.C. established itself as not only "different" from Chelsea A.F.C. but as, arguably, the fulfillment of township football's potential for cultural autonomy—achieved without denying the initial value of mimicry.

It's a Cape Flats Thing,
Try to Understand

Now on the Flats the frozen trees
dedicate their broken histories
—Donald Parenzee, "Uprooted"

Unlike white, English-speaking South Africans who supported metro-politan football clubs without the intention of replicating them, working-class coloureds engaged in a deeper cultural imitation. White mimicry was of a shallower and an occasional variety—enfranchised South Africans maintain a sharp distinction between English football institutions and their own domestic clubs. They support Manchester United but they do not attempt to "become" a local version of the English club—they do not call their sides, as coloured township teams do, "Leeds" or "Chelsea." White clubs are more blandly named, taking their identity from local geography rather metropolitan football inspiration. (They are in this way following the English tradition of naming—"Liverpool" takes its name from the city, as does "Leeds," "Sheffield Wednesday," "Sheffield United," and so on. This is the norm in English football; clubs such as Arsenal, from north London, are the exception.) The white club from the Cape Town suburb of Wynberg is called "Wynberg Amateur Football Club" (A.F.C.), Green Point's team is known as "Green Point United A.F.C." More frequently, white links to the metropolis are disguised, borrowing nicknames and sometimes the design of the English side's uniform. Wynberg A.F.C, for example, are also known as the "Magpies," after the English side Newcastle United, and their outfit is an imitation of the metropolitan team's black and white stripes.

White South Africans' highly mediated articulation of its metropolitan affiliation is remarkably similar to that of the (predominantly English-speaking) coloured middle class. Like their working-class counterparts, the coloured middle class supported English clubs passionately but they stopped short of outright mimicry.[6] They took their inspiration from the metropolis (a club such as Battswood, from the coloured section of Wynberg, adopted with tremendous success Liverpool's disciplined passing game as the football model for their team), but the coloured middle class named their clubs after local institutions such as schools (Battswood Teachers' Training College), churches (St. Johns, St. Raphaels, St. Lukes), or, in one instance, directly from the local Young Men's Organization (Y.M.O.). The smaller and more generally middle-class indian community also followed this pattern. They rooted keenly for Spurs or Manchester United, but their clubs were (like their middle-class coloured and white

South African counterparts) more likely to be named after local geography than English football institutions. (Leeds and Chelsea, however, have
a certain following in this community as well.)

Writing about post–World War I English football, Arthur Hopcraft
evokes many of the same sentiments expressed by Cape Flats residents
when they learned the results of metropolitan matches in the 1970s. By
"association with the [metropolitan] team," he writes, "positive identity
could be claimed by muscle and in goals. To win was personal success, to
lose another clout from life."[7] Hopcraft's grasp of the depth of fan identification, the vicarious accomplishment of making tackles and scoring
goals ("by muscle and in goals"), can easily stand as metaphor for the relationship between metropolitan player and a fan from the periphery. The
English writer's poetic tendency ("another clout from life") reveals a passion—if not a discourse—that would not at all be out of place in the
coloured township of Hanover Park where Liverpool results may not
quite be a "matter or life or death," but it is certainly of huge consequence. This kind of psychic affiliation with the metropolis would not be
as understandable in the black townships of the Western Cape. In Langa
and Guguletu, the latter quite literally just across the road from the
coloured township of Mannenberg, a different tradition held sway, one
that we might accurately label a hybrid of the postcolonial and the
"Africanist." Black township footballers cherished a set of cultural practices rooted in local communities and those Third World nations that had
thrown off the shackles of colonialism. Here, perhaps more than in the
coloured townships, it was a country such as Brazil that was admired for
the flair, spectacularity, and individual brilliance of its footballers: The
Brazilian icon Pele was a hero in both Mannenberg and Guguletu. But for
the most part, mimicry reflected a different visage in the black townships:
Pele rather than Dalglish, the Mozambican-born Eusebio (who represented Portugal in the 1966 World Cup) rather than Nottingham Forest's
John Robertson. (As a regional minority, Western Cape blacks also identified with professional football clubs from the north of the country, black
clubs such as Orlando Pirates and Kaizer Chiefs—based in Soweto, the
nation's "black capital." They adopted these cultural models, sometimes
calling their clubs "Young Pirates" or "Young Chiefs.")

As important as the ideological distinctions are that separate working-
class coloureds from their own middle class and from black, indian, and
white South Africans, it is equally difficult to account for these differences. The racially slippery distinctness (because it verges so closely on
indistinctness, the racially elusive that expresses itself culturally and politically) of coloured identity have assumed, predictably, a special pertinence in the postapartheid era. The coloured affinity (that goes beyond
the working class) with the English metropolis have persisted—at the ex-

pense, some would argue—of a deeper interpellation into (and more un-problematic affiliation with) the "new" nation. Nowhere is the resilience and vibrancy of those links more evident than in, ironically, South Africa's 1998 World Cup hero Benni McCarthy—a national icon. A product of the coloured township of Hanover Park, McCarthy's greatest ambition was, as he told a reporter shortly after returning from France, to play for Manchester United. (This from a player on the books of the Dutch champions Ajax, a club infinitely more successful than the English team in European competition.) McCarthy's cultural and athletic desire is telling, both because it speaks so volubly of the continued ideological investment of the coloured working class in English football, and, more important, because it marks the difference between apartheid and postapartheid potentialities. It was during the (extended) moment of apartheid, before the township hero McCarthy could dream of scoring goals at Old Trafford, that the local became a substitute for and an imitation of the metropolis. McCarthy is thus culturally salient, not so much as a player (talented though he is) but as a political sign. The Hanover Park native stands the representative par excellence of enfranchisement's possibilities, the coloured township footballer issued the historic license to legitimately imagine—and perhaps even realize—a cultural scenario his predecessors from the Cape Flats could only dream of. His Manchester United is an entire political epoch removed from the "Liverpool" (that conflation of admiration for the metropolitan institution with the township's capacity for footballing emulation) of the apartheid township. McCarthy's is the literalization, if not the realization, of "Liverpool" as cultural metaphor.

This is a metaphor that, as it turns out, requires a quite literal translation—from English into Afrikaans. Like the majority of working-class coloureds from the Cape Flats, McCarthy speaks Afrikaans rather than English as a home language. In the coloured community, language is a marker of class—as McCarthy's imperfect command of the language demonstrates. English is the language of the educated and financially successful and stable middle class; Afrikaans, often a hybrid version of it, is the lingua franca of the working class. (English-speaking township dwellers are not only in the minority, they understand that their mother tongue is read as an indicator of social aspiration—it articulates either a desire for or a history of a more elevated class position. To speak English is, in crucial ways, to situate oneself outside the dominant experience of the coloured working class. McCarthy's recent acquisition of the language coincides not only with the public demands of his newfound fame but also with his family's relocation to a middle-class suburb. But the choice of English was also, for some families, an anti-NP gesture that transcended class lines.)

The predominantly Afrikaans-speaking township residents are, para-doxically, culturally linked to the two "antagonistic" white ethnic com-munities—to the "Anglos" by sport, to the Afrikaners by language. Through their investment in English football, township residents are thus engaged in dual cultural translations: They convert (and adapt) the met-ropolitan practice into the terms of the periphery through a language that has no vocabulary, or empathy, for football. Working-class footballers must translate English culture into township Afrikaans, a process that in-volves changes in pronunciation (of English names), understanding cul-ture as geography (England as a collection of physical sites, as well as cites), and, most important, a telling instance of the hybridization of the Afrikaans language—a hybridization that is not unusual in township life.[8] In discussing football and their English heroes, township residents suffer the inadequacy of their mother tongue; this inadequacy and their limited formal education produce "football-speak," a language where sentences in English follow phrases in Afrikaans—or vice versa. ("Ek is 'n Liverpool fan" translates as "I am a Liverpool fan," for example.) The technicalities of the sport, however, are almost always described in En-glish so that the metropolitan cultural practice serves a pedagogical pur-pose—people learn to speak a specific kind of English because of their in-terest in the game, not because of the desire for upward social mobility. English football makes language (a second language, in this case) a mat-ter of culture, not class aspiration.

However, the most ironic aspect of the cultural identification of Cape Flats is that the English clubs so admired by the coloured working class were themselves proponents of racism.[9] Only since the mid-to-late 1980s players such as West Ham's Clyde Best (a fixture in the East London's team in the late 1960s) and Forest's Viv Anderson (a key member of the late-1970s championship side) were notable exceptions in a lily-white league. In this regard, the unique team was the West Bromwich Albion side of the late 1970s. Albion contained an array of black talent, with the gifted left winger Laurie Cunningham, the redoubtable striker Cyrille Regis, and the combative midfielder Remi Moses (one of the first black players to later join Manchester United) all regulars in an outfit that played attractive football. (But Albion's moment of fame was too brief and their success insufficient to win them fans away from Liverpool and Spurs. Racial identification could not counteract the tradition of support these other, predominantly white clubs, enjoyed in the coloured commu-nity.) Race and racism thus complicate the township-"Liverpool" cultural nexus. How could disenfranchised South Africans, so keenly aware of the racism in their own society, overlook metropolitan racism? Surely they could not have been unaware of it? How could they, as oppressed black subjects, idealize sports institutions to which they bore no physical resemblance? Was racism displaced racism eviscerated? Were the likes of Liverpool and Arsenal not simply offering an English version of sports apartheid? Was apartheid so heinous a system that it ameliorated all other forms of racial discrimination, especially one mediated (and palliated) by a passion for football? Or was Bill Shankley, read through the lens of Karl Marx, unerringly correct in his assessment of the sport's societal significance: Is football not only "more important than life or death," but so powerful an "opiate" that it invalidates (metropolitan) racism?

Because of the township's powerful "imaginary" bond to the metropolis, the Cape Flats was able to ameliorate the racism inherent to the English game. Because English football represents a certain politics of relief, the racism that should render "Chelsea" and "Arsenal" abhorrent to disenfranchised South Africans instead makes it not only palatable but desirable.[10] As oppressed members of a highly racialized and stratified society, they were well versed both in the obviousness and the nuances of race politics. (English football racism was familiar, but it was not immediate in the way that apartheid affected disenfranchised lives—geography muted the impact, passion rendered it largely insignificant.) Cape Flats football is, by virtue of history, an always already politicized space. From its roots as by-product of Group Areas social engineering, to the tensions with middle-class coloured clubs, to the intratownship team rivalries that mar(k) and sustain the practice, Cape Flats football has been intensely political. For this reason, identification with individual English players or clubs offers itself as a unique ideological space that serves a dual function. It is an athletic arena where narrow political debate is ruled offside, where metropolitan racism is (either tacitly or explicitly) acknowledged but is never allowed to dominate the debate. It is a cultural territory where passion rules, where argument about support for Liverpool as opposed to Manchester United is the norm, where there can be endless debate about the merits and demerits of metropolitan stars such Dalglish, Bryan Robson, or Paul "Gazza" Gascoigne. The symbolic and emotional affiliation with English football provides a relief from the constrictions of disenfranchised South African life: It allows for the heightening of the unadulterated joys of football without the political invocations that are inextricably bound up in it as township practice. Discussion about Liverpool's last performance or speculation about Manchester's chances of winning the league title regulates the political realities that so indelibly mark township life.

In this way the preoccupation with English football represents not only a temporary "escape" from the condition of township life, but fulfills a second political role—this time a more local one. Through their discussions about and their investments in the affairs of Liverpool or Arsenal, footballers from the various teams in the township league are able to converse and make community across local divides—Manchester United fans play for both Chelsea A.F.C and Leeds A.F.C. This complicated conception of community is important in a township environ where clubs are often fierce expressions of regional (sometimes gang-based), which is to say different, sections of the township (sometimes even gang-based) pride, identity, and loyalty. Intracommunity tensions are mediated through metropolitan affiliations because it "depersonalizes" (and in so doing, defuses) local disagreements. Disputes about the attacking merits of Spurs or the defensive shortcomings of Nottingham Forest offer a release for cultural (and political) tensions that would otherwise have no ready outlet. This depth of attachment to metropolitan clubs, rendered effective by its lack of immediacy, enables it to ameliorate local antagonisms. The township league thus derives an "overarching" cohesion from afar, a sense of community produced (incidentally) out of a shared affinity with the English institutions they idealize.

Scoring from the Cultural Rebound

The people who came to support were basically working-class people. . . . It sounds a bit corny but Liverpool really is the club of the people.[11]

—Kenny Dalglish, former Liverpool player and manager

There is a story about Liverpool F.C. in the 1970s that is culturally illuminating even though it is probably little more than apocryphal. The poster in a Liverpool church yard read: "Jesus Saves." Beneath it some wag, undoubtedly a Liverpool F.C. fanatic, scribbled: "And John Toshack scores from the rebound." Such is the passion that Liverpool F.C. aroused in the mid-1970s, when the team boasted talents such as Steve Heighway, Kevin Keegan, and Toshack, that one person's Saviour was merely the foil for another person's goalscorer. Located on the river Mersey in the English county of Lancashire, Liverpool is among the poorest cities in Europe. The "working-class" Glaswegian Kenny Dalglish describes when he got there in 1977 he was increasingly seeing its ranks depleted—as the docks stood more and more idle and the number of factories dwindled, so the working class shrank and the number of unemployables swelled. The elevation of football to the status of religion was thus easily made. Jesus may offer to save your soul, but Toshack, or Dalglish, or Ian Rush, or the current teenage prodigy Michael Owen, are far more likely to save your Saturday afternoon at the club's Anfield Road stadium. Or, as Arthur Hopcraft might have it, an Owen goal might spare you "another clout from life" on Merseyside.

John Toshack's spectacular feats were crucial not only to the economically depressed inhabitants of Merseyside: His accomplishments resonated loudly on the "sandy wastes of the Cape Flats."[12] John Toshack's ability to score from a goalkeeper's errant save transformed him into a cultural lodestar, a metonym for the coloured community's uniquely symbiotic relationship to metropolitan England: Toshack could stand at once as the individual hero, the Liverpool goalscorer, and the composite representative of all the English clubs and their (individual) stars. Toshack is only in the most nominal sense a cultural import. He is a measure of the integration into English football culture of the coloured working class and a marker of cultural transportability in the metropolis: Toshack is the metropolitan star made "native" in the periphery, claimed as hero because his successes and failures affect people's daily lives in the coloured townships.

As complete as the identification with and admiration for Toshack's footballing brilliance is, it also marks a point of cultural disjuncture. Like all metaphors, "Toshack" is a sign of approximation and therefore an indicator of incompleteness and aporias. Ingenious as the act of transporting the Liverpool player from Merseyside to the township of Mannenberg is, key components of metropolitan history do not make it to the other end of the cultural trade route. In South Africa, the journalism on English football is a limited genre, compensating for depth with a mild sensationalism. This mode of sports reporting concentrates on results, moments of individual brilliance and failure, occasional fortuitousness, and a cursory survey of a team's strengths and weaknesses. An "imported" journalism, it is shorn of the nuances familiar to a metropolitan audience—it rarely reflects upon the histories of class and religious caste so indelibly woven into the fabric of English football. It does not, for example, explain Arsenal's long affiliation with the Church of England or Newcastle's affinity with Catholicism; nor does this brand of journalism explore Manchester United's wealth, relative to, say, Southampton's shallow coffers—teams that compete in the same league, but that live in different economic universes. This is not to exaggerate the religious implications of an Arsenal-Newcastle game or to suggest that a Manchester-Southampton encounter is nothing but low-level English class warfare. Rather, these unspoken "conflicts" serve as a reminder of what is lost in the process of cultural translation—a number of subtle tensions are overlooked, vital components of histories are omitted, and the political aspects of football narratives are undermined. Transported to the Cape Flats, "Liverpool" is thus, for all its ideological import, a metaphor focused on cultural identity.

Of course, the lack of political familiarity with the class histories of English football clubs does not mean that the politics of class is not a significant component of township sport. Despite their lack of familiarity with the politics of class so central to Dalglish's description of Liverpool fans, township footballers still grasp his Merseyside populism. Township communities know, even if it is articulated more through inflection and suggestion than through informed critique, as much about the politics of Liverpool as they do about the city's football club. Footballers in Hanover Park understand the conditions of life in the metropolitan city because of the politics inherent to the sport. From its earliest roots in the newly urbanized British and French proletariat of the Industrial Revolution, football has always been, as it continues to be, grounded primarily in working-class communities. "The core values of the game as a professional sport, aggression, physical emphasis, and regional identity, meshed," according to Chas Critcher, "with other elements of that . . . working-class culture, elements carried within its network of small-scale organizations and supportive mechanisms."[13] These values were key to the formation of professional football in Manchester and Liverpool (key cities in the process of nineteenth-century mechanization) and are still manifest in these English institutions. Their "working class" roots make them understandable, if not always intellectually "knowable," to communities on the Cape Flats.

Geographically bounded by the apartheid law, the "regional emphasis" of township football was especially strong—supplementing, and sometimes exceeding, the "physical" elements so central to the sport as township practice. Cape Flats clubs were also "supportive mechanisms," social institutions where sections of a township gathered not only to play or organize for football but to construct a social identity that made them distinct in the township. In Hanover Park, for example, Lansur United A.F.C. supporters and players congregated at the "club house" (a wood-and-iron construction in the chairman's backyard) regularly for matters that were purely social—to play card games, darts, to drink, or simply to enjoy the company of those with whom they shared a cultural identity. For this reason, like their English counterparts, township residents were, on a microcosmic level (specific areas in a township as opposed to inter- or intracity rivalries) fiercely loyal. Such loyalty is commensurate with (and within) the circumscription of the Group Areas Act, which rendered the townships, more individually than collectively, "organic" cultural units; football gave fundamental shape to life in places such as Hanover Park or Heideveld. As cities and as coloured "areas," Liverpool and Hanover Park both used football—in different degrees, of course—as a cultural means to exceed their status as merely sites of labor for capital. Football enables the construction of an identity that transforms the "recreational" into the highly politicized practice. For Liverpool F.C. and its fans, it is a battle between the privileged South of England and the hard-bitten, industrial North; on the Cape Flats, of course, players also give a unique political substance to their "working-class" status. They are not only the South African equivalent of the Liverpool working class: Theirs is social oppression compounded by the realities of disenfrachisement. In the coloured townships (as in a predominantly black Liverpool neighborhood such as Toxteth), class is overwritten, or complicated, by race—even, of course, as metropolitan racism is refracted through (and overlooked because of) the passion of cultural affiliation.

English football's greatest cultural impact registers itself in a complex fashion: a negotiation between the ability of the metropolis to make its own names resonate on the Cape Flats and the capacity of township residents to appropriate those names for their own use. Not so much in the names of its stadiums, Liverpool's Anfield Road and Leeds's Elland Road are recognizable venues but they are ultimately sites impossible to replicate in a community where football grounds are shared by a dozen or so clubs and the very notion of property ownership is alien; people who live in rented "council" houses can dream but not conceive of having a football field belong exclusively to them.[14] The names of English-based players (they are as likely to be Scottish or Irish as English), however, are loaded with meaning. Liverpool's Dalglish and John Barnes, Manchester's Bryan Robson or Gordon MacQueen, or Spurs's "Gazza" set the mythical standard for township players—the intent is to "play like Barnes" or "Gazza." These are appellations adopted or given as nicknames, indicating admiration both for the metropolitan star and the local one. Most important, in a society where apartheid limited the ambitions of the township's residents and restricts their horizons, metropolitan names enable township footballers to express their talents through metaphor—township players become, if only for a single moment or a solitary game, the embodiment of the athletic excellence they so admire and covet. (Through idealization, township football becomes a metaphor for a more general sports condition: expressing what is culturally valuable and admirable through the desire to emulate it. Supporting Liverpool is only a mimetic step away from wanting to play like Liverpool's Michael Owen.) In that brief instance, scoring a brilliant goal or making an incisive pass, local footballers go from wanting to be "Gazza" to making like "Gazza." On this occasion township footballers offer their community, and themselves, a glimpse of what their talents, fully expressed, might look like, how the amateur dreams might be elevated in the stadiums at Ellard Road or Anfield Road. This is mimetic desire fulfilled: the rare occasion when the township and the metropolis conjoin, when the Cape Flats amateur and the English professional can be conflated. In that singular (but not necessarily single), exceptional moment, apartheid's restrictions are brilliantly overcome (as geography is transcended) and the

Saturday or Sunday afternoon encounter is transformed from cultural metaphor into physical (albeit transient) reality.

In his explication of the Scottish football fan's support for the country's national team, Stuart Cosgrove offers a reading that both reflects upon and differs from the kind of projection, identification, idealization, and displacement (of a thwarted football career) found amongst coloureds on the Cape Flats:

> Scottish fans are motivated by a dream, a dream that is past, present, and future . . . a dream that relates directly to the nation and its progress. The dream is one of Denis Law's bicycle kicks, it's Slim Jim Baxter making the ball talk, it's pulling on a navy jersey and it's King Kenny scoring through the English keeper's legs.

(The Scottish fans' "dream" is made all the sweeter by the accomplishments of Denis Law and Dalglish, Scotsmen who succeeded in the English league with Manchester United and Liverpool, respectively.) For the coloured player or fan from the Cape Flats, apartheid South Africa was too divided a country to invoke any discourse of the "nation," even as they struggled alongside other disenfranchised communities to effect that political construct; for this community the "past and the present" has been a seamless continuum of oppression and marginalization. The identification with English football is, then, a profoundly anti-National(ist) Party) gesture by township residents—a measure of their disenfranchisement and their distance from the regime, an all too brief triumph over the devastation of the Group Areas Act.

Although the Cape Flats fans, like their Scottish counterparts, appreciated brilliant ball skills and deft goalscoring, coloured passion and political antagonism did not have a ready cultural outlet, a stage on which it could express itself. Coloureds had no opportunity to do football battle against whites as Scotland did in its annual battle with England, its "Auld Enemy"; for these disenfranchised South Africans there was no satisfaction of witnessing Dalglish inflict the ultimate humiliation—a football practice called "nutmegging," "scoring through the English keeper's legs." Township communities, however, have developed their own highly local versions of adversarial football passion. The football grounds at Bonteheuwel were home to countless tough battles between Sea Point Swifts and Bluegum Wizards, Hanover Park hosted several exciting "derby" games between Lansur United and Surwood United, and at Heideveld fans witnessed many a rousing contest between Everton and Chelsea. The scale of the contest was greatly reduced, but both the intensity—the passion of Cosgrove's Scottish fan was matched on the Cape

Flats even if the terms of the game were markedly different—and some of the identities were instantly recognizable.

What's in a Metropolitan Name?

The name carries within itself the movement of a history that it arrests.

—Judith Butler, *Excitable Speech*

Most of the Cape Flats clubs that adopted names such "Leeds" or "Chelsea" were formed in the late 1960s and early 1970s. Displaced to townships that were being constructed by the Group Areas Act while they were moving in, deracinated coloureds found themselves in a cultural vacuum. When the residents of embryonic communities such as Heideveld and Hanover Park formed the first township football clubs, they did so with few resources. Located as they were in this interregnum, between the vivid memories of settled communities on the fringes of downtown Cape Town and the uncertainties of their new life on the Cape Flats, they reached outside their immediate geographical confines for cultural identity. In this moment of historical crisis and trauma (what Parenzee calls "broken histories"), the newly established townships of the Cape Flats resorted to what they, in the most complex sense of the term, "knew." Deeply acculturated in the ways of the metropolis, they accessed England, an ideological space that represented for them communal stability and geographical fixedness, sociopolitical securities so gravely lacking in their own experience. Amidst the multiple structural and psychic dislocations wrought by apartheid deracination, English football clubs became a symbol of community (and cultural) resilience. The very names of English clubs carried within them, in those early days when "community" was spoken of in the past tense (signifying the pre–Group Areas moment), the possibility of cultural and political survival.

These imported names spoke of the commitment to a history that they wanted to create and perpetuate because their other past had been so violently "broken" and decimated. Metropolitan clubs such as Liverpool, Leeds, and Chelsea had not always thrived but they had survived—all of them had overcome the disruption of the world wars, the chaos of internal crises, and the ignominy and humiliation of relegation to lower leagues. English football clubs became pivotal talismans, lifesaving and community-building institutions of the cultural variety for the unsettled—and struggling to adjust—residents of the Cape Flats. Without knowing it, apartheid's perniciousness transformed English football clubs into models of hope, of footballing prowess, of community creation and maintenance, and of social cooperation. "Liverpool" facilitated, in a small but culturally crucial way, the production of a community—and communal life in the township—in the face of apartheid hostility. The Group Areas Act was, after all, little more than a (racist) commitment to destroying organic social units—"Liverpool" and "Leeds" offered itself as an unexpected counter to the potentially debilitating effects of deracination.

However, as much as the township "politics of adoption" was a response to apartheid's "politics of disruption," so the choice of "Arsenal" and "Chelsea" as a cultural identity was also motivated by a more visceral and considered sense of footballing affinity. Township clubs assumed English identities because they, or at least some of the key founding members, admired the individual qualities, the "character," of these metropolitan institutions. The two most popular English clubs were Leeds and Chelsea, teams with contrasting styles but both of which appealed, for vastly differing reasons, to township communities. Leeds's outstanding feature was tough tackling, solid defense, and uncompromising style, appropriate for a Yorkshire city that valued hardness, resilience, and a no-nonsense approach to life and the game of football.[15] The late-1960s early-1970s Leeds side, a very successful team, boasted a series of "hard men" such as "Big Jack" Charlton, Norman Hunter, and their redoubtable skipper, the combative Scotsman Billy Brenmer. (Their strikers, Allan Clarke and Mick Jones, scored goals through grit and graft, only rarely through guile.) Leeds's salient feature translated well on the Cape Flats, where survival required the very qualities Leeds of Yorkshire embodied so fully in their football. In his essay "Football and Working Class Fans," John Clarke captures the spirit of Leeds and the working-class ethos it so unabashedly proclaimed:

> The worker, as breadwinner, could not afford to wilt under this pressure [of the factory], any more than the footballer could afford to give in to physical challenges on the field. Both in football, and in male working-class life, this idea of toughness sanctioned certain types of violence as normal.[16]

The kind of "toughness" that Leeds prided itself on was, as Clarke points out, always laden with the potential for "violence"—the kind of combative machismo that the Yorkshire club almost single-handedly transformed into a style of playing football.

Leeds's was an approach that found a willing constituency on the Cape Flats where township life required no small amount of "toughness" to get by. Leeds United A.F.C. of Heideveld and Hanover Park, to mention but two township derivatives, imitated the style of their English progenitors with astonishing success—to say nothing of the countless clubs that adopted the philosophy but not the name. With the occasional exception, the local Leeds players eschewed the dribbling and ball artistry so beloved by other township clubs. For them, football was a game to be played directly—they relished the "physical challenges" so innate to the Yorkshire team's (and their) game and dared other teams to beat them with fancy footwork and ball control. Leeds of the Cape Flats played the game according to a simple philosophy: the ball was cleared long and hard out of defense, their midfielders were bruising in the tackle, and their forwards aggressive in their quest for goals. In a cultural word, this was Jack Charlton, Billy Brenmer, and Allan Clarke come to township life. It was not that these local clubs could not pass the ball around the park, or "play football," as other clubs' fans would have had it; it was, rather, that they believed they were playing football the Leeds way, a style that most accurately suited to the conditions they lived under.

Chelsea, of south London, was a study in contrast. Defense was not its strong suit because this club prized slick ball control, deft footwork, and goals carved out of long, twisting dribbles—goals that left defenders helpless in the wake of Charlie Cooke and Peter Osgood's silky moves; or those moments when Alan Hudson stole goals out of nothing with a quick shimmy and a shake of his hips. In the absence of Leeds's stout defense there was the breathtaking goalkeeping of Peter Bonnetti, a man nicknamed "The Cat" because of his swift reflexes. (There was, however, one Chelsea defender who did relish protecting his 'keeper, the "hard man" Ron "Chopper" Harris. A central defender, he earned his sobriquet because of his ability to fell opponents ruthlessly as soon as he would tackle them fairly.) This was how Chelsea of Heideveld, of Bridgetown, and of the lower middle-class neighborhood of Lansdowne played. They moved the ball adroitly with swift, incisive passes; their teams were a collection of talented individuals who might not always play as a unit, but they always promised to enthrall the fan and mesmerize their opponents with flashes of skill. Unlike Yorkshire's Leeds, Chelsea of south London did not win many trophies but they played football with an abandon that enabled their township imitators to overcome the restrictions both of apartheid and of the sometimes stifling confines of the working class. Like their metropolitan namesake, township Chelsea(s) encouraged their players to aspire to the spectacular. They always tried to play, to use a phrased coined in August 1998 by ex-Newcastle manager Ruud Guulit, "sexy football"—Chelsea played to please the connoisseur of deft, intricate passing and long-range shooting; their defenders loved to go forward and attack even as they left themselves open to the quick counter from their opponents. They played a stylish game, preferring the ball at their feet, and always shirking the excessively physical challenges that was Leeds's very essence. You went to watch Chelsea for pleasure and excitement, not necessarily because you expected them to win. As Guulit, who himself played for and managed Chelsea, remarked: "I'd rather lose

5–4 than draw." Guulit was describing not only a scoreline, he was summarizing a football club's entire philosophy.

Like their namesake, township Chelsea(s) relied on the individual brilliance of their goalkeeper to keep them in the game. Indeed, Chelsea of Heideveld produced in Charlie Jongbloed, one of the two best goalkeepers ever to play football in the Western Cape. The local keeper too bore the appellation of "The Cat," and his long and illustrious career was studded with many an unbelievable save. After a while, however, the township "Cat" tired of being a one-man defense and he moved on to their neighbors, Everton, a team that (much more than their English "forbears") played brilliant football—without ever, like Chelsea local and metropolitan, shirking their defensive responsibilities.

Everton A.F.C. of Heideveld, a club with a valid claim to being the most successful township team in the history of Cape Flats football, demonstrates an important development in the working-class game. It is precisely because English models dominate the style of football, express a desire for a cultural identity, and articulate a series of relationships with the metropolis that Everton A.F.C. is such a salient township club. This is the team that shows how the process of cultural mimicry can be disrupted through redefinition: Everton of Heideveld demonstrates how idealization is transformed through township agency, how a metropolitan name can be hollowed out and reinvested with an autonomous identity; Everton shows how cultural appropriation can lead to a radical transmutation that renders the original model almost unrecognizable, the shared name the only remaining trace of the metropolis. Unlike England's Leeds and Chelsea, Everton of Merseyside (they are Liverpool F.C.'s neighbors) was not a club to inspire identification—and with good reason, many of their English opponents would add. Solid without being tough, hinting at stylishness without a full commitment to it, they are an institution marked by stolidness—moderate success, a club without any dramatic failures.

Loosely affiliated with the Anglican Church in Heideveld (much like the metropolitan club had early links to the Church of England, as well as to the Catholic church), the local Everton adopted the blue and white stripes of their Merseyside progenitors. From their origins in 1969, however, they have been a club committed to flair. Everton A.F.C.'s defenders, such as Errol Caswell, Colin Solomons, and John "Piggy" Richards, passed the ball as adroitly as their midfield—an area where Elroy Stokoe, Patrick Jooste, and Norman Philips were brilliant. Philips was articulate and incisive in his distribution, gifted in his ability to break down defenses; Jooste was an authoritative and commanding presence in the midfield, coupled with a lethal shot. Up front, Gerald Hartzenberg's speed and trickery, "Tickies" Caswell (Errol's brother) neat flicks and powerful shot, and Gary Arendse's ability to head the ball further than most players can kick it, wreaked havoc with many a defense. The Heideveld team played their football with a relish that was at once disciplined and full of bravado. Everton A.F.C. combined the township predilection for ball skills with the English insistence on "keeping your defensive shape." But the Heideveld club did not interpret this phrase in the prevailing English terms, which is to say, play dourly, take no risks, put a premium on not conceding goals. For them it was attack with responsible flair—threaten the opposing goal without leaving your own vulnerable.

The Heideveld club marks the point at which the metropolitan model recedes and township autonomy, not an outright rejection or complete disavowal of Everton F.C., becomes salient. As the Cape Flats amateurs produced their own distinct footballing style, they transformed "Everton" into an "independent" township name, and evacuated Everton of Merseyside from their identity—Everton A.F.C. represents the transmutation of metropolitan idealization into township originality. The amateur club's "declaration of cultural independence" demonstrates how, in Judith Butler's terms, the "history of the metropolitan name" can be "arrested"; it evinces how it is not only possible to "arrest" the metropolitan name but to create an entirely new and different history in the process of doing so. Metropolitan identification is not evacuated by a preferred local playing style, but it does mark the (partial) invalidation and transformation of the imported name. On the playing fields of the Cape Flats, "Everton" evoked only one identity: the local one, because Everton A.F.C. played a brand of football that was not only different from that of their English namesake, but one that was more highly regarded than the metropolitan model. The Cape Flats amateurs succeeded in wresting "Everton" from the county of Lancashire, unmooring it culturally, and then reinventing it. Everton A.F.C. made Everton F.C. a Merseyside institution that was not so much unrecognizable as "undesirable"—Heideveld boys wanted to play like "their" Everton, not the English model.

Everton A.F.C. is, however, an exceptional township club. For almost thirty years now they have been tremendously successful. They have a solid organizational structure (founder member Job Petersen has been there since the beginning, as chair, manager, and coach, a longevity rare in most township clubs), a tradition of winning (at the very highest level, boasting honors such as the Maggott Trophy and the Virginia Premier League), and a long line of talented players (several of whom have won the highest honors available to them). Of all the township clubs that have taken on English club's names, Everton alone has been able to convert the initial moment of cultural mimesis into a subsequent expression of cultural autonomy. They have established themselves as different from both their progenitor and their "fellow-mimics." Amongst the (understandable) proliferation of "Chelseas" and "Leeds" on the Cape Flats, "Everton A.F.C." registers uniquely; they can barely even be called mimics—or "idealizers"—in name. The Heideveld club is a symbol for township possibility, a marker of "difference." But it is their very exceptionalism that proves the mimetic rule: An autonomous cultural identity is extremely difficult to establish, footballing independence is hard to craft after the metropolitan name has been adopted. Everton A.F.C. is unique in that it has been able to resist the "burden of naming"; or, to put it differently, they have been able to effect a spectacular liberation from their "cultural arrest." Unlike other township clubs, they have not become local versions of their English progenitors; but Everton A.F.C. does show how loaded a metropolitan name is, how it carries within it a series of practices, a style, a complete ideology of football. Football is not only "more important than life," it is, if you assume the name of "Leeds" or "Chelsea," itself a way of sporting life. But so is Everton, that point where the township disarticulates the metropolis. The English city of Liverpool may have been where the process started but it is in Everton A.F.C. that the township expresses itself as an indigenous, unique, and autonomous cultural identity. The Heideveld club is what happens when Cape Flats teams translate themselves into, and ground themselves in, the (insistently) local. Everton A.F.C., in liquidating Everton F.C., marks the juncture where the township declares the metropolis redundant for its cultural purposes. The amateur club may contain within its ranks Liverpool F.C. fans, but they are undoubtedly Everton A.F.C. players.

Notes

1. Anthony Sampson, *Black & Gold: Tycoons, Revolutionaries and Apartheid* (London: Coronet Books, 1987), 155.

2. Ibid.

3. Alec Erwin, "Sport: The Turning Point," *Sport and Transformation: Contemporary Debates on South African Sport*, ed. Cheryl Roberts (Cape Town: Township Publishing Co-Operative, 1989), 44.

4. For a discussion of the working class roots of football and the identities that it has produced, see *Football Cultures and Identities*, ed. Gary Armstrong and Richard Giulianotti (Basingstoke, England: Macmillan Press, 1999). See especially the essays by David Russell and Udo Merkel. See also Giulianotti's *The Sociology of Football* (Basingstoke, England: Macmillan Press); John Nauright's *Sports, Cultures and Identities in South Africa* (Leicester, England: Leicester University Press, 1997); and D. Russell's *Football and the English* (Preston, England: Carnegie Publishing, 1997).

5. Homi Bhabha, "Of Mimicry and Man," *The Location of Culture* (New York: Routledge, 1994), 86.

6. Rare exceptions do occur to the middle-class practice of not naming their

clubs after English institutions, of which the suburb of Lansdowne's Wolver-hampton Wanderers (named after a struggling club from the English Midlands) and Factreton's Manchester United may be the most prominent examples.

7. Arthur Hopcraft, *Football Man*, as quoted in John Clarke, "Football and Working Class Fans: Tradition and Change," *Football Hooliganism*, ed. Roger Ingham et al. (London: Inter-Action Imprint, 1978), 42.

8. The kind of hybridization that football encourages is not unusual in township life because township residents are frequently involved in translation, of the cultural, political, and ideological variety. It has produced a language, indigenous to the Western Cape, locally known as "Kaaps." "Kaaps" was used in print, amidst considerable controversy, in the 1970s by the coloured poet and playwright Adam Small and has subsequently gained much wider political acceptance. "Kaaps," however, is a unique blend of English and Afrikaans and it has its origins in the townships.

From there it has gravitated out toward the middle-class coloured suburbs but is still a discursive form indelibly marked by—and therefore frowned upon—its class roots.

9. For a discussion of black metropolitan racism (as opposed to the surprising but explicable peripheral "indifference"), especially in relation to Leeds F.C., which is all too easy to overlook in this delineation of township football, see Note 15.

10. Black players were not just systematically excluded from the game, but the opposing fans barracked those black members of the other team. When Liverpool played against their neighbors, the Everton fans would wave cardboard bananas whenever the Jamaican-born English international John Barnes touched the ball. He was, they implied, a monkey, fit only for swinging from trees and eating fruit in the jungle, certainly not a suitable opponent for their all-white team. It took a considerable amount of time before black players' own clubs came, in any substantive way, to their protection. Black players too, as Paul Gilroy discusses in *Small Acts* in an essay comparing the boxer Frank Bruno to the footballer John Barnes, have rarely publicly engaged racism—West Ham's Ian Wright has arguably been the black player most prepared to take it up, both on and off the football pitch

11. Kenny Dalglish, with Henry Winter, *Dalgish: My Autobiography* (London: Hodder & Stoughton, 1996), 57.

12. Richard Rive, *Writing Black* (Cape Town: David Philip, 1981), 12.

13. Chas Critcher, "Football Since the War: A Study in Social Change and Popular Culture" (Birmingham, England: University of Birmingham, Center for Contemporary Cultural Studies, 1979), 161.

14. Built by the apartheid state for low income disenfranchised families, "council" houses are cheaply built structures designed to accommodate coloureds, indians, and blacks who had been deracinated by the Group Areas Act. With a bare minimum of facilities (unplastered walls, no running hot water), "council" houses were intended for rental purposes only. Although the model for these "council" houses was the post-World War II British Welfare State (where the construction was funded by local councils), there was none of the ideological commitments in the South African townships that motivated the local authorities in England or

Scotland. For the apartheid regime, the "council" houses were an inexpensive dumping ground for uprooted communities.

15. There is, in regard to Leeds United F.C., a remarkably different reception on the part of the metropolitan and peripheral "black" communities. Although the racism of English football was largely disregarded in the townships of the Cape Flats, it resonated very differently amongst the Afro-Caribbean community in Yorkshire itself. As Ben Carrington has demonstrated in his essay on the Caribbean Cricket Club of Chapeltown ("situated near an area of Leeds"), the local black community was removed from Leeds F.C. because of what it perceived as the club—and the city's—racism. Proximity to racist institutions, it is clear, determines the relationship of the local black—or disenfranchised communities to these cultural organizations. The experience of the black residents of Chapeltown could thus easily have been replicated in Toxteth, Liverpool or Brixton, London. See Carrington, "Sport, Masculinity, and Black Cultural Resistance," *Journal of Sport and Social Issues* 22, No. 3 (August 1998), for a fuller explication of this issue.

16. John Clarke, "Football and Its Fans" (Birmingham, England: University of Birmingham, Centre for Contemporary Cultural Studies, 1978), 40.

5

The Nation in White:
Cricket in a Postapartheid
South Africa

What know they of cricket who only cricket know?

—C.L.R. James, *Beyond a Boundary*

It is historically appropriate that a black cricketer from the Caribbean should bring into proper view the way the overwhelmingly white South African team is regarded by the rest of the postcolonial world. More than in any other part of the globe, the Caribbean is a community where the sport's ideological import is treated with the utmost seriousness. In the West Indies, "knowing cricket" is indivisible from a consciousness of history, colonialism, race politics, and socioeconomic conditions. It was in this spirit that West Indies cricket delivered its stinging indictment of South Africa's white team during the 1996 World Cup. The Caribbean critique leveled its criticism in the person of Brian Lara, the game's most eloquent ambassador today. Brian Lara is the éminence grise of the contemporary game: batsman extraordinaire, holder of the world record in runs scored in an international match, and among the youngest players to captain his native Trinidad and Tobago.[1] In the build-up to the World Cup quarter-final game between the West Indies and South Africa in March 1996, Lara showed that a critical awareness of the consequences of racism is as integral to Caribbean cricket as is brilliant stroke-making and ferocious fast bowling.

Interviewed by the Delhi-based magazine *Outlook*, Lara used this exchange as an opportunity to distinguish between the impact of a surprising defeat by a black African team and the prospect of losing to a predominantly white African side. The ignominious defeat by Kenya, a country boasting only a small amateur league and without any real traditions in the sport, seriously damaged West Indian cricketing pride. South Africa, however, was another matter altogether. Congratulating the Kenyans in their change room after the West Indies's embarrassing loss to the east African cricket minnows (in the preliminary rounds of the competition), the Trinidadian articulated a deep-seated resentment at the racial bias of his forthcoming opponents. "'It wasn't that bad losing to you guys [Kenyans],'" he remarked, 'Now, a team like South Africa is a different matter altogether. You know, this white thing comes into the picture. We can't stand losing to them.'"[2] Undoubtedly, Lara's pronouncement bore more than a trace of rationalization for the West Indies' humbling loss to a nation of cricketing rookies. Nevertheless, it stands as a courageous and scathing attack on the enduring inequalities of apartheid. International cricketing icon and then West Indies captain-in-waiting, Brian Lara broke with cricket's renowned custom of civility—a set of practices so sacroscant that, as C.L.R. James put it in *Beyond a Boundary*, a player would "cut off a finger sooner than do anything contrary to the ethics of the game"[3]—and spoke directly against the abiding legacy of white South African privilege. The consequences of apartheid were evident to Lara, no matter that it was no longer underwritten by institutional racism. The South African squad the West Indies were about to play in 1996 was composed of thirteen whites and a teenage coloured prodigy named Paul Adams.

Lara's attack on the postapartheid team anoints him as the most recent heir to the legacy of Caribbean cricket radicalism, a tradition that is several generations old. Outstanding among the earliest proponents of cricket activism were, of course, Lara's fellow Trinidadians, C.L.R. James and Learie Constantine. From the 1920s to the late 1950s, these Trinidadians were in the vanguard of the struggle against white administrative control of the game in the West Indies.[4] (Although black players had been dominating the West Indies team for decades by the 1950s, they had always done so under tutelage of a white captain. Black Caribbean cricketers and fans bitterly opposed this final vestige of British colonialism.) James spearheaded the public campaign to appoint Frank Worrell as the first black captain of the West Indies in 1959. In the words of former Jamaican Prime Minister Michael Manley, "C.L.R. James, his patriotic hackles no less than his sense of injustice aroused, led the assault."[5] More recently, James and Worrell's cudgels were taken up by the outspoken ex-West Indian skipper and Lara's batting predecessor, the Antiguan Viv Richards. In the wake of Nelson Mandela's 1990 release, the eloquent Richards cautioned that South Africa should not be (re)admitted to Test cricket until all of the nation's people could compete equally for a place in the team. Unless a gradual approach to the country's international reintegration was followed, Richards suggested, the South African team would reflect the constitutional and structural inequalities of apartheid. Richards's views are especially instructive if one recalls the historical precedent of Zimbabwe, a nation with the same racial cricketing profile as South Africa.

UDI (Unilateral Declaration of Independence), Rhodesia's national cricket team, was (like South Africa's national team) exclusively white. Until its independence in 1980, Rhodesia was an integral part of the South African cricketing structure; in the 1970s, their side was one of five teams that used to participate in the local interprovincial competition known as the Currie Cup. Following its independence, the new state was not immediately admitted to full international competition by the governing body. Instead, the International Cricket Council (ICC) adopted a policy of piecemeal admission to the world game for a country that was for the first time developing a nonracial cricketing tradition; the country had to nurture its postindependence players outside the South African environment. The Zimbabwe team, which was and still is mainly white, undertook and hosted second-tier tours designed to schedule matches against the second-string teams of countries such as England and Australia. One of the by-products of the ICC's ruling was that it facilitated the development of black and Asian players in Zimbabwe. After more than a decade, the southern African nation achieved full international cricketing status.

The ICC's response to the Zimbabwean situation is in sharp contrast to its historic protection of white South Africa. Both in its current and its previous guise (in 1961 the Imperial Cricket Conference dropped the "imperial" in favor of "international" as the reality of postcolonial India, Pakistan, and the West Indies made itself increasingly manifest), the organization has defended the right of the apartheid team to be included in its ranks. South Africa's cause has traditionally been championed by the lilywhite establishments of English and Australian cricket, countries whose administrative hierarchy bears a striking resemblance to that of the apartheid state—although England's on-field personnel has in the past fifteen years or so become more representative of a postcolonial metropolis. Because of England's status as founder nation of the world governing body and as the "home of the game," the country has exerted a tremendous influence on the politics of cricket. Despite the protestations and objections of the "newer" postcolonial members (who today outnumber England, Australia, and South Africa, the "established" ICC nations) about the country's racist policies, the apartheid team was allowed to participate in international competition until 1970. Of course, the South African team was not invited to tour the Caribbean or the Indian subcontinent nor did it extend invitations to those countries.

The apartheid side, which regularly played against England and Australia, demarcated the racial divide within the ICC. Supported by its ex-white colonies, postimperial England (which until very recently had veto rights within the organization) insisted upon the right of the apartheid team to enjoy a limited, but symbolically salient role, within the world body. England and Australia's position within the ICC is indicative of a particularly virulent racism because it had such scant respect for the domestic efforts of the nonracial cricket within South Africa. It seldom, despite concerted attempts by those in the nonracial fold, even paid lip service to the internal opposition; this strategic disregard explicitly established the white apartheid establishment as the guardians of the South African game. As objectionable as this stance was, it was adopted and vigorously defended despite strong postcolonial opposition. Not even its own public embarrassment in what became known as the "D'Oliveira Affair" (when Basil D'Oliveira, a coloured cricketer from Cape Town who had obtained British citizenship and selection to the 1968 England team to tour South Africa was rejected because of his race),[6] initiated a rethinking in English cricket policy toward South Africa. It took the efforts, in the early 1970s, of England's former black colonies, with the West Indies and India leading the charge, to isolate the apartheid team. And even then the success was greater on the cricket oval than in the boardrooms of Lords, the game's London headquarters. Because of South Africa's historic links to its traditional white rivals, it is not surprising that upon the eradication of legislative apartheid, the country was immediately welcomed back into the international cricketing fold. (The financial incentive of South African tours, to both the "traditional" and the postcolonial venues, also played no small role in the country's rapid return to the international cricket stage.) Clearly, Zimbabwe was not going to be a blueprint for the (re)admission of its southern neighbors into the ICC.

The relative success, however, of the Zimbabwean model, which Viv Richards may or may not have been invoking, only adds luster to the Antiguan's prophetic judgments on South African cricket. The inequities in the South African game have, six years after Mandela's release, become increasingly evident. On the eve of the 1996 competition, the former West Indian vice-captain Conrad Hunte "warned that it was time" for South Africa "to prove its commitment to a multiracial national team by selecting two nonwhites for the forthcoming World Cup side."[7] Hunte's plea fell on deaf South African ears. In the fourteen-man squad, Paul Adams was the lone representative of the traditionally disenfranchised communities.

It was at this state of South African cricketing affairs that Brian Lara aimed his ire, a criticism that evoked substantial turmoil. Apologies were called for by the South Africans and delivered by the Trinidadian player and the Caribbean management. But in typically Lara fashion, the furor did not deter him from scoring a majestic 111 runs in the West Indies's triumph over the South Africans. His riposte to apartheid inequality was as decisive on the field as it had been groundbreaking off it. As expected, however, the antiracism and opposition to historic structural inequality that motivated Lara's comments were addressed neither in the international cricketing press nor in the postapartheid society's media generally.

But for all those invested in South African cricket, supporters and critics alike, the controversy generated by Lara's *Outlook* interview offers a rare opportunity to reflect seriously upon the game—and all other postapartheid sports codes. An evaluation of apartheid, of how its residues have shaped the current condition of cricket and the future of the game in South Africa, is urgently required at this juncture in postapartheid society. Brian Lara provided the occasion for an intervention into South African cricket because he critiqued its racist formation. He has, just as important, inadvertently disrupted a narrative of emerging international sporting dominance that is developing in the newly democratized nation. South Africa is becoming a major power on the African continent in football (soccer) and an international force in cricket and rugby. An engagement with the complicated politics of South African sport could be no more timely and necessary than in this exceptional, euphoric, and nascent moment in the "new" country's cultural history.

Between May 1995 and March 1996, when the Lara-inspired West Indies eliminated South Africa from the World Cup, triumphs in sports arenas of all kinds flowed thick and fast for a nation just recently admitted to the international fold. Banned from the previous two Rugby World Cups because of apartheid, South Africa entered the competition for the first time with a bang. The country not only hosted the 1995 event, but "Amabokoboko" (as the rugby side is locally known) beat a highly talented New Zealand side to become the world champions. In January 1996, South Africa again served as the venue for an international competition, this time the continent's premier football competition—the Africa Nations Cup. The South African football team, "Bafana Bafana" (a Xhosa term that means energetic and youthful but is colloquially translated as "The Boys") is managed by whites—and was until mid-1997 captained by a white player as well—although it contains a representative mix of black, white, and coloured players.[8] This side triumphed over a young Tunisian squad in the '96 Nations Cup final. On both occasions President Mandela, draped alternately in the national rugby and football shirts, was in attendance at the stadiums and in the vanguard of the cheering. There was, quite literally, much flag waving and dancing in the streets. The leafy avenues of the traditionally white suburbs and the rutted roads of the townships alike were home to fans inebriated with the joys of athletic conquest. The Nations Cup football celebrations had barely subsided when the cricket team, skippered by the moderately talented Afrikaner Hansie Cronje, secured victory over England in the five-match test series. Played during December 1995 and January 1996, the first four matches ended in draws (ties) before South Africa manufactured a win in the fifth international at the Newlands ground in Cape Town. It was the cherry atop the new nation's resplendent sporting cake.

A Game of High and Difficult Technique

Cricket is a game of high and difficult technique. If it were not, it could not carry the load of social response and implication which it carries.

—C.L.R. James, *Beyond a Boundary*

In the midst of the nation's procession of athletic victories, the cricket accomplishments deserve special attention. Within South African culture, cricket has come to occupy a signal position. Located between football and rugby, respectively identified as the sport of the black majority and the old Afrikaner ruling elite, cricket is presented as a neutral ideological terrain. Untainted by an association with the dominant political formations of the present and the past, cricket is portrayed as an arena of unqualified, but benign, white control. It is presented as white authority made palatable, exemplary even, by the efforts of white administrators to recruit a new following amongst township residents. (The township dwellers are presumed to be primarily, but not exclusively, black. The game is more rooted within the coloured and indian communities, so that these disenfranchised sections represent a different target.) Unlike Afrikaner-identified rugby, cricket has traditionally been the province of English-speaking white South Africans. The sport is therefore, however misguided and simplistic the perception, imbued with the liberal and progressive strains of that constituency. The pioneering status of postapartheid cricket is captured in "Field of Dreams," a historically flawed—if evocatively entitled—account by *The Times* of London:

> South Africa's cricket organizers took a leap ahead. The cricket hierarchy, under Dr. Ali Bacher, began taking the sport to the black townships, establishing cricket clinics, training black schoolteachers to coach cricket. After the ANC returned from exile in 1990, a merger between the white and black cricket bodies allowed the sport to return to international competition in 1991. In November of that year, a South African cricket team visited India.[9]

All too quick to praise Ali Bacher as a cricket missionary to the townships, "Field of Dreams" disregards the long tradition of organized nonracial cricket—which it incorrectly refers to here as "black." Decades old, in one institutional formation or another, nonracial cricket was run by the South African Cricket Board (SACB) until the end of the apartheid era. (In an earlier incarnation this body was called SACBOC—the South African Cricket Board of Control.) Like all other codes that represented the coloured, black, and indian communities (and rare white individuals), the SACB functioned under the auspices of the South African Council on Sports (SACOS). Like their administrative colleagues in, amongst other codes, football, rugby, tennis, and swimming, the SACB was an underresourced organization charged with a dual social responsibility: It had to work diligently to keep alive the tradition of athletic excellence while simultaneously fostering and maintaining a culture of political resistance.

This was a struggle that SACOS conducted not only nationally but globally through its international arm, SANROC—the South African Non-Racial Olympic Committee. This nonracial sports organization was deeply committed to the principle that disenfranchised South Africans would never compete in sport with their enfranchised counterparts until a fully democratic society was achieved. Participation in SACOS was constructed as being in and of itself an act of political opposition. By foregrounding its nonracial principles and intervening wherever possible in the society's political debates, SACOS transformed the football field, the athletic track, the swimming pool, and the training sites for field hockey, baseball, and tennis: These cultural spaces were all reinscribed as venues of ideological resistance. The politics of cultural opposition established SACOS as a crucial vehicle for challenging the hegemony of the government.

In the mid-1970s, the effectiveness of SACOS and SANROC was demonstrated internationally and consequently attacked by the NP at home. The government's reply, however, constitutes a rare instance of apartheid legislative subtlety. The years 1976 and 1977 marked a crucial cultural turning point for white South Africa. The apartheid state found itself on the defensive, responding to local and global events that combined to effect a massive upheaval in South African society. Almost without any warning, mid-1976 found white South Africa confronted by a potent two-pronged attack: increasing black political resistance internally and the prospect of growing cultural isolation internationally. The Soweto student-led revolt of June 16, 1976 revealed patently the angry depths of the nation's disenfranchised. Black youth had claimed the classroom as *the* center of antiaprtheid struggle, an arena they would not relinquish for fifteen years. About a month after the Soweto uprising, in far away Quebec, Canada, the 1976 Montreal Olympics were marred by the specter of apartheid. Bitterly opposed to the tour that year by the New Zealand national rugby side (known, ironically, as the All Blacks) to apartheid South Africa, black African countries protested this visit by boycotting the Montreal Olympics. The marked African absence was so serious that British Commonwealth countries, seeking to prevent a repeat of the Montreal boycott, convened to sign the Gleneagles Agreement. This agreement prohibited international teams from touring the apartheid republic. Individual competitors in sports such as golf and tennis were exempted from this ruling because it interfered with their livelihoods; no matter, of course, that black South Africans would never have the opportunity to earn a living in this way.

The apartheid government's response to the political tumult was brutally swift and constitutionally tardy. The 1976 student revolt was quickly and violently crushed, but the spirit of opposition was by no means permanently quelled. Political disturbances in black high schools and universities became a regular feature of South African life, assuming a particular resilience throughout the 1980s. But it would take some fifteen years before the demands of the 1976 youth were met—it was only with Mandela's release in February 1990 that the country's black political leaders were freed and negotiations for a nonracial democracy commenced. The apartheid government's cultural rejoinder to the Gleneagles Agreement, however, was as rapid as that of its trigger-happy security forces of that era. In the middle of 1977, the Nationalists inaugurated a policy that Piet Koornhof, its Minister of Sport and Recreation, euphemistically referred to as "normal sport." It was a policy named without any sense of historical paradox: If sport was being "normalized," this very logic would surely render every other facet of apartheid existence "abnormal," not to mention immoral? It was an implicit, if unconscious, act of self-indictment. Rhetorically and ideologically, the term *normal sport* incriminated the entire edifice of apartheid. Recognizing this uncritical irony, SACOS picked up on the contradiction with a keen veracity. It replied promptly to the government's new legislation by coining a resonant slogan: "No Normal Sport in an Abnormal Society."

Moral self-incrimination, however, mattered less to the Nationalist government than did the prospect of participating again in international sport. The policy of "normal sport" demonstrates white South Africans's obsession with sport and its hunger for international competition. A preoccupation with sport is, however, by no means a province exclusive to whites as was evidenced by the widespread enthusiasm generated by the city of Cape Town's unsuccessful bid for the 2004 Olympics.[10] In the 1970s, however, sport was a cultural imperative so powerful for whites that it compelled the apartheid regime to repeal laws that were decades old and important, if not central, to the ideology of racial separation. (The "most damaging blow against apartheid," as Anthony Sampson pointed out, was indeed the sports boycott.) The introduction of this National Party policy marks an instance of creative apartheid legislation: It overturned the laws that forbade interracial athletic contests without endangering the basic tenets of apartheid. "Normal sport" allowed South Africans of all races to train and compete with and against each other, to belong to the same sports organizations, and it permitted them to share sports and other facilities such as hotels and restaurants. Apartheid circa 1977 was, however, strictly a sporting democracy. It was a cosmetic attempt to appease the international sports community while maintaining the pillars of apartheid. "Normality" was clearly circumscribed, it did not extend beyond the cricket boundary or the football sidelines. The apartheid laws that restricted personal relations and forbade the equality of education, housing, and health remained untouched. The franchise was, of course, still exclusive to whites. All these elements were integral to anti-"normal sport" platform of SACOS, a position that was supported by all but a minority of athletes in the coloured and indian communities.

Despite its nonracial principles, one of the major critiques leveled against SACOS was its racial composition. Like most other SACOS affiliates, the SACB drew the bulk of its membership and its leadership from the nation's coloured communities while remaining committed to making inroads into the black townships as well. SACOS' pronouncedly coloured profile was especially evident in the Western and Eastern Cape, where this community predominated; these two regions formed, not coincidentally, the SACOS base. In provinces such as the Transvaal, the black majority's support for the organization was tepid, at best. (In Natal, another region with a preponderance of blacks, SACOS's main constituency was the indian community.) The lack of black support for SACOS, especially in a sport such as football, requires a fuller explication than can be provided in this chapter.[11] However, suffice to say that there is an inverse proportionality between SACOS's administrative achievements in the black community and the popularity of the sport's code. The less popular a sport in the black community, the greater the nonracial body's success; the more popular the code the less SACOS prospered. The nonracial organization enjoyed most success in sports such as cricket and rugby, codes without significant cachet in the black community. On the other hand, it failed to convince the majority of amateur and professional black footballers to forswear the lure of "normalcy." In a Gramscian word, SACOS was insufficiently rooted in the black community: Its watchword, noncollaboration with the apartheid state in any form, was admirable, but the organization was neither ideologically nor racially organic to black South Africa. SACOS's signal achievement was its ability to isolate white South Africa internationally; its most notable failure was its inability to duplicate that success internally. Within the disenfranchised society itself, SACOS was always a principled but never a genuinely popular voice; SACOS could never substantively transcend its coloured roots.

SACOS's platform, however, did enable affiliates such as the SACB to take crucial political positions on sport. Those critiques, so innate to the SACB, are conspicuously lacking within the dominant narratives of contemporary South African cricket. The politics of cricket has been replaced by a trend toward restraint, so much so that commentators have become remarkably subdued about the root of the material disparities that distinguished the SACB from the overwhelmingly white South African Cricket Union (SACU). This cultivated silence encourages an omission of SACB history, quietly sanctioning a neglect of the SACB's tradition of resistance. In its stead a piece such as "Field of Dreams" foregrounds a trajectory that is not only philanthropic and colonialist (Bacher "began taking the sport to the townships"), but one that is problematically singular in its reading of the disenfranchised's cricket traditions. It does not explore how cricket was deeply grounded within the coloured and indian communities and more sparsely and shallowly rooted amongst black South Africans. The coloured community's cricket culture is rich and filled with milestones. One of these is the achievement of Mohammed Idris Yusuf. In the 1936–37 season Yusuf, playing for Government Indian Schools Cricket Club against Star Cricket Club in Bulawayo, Southern Rhodesia, scored an undefeated 412. Cricket's holy book, *Wisden* (which records all the first-class matches of every season), noted that this was the thirteenth highest score in the history of cricket at that time. Nonracial cricket's limitations aside (its ideology, its racial formation, or its material deprivations), the history of the SACB enunciates clearly that the disenfranchised's cricket is not a cultural practice in its genesis; contrary to perceptions that presently dominate, township cricket is a sport with an a priori history.

Without many resources, nonracial administrators such as Hassan Howa and Stan Abrahams worked diligently in the working-class black, coloured and indian townships, the middle-class suburbs, and the schools to nurture a cricket culture commensurate with SACOS's political philosophy. The SACB ran cricket clinics in the coloured townships of the Cape Flats and it initiated programs in the adjoining black areas. Today those SACB accomplishments are seldom acknowledged, Hassan Howa's political memory and Stan Abrahams's administrative astuteness are rarely invoked. This trend extends naturally to the cricket oval itself. The exploits of SACB players such as the mercurial spin bowler (a slow bowler who makes the ball spin in both predictable and unexpected ways) "Lefty" Adams, the fast bowlers (or speed merchants, as they are sometimes known in the game) Vincent Barnes and Jeff Frans, the exciting Majiet brothers, Rushdie and Saait, both high-caliber all-rounders (players who bat and bowl with equal skill), and brilliant batsmen such as Ivan Dagnin, Khaya Majola, and Michael Doman, are seldom remembered. (Vincent Barnes, at the end of his career when apartheid ended, made a brief appearance for his provincial team. A 42-year-old Majola captained an all-black Soweto team that toured England in 1995.)

The achievements of these players and the traditions of their various clubs and provinces demonstrate that nonracial cricket is of an old vintage. The cricketing culture that produced the talented Paul Adams is not the result of a sporting message brought by well-meaning white administrators such as Ali Bacher. It is a culture that was carefully administered by the likes of Howa and honed in the cricket nets and on the playing fields by "Lefty" Adams, Vincent Barnes, and Saait Majiet. Paul Adams traces his cricket roots to a tradition independent of and oppositional to that of Bacher, now executive director of the United Cricket Board of South Africa (UCBSA). When the Bacher-like philanthropists came, they brought with them more than shining red balls and carefully oiled bats. They were missionaries of apartheid acquiescence and unabashed advocates of "normal sport."

Goodbye Dolly,
Hello Isolation

Like the matured Gary Cooper
In 'High Noon'
He played the hand
From where he stood, solo.
—Irene Murrell, "A Tour in the Game"

One cricketer, of course, from the nonracial fold has achieved a prominence that has interrupted the dominant narrative for almost thirty years. His position is exceptional, his skills so tremendous that apartheid law could exile him but never thwart his ability. His accomplishments have assumed such legendary status that his name has been etched indelibly into the annals of apartheid history: Basil D'Oliveira, or "Dolly" as he is more commonly known on the hardy cricket fields of the Cape Flats and the manicured ovals of England. More than any other single individual, Basil D'Oliveira was responsible for South Africa's sporting isolation. A coloured player who came up through the ranks of St. Augustine's of Cape Town, one of nonracial cricket's most established clubs (which also produced Paul Adams), D'Oliveira was sponsored by his community to try his hand at the mid-level professional game in England. Dolly worked his way through the professional ranks in England, making his debut for Worcestershire in 1960 before being selected to represent his adopted country in 1966. Largely presumed to be an automatic choice for the 1968 England team to South Africa, "Dolly" was initially omitted from the squad by a pusillanimous selection committee who knew that the tour would be jeopardized by the inclusion of the coloured immigrant from Cape Town. A great controversy erupted in English cricket following "Dolly's" exclusion but he was picked at the very last minute as a replacement for the injured Tom Cartwright. The South African Prime Minister, B.J. Vorster, refused to admit an England side that he described as the "team of the antiapartheid movement." The 1968 tour was called off and South Africa's cricketing wilderness was only two summers off. Bill Lawry's 1970 Australians were the last official visitors until the 1990s.

Basil D'Oliveira returned to South Africa in January 1996 to watch the fifth test at Newlands, in which the country of his birth beat the country he has called home for more than thirty years. During the match, the UCBSA arranged a luncheon to honor "Dolly." Bacher, who would have played against him had the 1968 series taken place, was characteristically full of hubris during the proceedings. He hailed the ex-England allrounder "one of the most famous people in South Africa's nonracial society" and thanked him for "transforming"[12] the apartheid state. Always a man of few words, and flanked by the irrepressible Archbishop Tutu and Bacher, the stoic, "Gary Cooper-like" D'Oliveira was too moved to reply. Had he been able to respond, however, one wonders whether he might have recalled the poet Arthur Nortje's "Song for a passport." Like much of Nortje's poetry, "Song for a passport" ruminates on the condition of exile from South Africa. This poem, however, possesses a poignance that is striking because it is overwritten by the determination to remain permanently outside the experience of apartheid South Africa:

> *Now interviews and checks are in the offing:*
> *O ask me all but do not ask allegiance!*[13]

These final lines from "Song for a Passport" provide an especially apt metaphor for D'Oliveira, an exile whose "allegiance" to his adopted country has remained constant despite the postapartheid South African cricketing establishment's recent attempts at reappropriation. At the UCBSA luncheon, Bacher enthused, "deep down we will always regard you as a South African."

The D'Oliveirian moment is instructive within postapartheid cricket for a variety of reasons, not least of which is the way his reclamation has been so different from the reintegration of a white player. The reinscription of D'Oliveira has been a national project, one that provides a sharp contrast to the unproblematic ways an exiled white cricketer quietly assumed a leading role on the postapartheid playing field. An Afrikaner from the heartland city of Bloemfontein, Kepler Wessels was a talented left-handed batsman who moved to Cape Town to play for Western Province before leaving to represent the English county of Sussex; his career in England lasted from the mid-1970s through the early 1980s. Frustrated with South Africa's isolation, he decided to look elsewhere for a national home. Migrating to Australia and marrying a woman from Down Under, he qualified for his new country's national team. While making his new home in Australia, the Bloemfontein native pledged, expediently as it turned out, undying allegiance to his adopted country. Wessels's career in the Australian team lasted about five years; he failed primarily because he was unable to play West Indian fast bowling; after his Australian sojourn, he promptly returned to the land of his birth. Because of his subsequent disloyalty to Australia, Wessels's notoriety down under has taken on a markedly (un)popular aspect. A subplot of the mid-1990s Australian movie *Muriel's Wedding* parodies the Wessels scenario. It depicts a white South African swimmer so desperate for international competition that he offers to pay an Australian woman to marry him so that he could participate in the next Olympics. Physically and ideologically, the swimmer is a dead ringer for the dour-faced Wessels.

Wessels was, however, only one of a number of white South Africans who tried to overcome apartheid-inspired isolation by becoming athletic mercenaries. Their talents blunted by a lack of competition, enfranchised South African sportspersons introduced a whole new commercial dimension to international athletics. They traded their talent for a new passport, if not a new national identity; countries such as Britain were all too willing to barter. Most famous amongst these South African sporting "expatriates" is the middle-distance runner Zola Budd. A Bloemfontein native like Wessels, the barefoot wunderkind with the pronounced Afrikaner accent assumed British citizenship so that she could compete in the Los Angeles Olympics. Americans remember Budd only too well. In her (unsuccessful) effort to win a medal for Britain, she literally (if inadvertently) pushed the Olympic favorite Mary Decker Slaney right out of the race. When Wessels made his debut for Australia in the 1982–83 series against England, his opponents included his old Western Province batting partner Allan Lamb, an Englishman of very recent standing.

Wessels's decision to quit the Australian team turned out to be a timely departure, as political changes would have it. He was barely back in South Africa when the postapartheid era arrived and he was appointed captain of a side sorely lacking in international experience. Wessels's South African-ness, his loyalty to the country of his birth, was always already presumed. His brief stint as "Australian" represented only a hiatus enforced by the international ban on competition with the apartheid state; Wessels's true national status was as valid in an apartheid South Africa as it was in a postapartheid society. D'Oliveira's South African-ness, no matter how liminal or nostalgic, required a greater effort to reconstruct. White South African's expedience was never scrutinized, nor were the different motivations for "Dolly" and Wessels's "foreign" cricketing experiences explored.

Unlike Wessels, the old St. Augustine's cricketer resists easy reinterpellation into postapartheid history for a complex of reasons that range from the political to the personal. The least important of these is his renowned reticence. The most significant is that his 1968 selection put a firm end to the notion that racist politics could be kept out of South African sport. Constitutionally denied the right to represent his country, he was exiled by apartheid; in his turn, his selection by England exiled South Africa. Today, white South Africans can praise "Dolly" fulsomely, but they cannot bury the painful memory of the isolation their sport endured because of his selection. Apartheid society's refusal to acknowledge the legitimacy of his new national identity and his status as English cricketer propelled them into the international sports wilderness. Not withstanding the glossy efforts of postapartheid cricket's administrators to reappropriate this (once rejected) native son, Basil D'Oliveira remains a silent rebuke to the injustice of apartheid sport. Much of the tacit admonishment that D'Oliveira represents derives from his historic standing: He is a reluctant symbol of the talent and the skills that flourished in nonracial cricket. Because he is the exceptional cricketer who escaped apartheid oppression and thrived outside it, he is simultaneously a reminder of the cost of white racism.

The symbolic Basil D'Oliveira has been reclaimed in toto, transformed from metaphor and metonym of nonracial cricket into icon of an egalitarian postapartheid sport. D'Oliveira has had to assume the burden of overrepresentation, the exceptional cricketer who stands in place of and replaces the entire disenfranchised community. Overrepresentation functions here like *erasure* in that the sign *Dolly* marks an attempt to prevent a series of pointed political inquiries. The elevation and celebration of the old St. Augustine's all-rounder represents a crucial instance of postapartheid cricket's effort to orchestrate amnesia about its own racist past. The UCBSA does not want to engage the following questions: How many other "Dollys" did nonracial cricket produce? What would the status of nonracial cricket have been had more players achieved Dolly's success? How is apartheid's culpability for the waste of nonracial talent to be measured? How different in racial composition would the South African cricket team have been today if the SACB had not been so structurally underresourced? How many more Paul Adamses would there be in the current squad? These issues have to be taken up by reconstructing the D'Oliveira-Adams genealogy. Paul Adams is "Dolly's" heir, as the media is quick to claim, but a removed one. The lineage from "Dolly" to Adams extends through "Lefty" Adams, Ivan Dagnin, the Majiet brothers, and Michael Doman. The teenage spinner is the England player's great-grandson, the two St. Augustine's cricketers bookend the unheralded SACB generations who came in between.

The complex repercussions of D'Oliveira's exile, his inability to return as an English cricketer, and his ambiguous status today (local hero and insistent Englishman), demonstrate the burden of postapartheid nation building through sport. (Cricket's responsibility is especially onerous because rugby and football have no "Dolly" to be accommodated.) Assuming this task, the South African cricket community has attempted to produce a complicated and layered discourse that can address the demands of this historic conjuncture. Administrators, players, and the media are forging a discourse derived from the sometimes contradictory and occasionally complementary vocabularies of rationalization, apology, deferral, silence, and naturalization. In D'Oliveira's case, the language of apology and an all too spirited attempt at (re)naturalization are at work. But "Dolly" is the unusual case: His historic status demands a self-consciousness about the effects of apartheid. No such attention is paid to the consequences, past and present, of racist sport.

The Triumph of
White Culture and Capital

The traditions of all the dead generations weighs like a nightmare on the brain of the living.

> —**Karl Marx,** *The Eighteenth Brumaire of Louis Bonaparte*

In negotiating between apartheid and postapartheid, the transformation of the antagonistic SACB and SACU into the UCBSA, the nation's cricketing community is clearly privileging only one version of the past. The history of whites in the game has assumed, through the absence of a sustained counternarrative, *the* status of South African cricket. The conflicts that marked SACB and SACU relations are not so much ignored as they are hegemonically rendered. History is written by the victors—SACU claims the honors on that score. (The SACB's "traditions" do not "weigh" at all as the "brain" of postapartheid South African cricket—Marx, it appears, underestimated the power of white cultural capital.) This particular formation of the UCBSA is in itself a telling commentary on postapartheid cricket, and South African society as a whole. As the UCBSA is currently constituted, in control of the sport's resources, editing and censoring its past, and selectively writing its traditions, there is no possibility for challenging the cricket accounts it presents. There lies an instructive cultural tale.

A counternarrative depends on the willingness, the historical capacity, and the resources to provide an alternative history. The unification of the two ideologically opposed cricketing bodies (in a climate of national reconciliation) did not lend itself to remembering, celebrating, or enshrining the ideological imperatives of SACOS resistance. (The "United" in UCBSA reflects the ideological tenor of the times, the spirit of political reconciliation without a commitment to equity.) The "United" Cricket Board's priority is international competition, not a comprehension of historic differences. The SACB never possessed the means to challenge the white cricket establishment publicly, to offer playing or training facilities comparable to that of SACU. Nonracial cricket administered a moderately successful interprovincial competition but it could not organize international tours; the SACB did not include in its brief, however, the development of an international cricket program. Nonracial sport's main asset was its awareness of racism and injustice: Politically principled, SACOS believed it had (postcolonial) History on its side. In the "new" South African society where national unity is the dominant narrative of the day (although that account appears to be showing increasing signs of coming under public pressure), no longer is it possible to invoke the high moralism of antiapartheid to combat the reductive and inaccurate accounts of township cricket currently in vogue. The ANC government's commitment to national reconciliation, at considerable cultural and political costs to the black community, renders unlikely the possibility—at this too late stage—of a Zimbabwe-like probation. The moment for inaugurating such a policy has passed. At this juncture the best that can be achieved is the reappropriation and refashioning of the SACB platform, tailored to suit the contemporary terrain. Unless such an intervention is made, the disenfranchised's history will be distorted and disfigured beyond political recognition. Already it is but a minimal heave from the scrap heap of (anti)apartheid history.

The SACU hegemony within the UCBSA was achieved via a dual strategy. The evacuation of SACB history and, more strategically, the absorption of nonracial players and administrators, sans traditions. Nonracial players and clubs have had to accommodate themselves to new cricket infrastructures that bear no evidence of their struggles, their customs, or their past. Administrators have been assimilated, for the most part nominally, into the official structures of the SACU, in the guise of the UCBSA. Hassan Howa's successor as SACOS chief, Krish Mackerudj, is currently the president of the UCBSA, an office with more ceremony than clout.

Khaya Majola, Vincent Barnes, and Rushdie Majiet, outstanding SACB players and administrators, are among the few nonracial cricketers appointed to full-time positions in the new structure.

The story of disproportionate resources, the main reason for ten white players on the national team, has to be retold.[14] In the pre–Paul Adams era, just a few short years ago (the spinner made his international debut in 1995), all eleven were white. (Depending on the condition of the pitch, whether or not the management thinks it will be conducive to his type of bowling, Adams is sometimes omitted.) But like D'Oliveira, Adams should not have to bear the burden of overrepresentation. He should be one of several black—in the broadest sense of the term—players on the team; he isn't because apartheid inequities mitigated against the disenfranchised community. The schools lacked facilities, if not committed teachers, the townships and the suburbs suffered from a lack of playing fields. If the national team is to assume any semblance of the society's racial composition, the SACB platform has to be recovered. Because of apartheid ideology, such SACU training facilities as Newlands in Cape Town, Kingsmead in Durban, and the Wanderers in Johannesburg dominate South African cricket. They now host the international contests, monuments to superior white capital—a currency easily converted into white cricketing dominance. In and of themselves, these plush stadiums boldly attest to the triumph of SACU. At no point did the SACB possess comparable capital. Consequently, there are no memorials to the struggles of nonracial cricket, no SACB archives, no acknowledgment or incorporation of its struggles.[15] Moralism seldom converts into hard currency. It does, however, provide a ready counter to fictitious renderings of history.

One such attempt to reconstruct history is the SACU rendering of the "rebel tours" it organized from the mid-1980s to the very beginning of the 1990s. Frustrated by its international isolation, the SACU decided to embark upon a new strategy. They put together their own series of tours by attracting groups of players from other countries who were prepared to contravene the Gleneagles Agreement. Using funds secured from the government and South African Breweries, Ali Bacher was the SACU point man in these operations. He lured these players with exorbitant amounts of money (by cricket's standards, anyway) and put together squads of renegade English, Sri Lankan, West Indian, and Australian players. These cricketers either were just past their prime or were a little too young to have yet made their mark upon, say, the Australian or Sri Lankan game. These rebel tourists competed against the cream of white South Africa's talent.[16] (The West Indies and the Sri Lankan authorities banned their "rebel" players for life; the other two nations imposed bans of under three years.) The SACB and SACOS spearheaded the opposition to these visits, a resistance that was shared by a significant segment of the disenfranchised population.

Yet in October 1995, Bacher had the temerity to suggest that he did not grasp the depth of black resentment:

> If we knew then what we know now about the bitterness those rebel tours were going to cause, we would have thought twice. This may sound a bit naive but the fact is that in those days the blacks were not allowed to demonstrate and it simply did not occur to us how strongly they felt.[17]

Bacher, of course, has long since proved himself too shrewd an administrator to be ideologically "naive"; he simply has a cynically selective political memory—the "weight" of SACOS's history has had little impact upon his expedient philosophy. He is also in a position of cultural authority from which he can insert massive silences into black South African history. Whether or not blacks were "allowed to demonstrate," they had been doing so for centuries and with a particular intensity for more than fifteen years by the time the "rebel tours" came around. The Soweto protest of 1976 was certainly not sanctioned by the apartheid state, nor were the insurrections of the mid-1980s.

The public conception and the representation of the game, however, is most disturbing. The disproportionate racial representation, the retention of the team's (nick)name, and, most important, the ease with which a continuum between the apartheid side of 1970 and the postapartheid side of the mid-1990s has been established demonstrate how little has changed. But this surely cannot be the case? Have the political conditions not changed so dramatically as to call for a major reconceptualization of the national cricket team? Isn't there, after all, a huge difference between the government of Nelson Mandela and the apartheid regime of B.J. Vorster? The public discourse, however, for which the white press is mainly but not exclusively responsible, is one of insistent continuity. Black and white journalists, radio and television commentators such as Heinrich Marnitz, Omar Henry, and Trevor Quirk consistently invoke the skills and accomplishments of the apartheid era's renowned players. The media recalls Eddie Barlow, Mike Procter, the Pollock brothers, Graeme and Peter (Peter is currently chairman of the national selectors), and Barry Richards—some of the finest cricketers in the world at that time. Hansie Cronje, who captains a team in which he cannot properly command a place on individual merit, leads a side that is regularly measured against that of its "predecessors," the 1970 Springboks—skippered, incidentally, by one Ali Bacher.

In pure cricketing talent, of course, there is no real comparison. Bacher's team boasted several world class players. Richards and

Graeme Pollock were among the best batsmen of their generation; Barlow was an inspirational opening bat and a medium pace bowler of ingenuity and verve. Mike Procter and Peter Pollock were menacing quick bowlers, and Procter was no slouch with the bat either. Of the current squad, only the all-rounders Jacques Kallis and Lance Klusener and the fast bowler Allan Donald are recognized as players of international stature. In racial composition, however, the parallel is apt. The South African cricketing universe circa 1999 is not markedly different from that of two generations ago. There are now thirteen white players in the national squad as opposed to fourteen. Only the unexpected rise of Paul Adams, the young spin bowling prodigy from the coloured lower middle class, distinguishes Cronje's team from Bacher's.[18] The pivotal aspect of the comparison between the 1970 and the 1990s sides, however, is that it reconfigures white South African cricket history: It eliminates the twenty-year hiatus between the apartheid society's enforced isolation and the postapartheid state's readmission to world cricket. The "lost years" of the 1970s and the 1980s, alleviated only in part by "rebel tours," cannot be recovered but they can be written out through an imaginary continuity.

Now that the postapartheid nation's (white) men have taken to the field again, resplendent in crisp white flannels, shirts, and pullovers and topped with the green-and-gold hat of the old apartheid team, the blow of two decades in the cricket wilderness has been ameliorated; at worst, it has been rendered a vague memory. It is apropos that Wessels and Cronje's teams should, like Bacher's and Peter van der Merwe's before them, take the traditional apartheid nickname of the Springboks. For in truth the Springboks have returned to international competition—which of course begs the pivotal question: Is the postapartheid team *returning* to international competition or is the nation competing for the first time? If the postapartheid society is indeed a new and democratic one, 1991 should mark South Africa's *entrance* into the international cricket arena. The all-white teams that competed before this moment should be acknowledged as cricketing footnotes, a testament to a racist past that should be neither hastily recalled nor easily invoked. There are, after all, significant differences between the two epochs. During the apartheid era, black countries in the ICC, led by the West Indies and India, refused to play against white South African sides. Today, the West Indies, India, Pakistan, and Sri Lanka are part of the South African cricket schedule. When the Springboks played against Australia and England in Cape Town or Durban in 1970, the grounds were strictly segregated, coloureds and blacks occupying the worst seats in the stadium. These seating arrangements have, survived the demise of apartheid. At Newlands in Cape Town, coloured spectators still flock to their old places under the famous "Willows," named after the tall willow trees that provide shade from the summer sun in this southwestern corner of the ground. Although largely replaced by a new stand now, the "Willows" are still favored in part because of economics, but largely because of a tradition that goes back decades. Much like the "Hill" in Sydney, Australia, the fans in the coloured section are full of witticisms and easy banter. The legacy of physical separation is stronger than the fledgling reality of postapartheid structural changes.

Locally and internationally, however, the dominant designation of South Africa's postapartheid participation in international cricket is written as the country's readmission into the world fold. In and of itself the use of such terms as *readmission* and *return* are tantamount to legitimizing the apartheid past; it implicitly authorizes white postapartheid hegemony. It invalidates the SACOS struggle, obliterates the history of nonracial cricket, and anoints the achievements of white players. Furthermore, such a conception of postapartheid cricket situates the likes of Basil D'Oliveira as the exceptional token, black cricketer of merit and repute. There is as much at stake in the language of "return" as there is political significance embedded in the name "Springbok."

It is not surprising that half-hearted efforts to rename the national side the "Proteas,"[19] a rare South African flower indigenous to the Western Cape, have fallen on deaf ears. A renaming of the national cricket side is dependent upon a major ideological refashioning, a substantial project that requires rethinking a society's past, how its cultural signifiers function, and how political histories (of oppression and resistance) are inscribed within those signs. To rename is to critically appraise the past: It necessitates a realignment of political forces, the replacement of offensive old symbols with ones that are new and in ideologically good repair. South Africans, restricted as they are by the ANC government's policy of reconciliation, do not have such an option at their disposal. They trek into the postapartheid future emblazoned with the symbols of the apartheid past.

He's Got Them in a Spin

The word 'googly' was first used in a newspaper article in New Zealand in 1903 to describe Bosanquet's new ball. The word means uncanny, weird, ghostly, and is supposed to be of Maori origin.

—R.W. Cockshut, "The Googly and Lewis Carroll"

The issue of naming assumed considerable ideological salience during the selection of Paul Adams. Selected as the youngest and the newest member of the national side in December 1995, the media displayed a disconcerting lack of irony and self-reflexivity when they uncritically took to dubbing the coloured Adams the "SpinBok." He is certainly a spinner, a slow bowler with the ability to make the ball move in surprising ways. But a Springbok? As a coloured he is surely excluded by the apartheid-derived definition that links Kallis to Barlow. How is his lineage akin to the lineage that connects Allan Donald to Peter Pollock? And how can the history of the Springboks be made to accommodate Adams? How does he reconfigure, or configure, Springbok history? Does he simply disrupt it or can his selection be deployed more strategically?

In the initial media coverage of his selection, Adams's cricketing style provided an easy answer. He was exceptional, not so much in race or talent, but through his unorthodox bowling action. Adams's style of bowling is indeed unconventional, to say the least. In a sport where smooth physical action and unadorned athleticism are prerequisites, Adams breaks all the rules. His delivery of the cricket ball is full of awkward contortions, so eye-catching that commentators such as Eddie Barlow have likened its ungainliness to that of a "frog in a blender." Journalist Jon Swift was equally imaginative, describing the delivery as the "strangled action of capsized terrapin." The animal imagery persists among Adams's cricket friends from the Cape Flats. Lapsing into the colloquial, they labeled him "Gogga," an unflattering but affectionate term for an insect.[20]

When attention did switch from Adams's style to his race (without ever relinquishing the former as spectacle), the trope of exceptionality intensified. (The "otherness" of the Maori term, an origin long since lost and obscured through regular cricket usage, has returned in the "uncanniness" of the "Cape Coloured." Adams, no slouch at bowling the "googly" himself, is connected by his "weird" skill to a substantive history of cricket racism, however coded or poetic the description might be.) Despite being the youngest player ever to be selected for apartheid or postapartheid South Africa ("Paul Adams became the youngest player to wear cricket's green and gold at 18 years and 340 days."),[21] that distinction was overshadowed by his racial status. In one of the more considered pieces on Adams's race and background, English cricket columnist Peter Johnson writes: "He is what was once dismissively known as a Cape Coloured, brought up in an area where . . . equality is a word they are just beginning to understand."[22] It is paradoxical, but telling, that Adams was at once touted as a symbol of postapartheid cricketing hope and as a vision of the society's cricketing future—reporter Mark Nicholas claimed him as a "torch for the new South Africa"[23]—while being interpellated into the hegemonic structures of old.

South Africa is psychically torn, the memories of inequality and injustice deeply ingrained; yet democracy is so novel and invigorating an experience. There is a predictable commensurability between the psychic ambivalence and the immense importance that accrues so quickly to new symbols such as Adams. South African rugby has produced its second generation of this phenomenon in the coloured winger Chester Williams, quite literally (and expediently) the poster boy for the 1995 World Cup. The winger, and before him Errol Tobias, a scintillating coloured flyhalf who played "normal sport" (and currently mayor of his home town of Caledon), for the past few years has been fulfilling in rugby the same role that Adams is in cricket. Cricket, in fact, has long been looking for its own "Chester Williams," a camera-friendly black body that bears testament to the bona fides of white dominated sports codes and their administrators. The lone, alien(ated) black representative's highly publicized presence reflects the "successful" transition of all aspects of postapartheid society, not just sport or culture. Adams and Williams are both young coloured athletes who bear the burden of overrepresentation. The traditionally disenfranchised communities' national standing in cricket and rugby is contingent upon every performance of their single representative. Sporting success translates all too easily, understandably so, into communal achievement; failure by Williams or Adams is inconceivable. This is an unfair burden, but one enforced by a status that is multiple in its contradictions: the historic condition of being a black athletic minority in a white dominated sport in a black majority society.

Overrepresentation has transformed Adams from gifted cricketer into a loaded sociopolitical symbol. He has become a figure worthy of emulation for the society's traditionally disenfranchised communities, a lodestar for the country's cricketing future. Paul Adams is a metaphor of possibility and transition. The young cricketer is a sign of potentiality, representing the hope that a society with a racist past can overcome its discriminatory history and meld into a nonracial and egalitarian society. Ideally, of course, the "equality" his community has just acquired constitutionally will not just be rhetorical but a transformative material experience. In that respect he becomes a figure of transition, the exceptional player through whom the future becomes racially distinct from the past. The next generation of South African cricketers, as prefigured in Adams, will look less like Hansie Cronje and more like the coloured spinner. The nation will still be clad in white, but those flannels will adorn black and coloured and indian bodies, as well as white ones: the nation re-presented. But in reality, Adams's selection inaugurates only a tentative new era, one that negotiates with the old edifices of representation and organizational dominance from a position of symbolic promise but structural disadvantage.

For this reason Adams can be so effectively interpellated as the "youngest player to wear cricket's green and gold." In this rhetorical sleight of hand, he is both naturalized as national cricketer and subsumed under the sign of the Springbok. Adams's designation of Springbok appropriates him through writing him into and against a history of oppression antagonistic to the teenage spinner. Apartheid is solely responsible for Adams's lack of racial predecessors. He is being asked to make history bereft of basic resources such as cultural memory or the ideological traditions of his embattled community. He is expected to be a cricketing pioneer without a political past. He is deprived of his own community's history, and he is unable to acknowledge how apartheid laws denied him a lineage that is rote to his teammates Kallis and Donald.

The teenage spinner is, like D'Oliveira, a bad fit with white traditions, yet the postapartheid nation in white flannels is symbolically dependent upon him for the maintenance of its racial dominance. Adams functions as a figure of possibility and as a marker of limitation. He affirms black potential while simultaneously confirming white hegemony. Through D'Oliveira's postapartheid reinscription and Adams's inclusion in the Springbok team, white South Africa is symbolically absolving itself of its racist history without having to relinquish the privileges it has accrued via apartheid. The nation in cricketing whites is a powerful metaphor for white South Africa's postapartheid sporting dominance, an authority no longer fettered by the prospect of international or local cultural sanctions. The South African cricket team is an emblem of a rare postcolonial victory, a triumph untempered by an ICC probation, a radical disruption of the apartheid structures, or the memory of oppression. The major achievement of the nation in white is, appropriately, that it has won a widespread postapartheid approval without being considered offensive. Except, of course, for those to whom the game signifies a great deal more than just cricket.

Notes

1. In the wake of the West Indies's unsuccessful World Cup in 1996, the then-captain Richie Richardson was replaced by the Jamaican fast bowler Courtney Walsh. Following Walsh's decision to step down as skipper, but not as player, the Jamaican handed over the reigns to Brian Lara. The Trinidadian has, in his brief stint as captain (he took over in 1998), seen the steady decline of both the West Indian team and his own form. Under Lara's leadership, the West Indies team performed badly at the 1999 World Cup in England, failing to qualify for the second (knockout) round of the competition.

2. Lara Sorry for His Slip-Up," *Daily Mail* (London), 9 March 1996.

3. C.L.R. James, *Beyond a Boundary* (New York: Pantheon, 1983), 248.

4. For an in-depth discussion of Caribbean cricket see Hilary Beckles and Brian Stoddart's (eds.) *Liberation Cricket: West Indies Cricket Culture* (Kingston: Ian Randle Publishers, 1995), a series of essays that explores many aspects of the game in the region. A collection deeply influenced by C.L.R. James, *Liberation Cricket* owes its critical focus to the Trinidadian doyen's seminal work, *Beyond A Boundary*.

5. Michael Manley, *A History of West Indies Cricket*, rev. ed. (Kingston: West Indies Publishing Company, 1995), 148. See also James's *Beyond a Boundary* for a fuller account of the movement to appoint Worrell captain.

6. See a two-part series on the D'Oliveira affair titled "D'Oliveira Affairs Shameful Secrets" (15 February 1999) and "What REALLY Happened with D'Oliveira" (22 February 1999) in the *Weekly Mail and Guardian* (South Africa) for a historically adept account of the event.

7. "Hunte Speaks Out," *Daily Telegraph* (London), 18 October 1995.

8. Following the 1998 World Cup in France, South Africa appointed Trott Moloto as its first full-time black coach. After Barker's dismissal in late 1997, Jomo Sono was appointed interim coach—at his own behest, it should be noted. The white skipper, Neil Tovey, was succeeded by the black defender Lucas Radebe, who has served four coaches as captain—Barker, Sono, Phillipe Troussier, and Moloto.

9. "Field of Dreams," *Times* (London), 20 May 1995.

10. From mid-1998 until the 2004 Games were awarded to Athens, a local anti-Olympic movement has been developing in Cape Town.

A grassroots organization linked to left political groupings has been spearheading this drive because they believe more urgent issues should be confronted in South African society. Graffiti ("Why spend R1.8 billion on the Olympics? Build Houses!") has become a feature of life on the predominantly coloured Cape Flats. A fair measure of (tacit) support is presumed for the anti-Olympic movement and the entire South African sporting and political community is watching these ideological antagonists do battle over sport.

11. The relationship between SACOS and the black community was so complex that it could not be accounted for by any single factor. SACOS's lack of resources prevented it from making significant inroads into the community, its ideological and political roots lay outside of the ANC (the organization with the greatest purchase in the black community), and SACOS's principles could not accommodate the cultural–real politics schism that characterized black sporting life in the "normal sports" era. The black community was able to reconcile the privileges its players accrued from participating in "normal sport" with the ability to oppose politically the very National Party government that oversaw this cultural practice. It was a contradiction that SACOS could address, an expediency beyond its ideological ken. These are some of the issues that have to be engaged as a crucial part of the cultural history of disenfranchised South Africa.

12. "D'Oliveira Remains on England's Side," *Times* (London), 3 January 1996.

13. Arthur Nortje, *Dead Roots* (London: Heinemann, 1973), 30.

14. The February 1996 issue of *Sports Illustrated* (7 February 1996), carefully documented this phenomenon. Touring the townships of South Africa, the magazine

captured the continuing material deprivations that prevent black youth from competing on a level playing field with their white counterparts.

15. Since the mid-1990s, a community-inspired movement, "The District Six Museum," has been established.

This organization intends to document, as part of an ongoing process, the history of deracination in Cape Town. The museum has been open for almost five years now and on 31 August 1996 it hosted a program titled "(Dis) Playing the Game: A Celebration of More than a Century of Sport," a testament to the history of nonracial sports organizations with their roots in the community of District Six. My thanks to Mr. Leslie Van Breda for this information.

16. Omar Henry, one of a small minority of coloured players who participated in "normal sport," represented South Africa in a few of these "rebel" tests.

17. "England's Trip of Hope," *Mail on Sunday* (London), 22 October 1995.

18. As I mentioned in the Introduction, the black fast bowler Mhkaya Ntini was briefly Adams's teammate on the national team. However, Ntini was found guilty of rape and although he is still supported by the cricketing authorities it appears unlikely that he will be able to fulfill the charismatic role Adams has since 1995. Since this chapter was first published as an essay in 1997 in *Social Text*, several more players of color have represented South African provincial sides. Roger Telemachus, a medium fast bowler from the province of Boland, has even made the national team on the odd occasion. For the most part, however, the "nation in white" has remained precisely that: predominantly white. So much so that Paul Adams was not even included in the squad for the 1999 World Cup in England, replaced by a singularly untalented—and hugely ineffective—white spinner Nic Boje.

19. "Proteas" is, however, itself a name sullied by the apartheid past. During the early days of the "normal sport" era, the rugby team that represented the coloured community was known by this name; the black side was called the "Leopards" and the white team was called, predictably, the "Springboks."

Errol Tobias, as I noted in the essay, is among the best-known rugby players to come up through the ranks of the "Proteas." Note, though, that the emblem on the national cricket cap bears an image of both the Springbok and the Protea; the latter, however, is almost never invoked as a national symbol.

20. These commentators all revived an old colonialist trope in their depictions of the young bowler. At the height of nineteenth-century British colonial rule in the Indian subcontinent, talented local cricketers were groomed for incorporation into the racist structure. Indian cricketers such as the great batsman Ranjitsinhji, his nephew Duleepsinhji, and the first Nawab of Pataudi, were manicured by a certain kind of orientalist discourse for English consumption in those days. They were presented as honorary Englishmen, so gifted as cricketers that they were elevated to a level exceeding that of ordinary colonial subjects. On this basis, they were selected to play for the imperial state. Ranjitsinhji, who played during the era C.L.R. James labels the Golden Age of Cricket, ranks among the most accomplished batsmen ever. During this epoch, Indian spin bowlers were frequently described as "wizards," cricketers whose performances conjured up visions, as Ken Surin put it in a recent conversation, of "snake charming and rope tricks in a Kiplingesque bazaar." All because of the in-

scrutable and unpredictable ball movement these bowlers could induce. In the 1920s and 1930s, the aborigine fast bowler Eddie Gilbert was called for throwing and some twenty years later the Barbados speed merchant Charlie Griffith was similarly accused.

21. "Breathing New Life into an Old Game," *Mail and Guardian* (Manchester), 5 January 1996.

22. "Weird Magic of a Boy with a Sting in his Wrist," *Daily Mail* (London), 26 December 1995.

23. "Whirling Adams Carries Cape's Good Hopes into Port Elizabeth's Lion's Den," *Daily Telegraph* (London), 23 December 1995.

In much the same vein, Eddie Barlow ebulliently pronounced that the young spinner would "change the face of South African cricket," *Jerusalem Post*, 26 December 1996.

6

McCarthyism, Township Style

Symbols are mental constructs: they provide people with the means to make meaning. In doing so, they also provide them with the means to express the particular meanings which the community has for them.

—A. Cohen, *The Symbolic Construction of Community*

We don't need another hero.

—Tina Turner

Hanover Park Hero:
But Not Everyone Knows
What That Means . . .

Contrary to Tina Turner's brassy claim, what "new" nations need more than anything in the moment of construction, that most arduous but exhilarating of political projects, is heroes. These figures represent, to the outside world and the nation, the current promise and the future potential of the society. Societies previously divided along the lines of race or ethnicity most urgently require, to accelerate and solidify the process of nation-building, symbols of transcendence, heroes who can overcome the bitter disjunctures of the past and signal a new, egalitarian beginning; in a fin de siècle world, this has come to be imagined—if not realized—as a nonracial, nonsexist, nonhomophobic, and democratic social arrangement. Most often these figures belong to a mythic past (in both the long-range and the more immediate senses of term), men and occasionally women who gave unstintingly of themselves to achieve the freedom or liberation of the present. Most frequently these heroes are identifiably political, veterans of anticolonial, anti-imperial, or anti-invasionary struggles, figures instrumental in the production of this new historical mo-

153

ment. It is far more unlikely, but not unprecedented, for cultural icons to perform the same role as political leaders. Artists, musicians, sportsmen, and sportswomen may speak of and for the nation, but they are seldom conceived of as—or expected to be—emblematic.

Postapartheid South Africa[1] is not unusual, then, in either its adulation for heroes or its privileging of the political in composing its pantheon of heroes. In the wake of apartheid's demise, a polyglot of South Africans with a history of political involvement have been reinscribed in the national imaginary. Blacks, whites, indians, coloureds, men, and women, have been included in this newly constructed pantheon. These figures range from Sol Plaatje to Archbishop Trevor Huddleston, Clements Kadalie to Fatima Meer, Harry Gwala to Winnie Mandela (whose place on this list is more contentious than most), Albertina Sisulu to Ruth First, and Joe Slovo to Chris Hani. This roll call of heroes culminates, predictably, in that ultimate of South African icons, Nelson Mandela. Powerful as these figures are, however, they all signal (to varying degrees), more the present than the future, less the present than the past. For all his efficacy as a national symbol (beloved by the historically enfranchised and disenfranchised alike), Mandela is intensely a sign of the current, the embodiment of the victory of the postapartheid present over the intense racial conflicts of the past. A leader who imbued the interregnum with a rare stability, a man who contributed greatly to the in-formation (the exacting transition from racism to democracy) dispensation, he will soon be available only as a figure who can be projected onto—and not into—the future.

It is doubtful whether he can, despite his iconic authority, sustain the nation indefinitely beyond his presidency. He will, of course, be ceaselessly invoked in moments of national celebration or crisis—though one expects the end of his reign will see more of the latter than the former. His retirement from office might mark the first such instance of national uncertainty, much as his political departure will mark a rare instance of national (and international) acknowledgement and unity. Indeed, this process may have already begun. When he took his leave of parliament in March 1999, centrist-left political allies and right-wing foes alike expressed their acclaim and gratitude for "Madiba" ("father of the nation"), their praises doing little to disguise their concern about the future. Such gestures, of course, do nothing but beg the question: What will post-Mandela life look like for this society? As South Africa heads into its second democratic elections in mid-1999, political leaders who can instill a sense of optimism about the future are in short supply. Not surprisingly, given the growing economic uncertainty, increasing violence, collapsing infrastructure, and ill-conceived and underfunded educational policies that have marked the first five years of ANC rule; moreover, South Africa is a nation warily anticipating the ascension of the current vice president, Thabo Mbeki. Mandela's successor is a dour, heavy-handed, uninspiring bureaucrat, a man without either "Madiba's" charisma or his credibility.

If contemporary South Africa's political heroes represent the "residual" moment, in Raymond Williams's sense of the term where traces of the past manifests itself in the practices of the present, then the new society's cultural icons belong unambiguously to the mode of the "emergent." The "emergent" cultural hero stands as a new kind of figure, attentive to history and current development but more invested in reconceptualizing how culture functions in the present and how it might be reconfigured in the future. No cultural figure marks the "emergent" more than Benni McCarthy, the talented young footballer who belongs to the first generation of South Africans to come of age in a postapartheid society. Raised in the township of "Hanover Park, on the Cape Flats,"[2] the twenty-year-old striker fired the imagination of his countrymen and women with a stellar performance at the 1998 African Nations Cup. How could one not sit up and take notice of this flamboyant township kid? He did, after all, announce his arrival on the national scene spectacularly by scoring four goals against northwestern neighbor Namibia in the qualifying rounds of the tournament; no small feat since it set the record for the most goals by a South African in an international contest. All this, in the space of "less than half an hour . . . catapulted McCarthy into the status of South African superstar."[3] He was transformed, within the brief period it took him to devastate the Namibian defense, from "anonymous" young player into national hero, from township dweller into lodestar for the hopes of the postapartheid moment.

By virtue of his youth (half his two decades were lived under apartheid, the other half either anticipating or under the auspices of the Mandela government), he became a symbol of a "retrospective continuity" (how the past can be overcome in and through the present, signaling a "continuous" future), transcendence, and the "future-present." McCarthy's achievements signal the triumph of "black" South Africa over the deprivations of apartheid and the imagining of his Namibian performance as normative within the coming postapartheid epoch. He is the "future," if only metonymically, of the township come to dramatic fruition in the present. In a society where the past is still all too pressing and raw a psychological wound, the culture of the present has to offer itself as an antidote, prescient and pregnant with a vision of the future. Not surprisingly, McCarthy and his cricketing equivalent Paul Adams have inspired an entire generation of black, coloured, indian, and even white schoolboys to envisage careers in professional sport. So much so that none of these schoolboys, writes a local journalist, "thinks he will become a doctor, a lawyer or a teacher. They all dream of becoming footballers and doing even more than McCarthy has done for his country."[4] Every South African boy, to both invoke and exceed basketball superstar Michael Jordan, not only wants to be like Benni, he wants to leave his hero in the footballing dust. The present inspires the future, on a grand scale. For these kids, the present is only potential; they will be its realization. In these schoolboys' youthful estimation, Benni is only a foil for their future feats; he is not the nation's footballing fulfillment.

Appropriated by all, from township schoolboys to leaders in government, who the new national hero is has been (understandably) lost amidst this footballing furor. How Benni McCarthy has been read and politically situated cannot be engaged, this final chapter will argue, without recalling that he is from Hanover Park. He is not simply a "township" player, he is a coloured kid from a coloured township in Cape Town, a footballer whose cultural significance varies from one South African constituency to the next. "Benni McCarthy" registers differently in coloured Hanover Park than he does in black Soweto or indian Chatsworth. A coloured player starring in a predominantly black sport, McCarthy's racial background has been largely ignored in favor of class analysis. "I am proud to represent the people in the township, I will try and score as many goals as possible for them,"[5] the national hero told reporters on the eve of his departure for World Cup '98 in France. The "township" has become, through this mode of articulation, a cryptic, incorporative sign: It designates all of historically disenfranchised South Africa, a class-based rhetorical gesture that eliminates racial difference. The "township" stands as an uncritical code for broader "black" poverty and deprivation, emphasizing an (imaginary) shared class identity uncomplicated by the fissures of apartheid's racial categories. Claimed indiscriminately by his fellow South Africans, McCarthy's own racial trajectory and past has to be reduced to an elliptical "township," making the Hanover Park experience commensurate with Soweto with Chatsworth (which it is not). The "difference," as Toni Morrison so incisively reminds us in *The Bluest Eye*, "is all the difference there is."

For a community with such a long history of racial, cultural, and ideological ambivalence, coloured South Africans understand Benni McCarthy differently, appropriating him in a way that is distinct from other disenfranchised constituencies. A product of the Western Cape, the only region in the country to return the party of the apartheid regime, McCarthy has been claimed as a "local" hero whose national triumphs speak of a complicated admixture of pride in, alienation from, and partial affiliation with the new nation. A community that frequently sees itself as situated on the margins of postapartheid South Africa, McCarthy functions as a symbol of partial or momentary integration: Through his triumphs, coloureds vicariously, if only fleetingly, become members of the new nation. Politically "different" because of their voting patterns and their particular political and cultural history, international football contests enable them to temporarily overcome their remove from the new dispensation. McCarthy's goalscoring metaphorically ameliorates their support for the traditional oppressor, undermining their "political" (reduced to participation in elections) affiliation with the National Party and drawing them closer to the country's predominantly black football team; his swift strikes against Namibia and Denmark, too, situate them, if only for the duration of the game, as "South Africans"—coloureds are transformed into transient members of the new nation.

In these moments, the cultural triumphs over the ideological, the tentative national identity, takes precedence over a "hybrid" racial one. The resilience of the cultural, however, is dubious and unreliable in the hardened face of political alienation. Such unreliability, of course, provokes the question: Is the coloured community capable of partial affiliation only, of integrating itself through vicarious cultural triumph? Will Benni McCarthy, and to a lesser extent Paul Adams, have to bear the burden of coloured interpellation into the postapartheid state? Represented by a nationally recognized hero, coloureds have been offered an opportunity to see how they might be vital to the composition and success of postapartheid society, how the nation's cultural accomplishment (especially in so racially coded a sport as football) might (vicariously) depend on "them." McCarthy's capacity to momentarily draw "his" community—and he does acknowledge Hanover Park as his "home" even though neither he nor his family still lives there, thereby implicitly naming himself coloured—speaks of an especially complicated ideological location. He is a particularly vexed kind of "national" hero because his own constituency is only precariously attached to the nation.

McCarthy's iconic standing, moreover, at once obviates and throws into sharp relief the contributions of other coloured players to the success of the national football team. Because he is not the first coloured footballer to succeed, his status has to be interrogated more closely. For instance, Mark Williams, another township footballer who was crucial to South Africa's victory in the 1996 African Nation's Cup, has never "signified"—in Henry Louis Gates's sense of the term—in the ways that McCarthy does. Quinton Fortune, currently one of McCarthy's national team colleagues and a technically superior player to the Hanover Park striker, is a possible candidate to succeed the current sweeper (central defender) and captain Lucas Radebe when the defender steps down as leader. Compared to McCarthy, however, the talented Fortune labors in relative national obscurity. To account for the "Benni phenomenon" or "Benni fever,"[6] as his hometown newspaper dubbed it, we have to explain why so much cultural weight has accrued to McCarthy. This chapter will engage the issue in terms of generation, the position he plays, and the economic and social opportunities available to him. His ability to represent both the coloured community and the nation depends, in some ways, as much upon what is articulated as upon what is silenced—or simply left unsaid in one venue and informally disseminated in another.

More than anything, McCarthy is a symbol of coloured integration into the nation. His colouredness has to be, in the same rhetorical maneuver, acknowledged and denied: It has be implicitly recognized so that, through him, his community can be incorporated into the nation. It has to remain, however, an unspoken—and unspeakable—identity because to publicly emphasize it would be to remind the nation of his racial difference, of his liminal blackness and of the marginal, conflicted relationship the coloured community has to the postapartheid state. McCarthy, after all, traces his roots to the coloured townships of the Western Cape, that idiosyncratic political domain where the National Party still rules. McCarthy's status as national icon is complicated, an amalgam of cultural affirmations and racial contradictions that render his public representation such an engaging palimpsest of a political text. He is the national symbol whose community has a tenuous relationship to the nation, he is the icon whose background has to be rhetorically nuanced for fear of accentuating his racial difference, he is the recognizably black body whose blackness is truncated—at the very least, complicated—by an accent that speaks of a particular region and a community whose blackness is hybrid. And his accomplishments enable, for significant constituencies of coloured people on the Cape Flats, that rare moment when they can say, with something approaching Richard Rive's "full conviction," "I am, at this particular conjuncture, a South African." McCarthy, in other words, makes South Africans out of township (and some middle-class) coloureds.

For a complex of reasons, McCarthy's status as icon does not derive only from his skill as a footballer. Because of postapartheid economic opportunities, he has been able to self-consciously mold himself as a glamorous athlete. In addition to his copper-dyed hair, he has "gold in his teeth, diamonds in his ear"[7] and he aspires to drive a Mercedes Benz.[8] If Paul Adams, contorted in his bowling actions but reticent in his off-field demeanor, represents the slow transformation of cricket (a predominantly white sport), then the flashy McCarthy stands for the rambunctious energies and stylized individuality that characterize football, the country's most popular social practice. Football is, as argued in Chapter 4, the sport's code most unambiguously associated with South Africa's disenfranchised communities.

Forwards Know How to Have Fun

Ian Rush is a natural. Its as simple as that. The man is a fine player who can take the ball from either side, has the pace to bury defenders and believes he is going to score whenever he gets half a chance.

—Kenny Dalglish, as quoted in *Shoot Magazine*, February 1978

When South Africa won the African Nation's Cup in 1996, the victory over Morocco was secured by a brace of goals from Mark Williams, a thirty-year-old coloured striker. In the wake of this triumph, Williams went on to star for South African glamour club Kaiser Chiefs before enjoying a brief and unsuccessful stint in Brazil. Even though the 1996 Nation's Cup was South Africa's first accomplishment in international football and wildly celebrated in the presence of the newly-elected President Mandela, neither Williams nor any of his teammates garnered the kind of media attention that McCarthy has. A graduate of nonracial football (he learned his trade with the amateur club Clarewood), Williams went on to "defect" to Hellenic, a white-owned professional club in Cape Town. (In the apartheid era, "defection" meant leaving the nonracial SACOS ranks to play "normal sport": This decision carried considerable social sanction, effectively rendering the defector persona non grata to his former teammates, his community, and the broader nonracial community. "Defection" was, in SACOS terms, the ultimate ideological crime: abandoning the nonracial code in favor of "normal sport" was legitimately understood as giving tacit endorsement to the apartheid state.) A deft striker with a nifty turn of pace, Williams only came to prominence in the final stages of the 1996 tourney. Before his goals in the semifinal and the final, the ex-postman from the impoverished Cape Flats neighborhood of Parkwood was simply one of four strikers competing for a starting job in coach Clive Barker's squad. Williams is, however, a complex figure, a player both reluctantly embraced and rejected by the coloured townships, simultaneously a villain and the compromised, implicit champion of the SACOS cause.

After Williams's brief flirtation with national glory, he was succeeded in the South African team by a number of strikers, none of whom were able to find the back of the net with regularity. Phil "Chippa" Masinga, a bruising journeyman of a forward, did enough to retain his place but seldom set the world alight; Jerry "Legs of Thunder" Sikhosana promised much but delivered little; and Shaun Bartlett, another coloured player from Cape Town, showed poise but scored infrequently. (Bartlett did, however, perform admirably at World Cup '98, scoring two goals in the final game against Saudi Arabia.) The player who invites the most comparison with McCarthy, however, is Quinton Fortune. Only two years older than the Hanover Park striker and from a similar background (he grew up on the mean streets of Kew Town, a gang and drug-infested coloured neighborhood in Cape Town), Fortune is a midfielder who also plies his trade in Europe. However, while McCarthy cannot force his way into the staring lineup at Dutch champions' Ajax, Fortune is a regular with Atletico Madrid in the Spanish *Prima Liga*. A gifted and intelligent player, Fortune is that rare combination of midfielder: combative in the tackle, a redoubtable player who executes his defensive responsibilities with aplomb and relish, superior in his vision (he can "read" the game, as football pundits say, which is why he is a natural to succeed current national skipper Radebe), a brilliant passer of the ball, and occasionally capable of scoring breathtaking goals. Physically stronger than the slight McCarthy, Fortune is supremely conditioned and durable. He takes knocks as easily as he hands them out. But Fortune's job is in the "engine room," the place where the game is won or lost but not where most of the kudos go at the end of the contest. Fortune's is not the "glamour" position that is reserved for strikers such as McCarthy. The discrepancy between McCarthy and Fortune's national status serves to reveal the "midfielder's rationalization" that girds Paul Ince's recent claim: "Tackling," the authoritative ex-Liverpool F.C. skipper announced in 1998, "is better than sex." Undoubtedly one of the best midfielders playing in the world today, in part because of his bone-crunching combativeness, Ince suggests through hyperbole that the great tackle (a defensive intervention that potentially prevents the loss of the game) is the—orgiastic—apogee of the game for those who play his position. Glory is the reward for goalscorer, the ultimate offensive gesture in football.

McCarthy, however, is different from Williams not only through his ability to cement his place in the team for the foreseeable future or from Fortune simply by his position on the football field: Unlike Mark Williams, a symbol of the difficult cultural interregnum, Benni McCarthy is "fully" representative of the new South Africa. Unlike Williams, he does not represent the difficult, contorted transition of the apartheid past into the postapartheid present. Williams's career can be taken as emblematic of a historic cultural conflict, nonracialism versus "normal sport," a principled SACOS membership against white-dominated sport; and, though this critique was seldom articulated, SACOS against an "expedient" black footballing community that was implicitly underwriting the ideology of apartheid by participating in "normal sport."[9] McCarthy is, in a loaded cultural word, largely unmarked by an affiliation with SACOS (having only played his football there as a young boy), an organization that represents an unequivocal difference between coloured footballers from the Western Cape—a community where the politics of nonracialism held sway—and their black counterparts in other parts of the country. (Committed to noncollaboration with the Afrikaner regime, SACOS players did not, unlike black South Africans, participate in the multiracial professional league—the same one where Williams played for Hellenic after his defection from Clarewood.) It is one of the reasons why the ex-Clarewood striker was not adopted wholeheartedly by the township community. Despite his 1996 exploits, his disloyalty may have rendered him unpalatable as icon; he was soiled ideological cultural goods, a figure who had once betrayed the trust and the political integrity of his community.

Unlike Williams, who came to national prominence at the tail end of his football life, McCarthy's 1998 triumph (which did not culminate in national success but in a loss to Egypt in the final) marked the beginning of his career. Like the postapartheid society, McCarthy is youthful and he does not speak of nor does he ever suggest that he is aware of the cultural contentiousness of the past; like the "new South Africa," he sets his eyes on the prize that is the future. However much McCarthy and Williams are distinct, there are also ways—the Hanover Park striker is the ex-Hellenic player's successor—in a narrow, strictly racialized sense, one coloured striker replacing another. Also, Williams's timely goals in the 1996 Nation's Cup tournament established an important national precedent: A coloured player could spearhead a South African victory. More than that, however, Williams demonstrated the strategic value of the (politically complicated) residual and the transitional nature of his particular conjuncture. Players who had graduated through the SACOS ranks showed, through Williams, how the talent of the disenfranchised could triumph at the highest levels of the game. In spite of the impoverished conditions under which they participated, SACOS footballers metonymically proved themselves the equal of players on the African continent. Williams's goals demonstrated the tremendous talents, nurtured in the coloured townships by SACOS, that had been legislatively denied by apartheid. In a "normal" society, that is, a just, democratic, equitable state, "Williams" could compete against anyone. The "defector" was also, paradoxically, a representative of SACOS's achievement: In a small, complicated way, his African Nation's Cup goals marked the triumph of (compromised) "principles" over "expediency."

In the newly postapartheid society, the 1996 triumph represented a crucial moment of accomplishment. Football, the sport of the black majority, came to international prominence on that late-January day when South Africa was crowned champions of the continent. The "sport of the people" showed itself to be not only populist, but triumphant. But the team, despite its victory, seemed makeshift, patched together by coach Clive Barker, not quite a motley collection of individuals but certainly not a side fluid or fluent in their communication with one another. The 1996 champions seemed, much like the nation, to be a work in progress, borrowing the resources of the old—players such as Williams and the then-captain, Neil Tovey, appeared past their prime but not yet ready to be replaced—to produce the new. The significant difference, however, was that political coherence of the nation seemed to exceed its footballing unity. Bafana Bafana was still finding its way, attempting to craft an identity in the midst of tumultuous sociopolitical changes.

But by the time the 1998 Nation's Cup came around the South African team members appeared more unsettled than their predecessors. Football legend Jomo Sono, who had starred with the black Soweto-based club Orlando Pirates in the early 1970s, had replaced Barker on an interim basis before a new coach (Phillipe Troussier) took the team to the World Cup in France. The team was, however, still too full of older players, still bore the imprimatur of the interstitial Barker era. Recognizing this, Sono presciently selected Fortune, the Kaiser Chiefs goalkeeper Brian Baloyi, and the young McCarthy in his bid to build the nucleus for the future. (On the team's return from Ougadougou, Burkina Faso—where the tournament was held, South Africa's chief football executive Danny Jordaan anointed these three the representatives of the "new generation"[10] of footballers.)

Sono's most inspired move, of course, was introducing the striker against Namibia. McCarthy's fame was inconceivable without Sono's vision, the coach's preparedness to dismantle the old guard and install the youth brigade. Consequently, the Hanover Park player felt a special affinity with the rotund coach who, like him, had found fame abroad. The heady environs of late-1990s Ajax Amsterdam, which boasts a tradition that includes great players such as Johan Cruyff, Ruud Gullit, and Frank Rikjaard, recalled for both the Hanover Park striker and older South African football aficionados Sono's exploits in the United States in the mid-1970s. Already a star in South Africa, Sono had left to play with the Brazilian great Pele for the New York Cosmos some twenty years before. Pele was past his prime, but it was an unprecedented honor for Sono to line up with him every week on Randall's Island, the Cosmos's home stadium. Player and coach also bonded around their mutual flamboyance, the "natural" striker's hunger they shared for public acknowledgement. Proclaiming his debt to the ex-Orlando Pirates striker, McCarthy said, "'I was like a son to Jomo.'"[11] McCarthy's was a magnanimous gesture, thanking his coach for the opportunity to represent his country. The young striker was, however, an articulation considerably more loaded than that, impacted as it was with political significance.

McCarthy's proclamation was a telling moment, a newly created bond that transcended generations (Sono was at his peak before McCarthy was born), race (the coloured player tracing his lineage to the black coach, fulfilling the "reconciliation" premise of the postapartheid society), and, most important, history. The differences of the past, which separated Sono's community from McCarthy's, one cultural tradition (athletic accommodation with the apartheid state) with another, previously incompatible one (sustained and principled noncollaboration). In its stead, an imaginary patrilineal line was established, a "Jomo-Benni" link that invalidated previous ideological incommensurabilities, reinscribing the past as a seamless continuum so that it coincided with the prevailing political ethos—the need to write national unity publicly at every opportunity, the reluctance to engage the complications of the past for fear that it would undermine the project of nation building. In a historically perverse way, the apartheid ideology of divide-and-rule had succeeded, not once, but twice—"posthumously" the second time. The apartheid state, according to its policy of dividing the disenfranchised, worked strategically to distinguish the three racial groups separate from each other. With the founding of the postapartheid society, the history—and the historic consequences—of those divisions have been sublimated, articulable only through the ballot box when coloureds mark themselves off from their black counterparts. Historical division has found a new and potent ally: silencing the disenfranchised cultural differences of the apartheid past. Postapartheid unity has to be publicly willed into existence through the repression of past differences.

There is little possibility of the new national formation's being publicly discoursed, discussed, debated, and wrangled over. McCarthy and Sono have become patrilineally related, the metaphoric father has found a precocious son, postapartheid disenfranchised "oneness" writ spectacularly in the persons of the ex-striker and the current one. But the interrogations the spectacle of these two bodies, the one (Sono's) only slightly darker than the other, obscures is vital: What is it that distinguishes McCarthy from Sono, Radebe from Fortune, John "Shoes" Moshoeu from Bartlett? How does the cultural unity of the team stand in relation to larger political and regional differences? Is sport the least fractious, and therefore least efficacious, expression of the imaginary unity of postapartheid society? Does national unity only exist when publicly performed? If the new nation is not aware of how McCarthy's past is not Sono's, what kind of future can be conceived? What are the costs of public silence?

Privileging the rhetoric of unity reveals its discursive limitations. It precludes an investigation of the very basis of that nation, the nature and the processes by which it is being constructed; it deliberately undermines the aporias and schisms of the past, refusing to acknowledge hybridity; it endorses a sameness that is more projection, wish fulfillment, than substance. Succinctly expressed, Benni McCarthy is not Jomo Sono, nor should he be expected to articulate himself publicly as though he were. If Paul Adams has been made to bear the burden of overrepresentation, then McCarthy has endured a more exacting experience: He has had to bear the burden of deliberate misrepresentation. However Adams has been positioned, read, and disseminated, his status as historically coloured subject has never been drawn into question. His body is, within the South African cricket context, sufficiently representative of the disenfranchised. (Of course, set alongside Makhaya Ntini, a black fast bowler who recently had a brief stint with the national team, Adams is indisputably coloured. His racial difference from his white teammates is obvious enough.) Although his accent (a native Afrikaans speaker in the process of making English his primary public language) and his geographical origins (the coloured-dominated Western Cape) mark him as identifiably "coloured," the Hanover Park footballer has been appropriated as the generic new "black" South African cultural icon. In this way, McCarthy's colouredness is not so much ignored as it refracted. His accent and his Cape Flats origins become muted codes for his colouredness, the identity that dare not speak its name, except through innuendo.

He has become "everyone's Benni"; in part he has succeeded in the nation's most populous (that is, numerically dominated by blacks) sport, but also because to suggest he might belong more to some constituencies than to others is to publicly register the extent to which "blackness" is a fractured identity, one with different kinds of purchase in different communities. If McCarthy were overly identified with Hanover Park, the disjuncture between his status as national icon and his community's remove from the postapartheid society would require a political accounting that does not seem possible at this moment.

A South African,
in Those "Benni" Moments

All that I know most surely in the long run about morality and the obligations of men, I owe to football.

—Albert Camus, *Faber Book of Football*

The 1998 World Cup in France was an intoxicating moment for South Africans. After the isolation of the apartheid era, the country made its World Cup debut against the hosts France in mid-June. Expectations seemed inordinately high for a team so new to international competition, but the team performed credibly, drawing with (tying) Denmark (1–1) and Saudi Arabia (2–2) after losing convincingly (3–0) to eventual champions France in their World Cup opener. After his seven goals in the African Nation's Cup (making him joint top scorer with the Egyptian veteran Hossam Hassan) earned him the honor of "Player of the Tournament," McCarthy became the focus of the South African attack—the striker expected to carve goals out of nothing, to make do with a paucity of possession and to convert that into improbable victories. There would be no South African wins in World Cup '98, but McCarthy left his mark on this tournament in a way that was internationally insignificant but locally resonant.

Unlike the Nation's Cup, McCarthy finished at the bottom of the list of goalscorers in France. The brace of goals by his fellow Cape Townian, Shaun Bartlett, was double McCarthy's. However, the one strike the Hanover Park player managed was historic. Netting the ball awkwardly through the legs of the splayed Danish goalkeeper Peter Schmeichel, McCarthy scored the first goal by a South African in the World Cup. Long a fan of the Danish 'keeper (who until the 1999 season played his club football for the English Manchester United, who the Hanover Park striker supported as a boy), McCarthy could barely contain himself after the game. "'This was a great game for myself and my country,' he said, 'I'm really happy to have scored because it's the first goal for South Africa in the World Cup. . . . To score against that man [Schmeichel], it was a dream for me.'"[12]

In the entanglements of McCarthy's euphoria it is difficult to decide which accomplishment takes primacy. There seems to be a telling conflation, the honor of scoring the "first goal for South Africa" with the feat of doing so against "that man." In this salient cultural moment, McCarthy seems to be at once national hero and township coloured, South African striker and Manchester United fan. Measuring the import of the goal by the player it was scored against rather than by simply celebrating the "first" goal as a feat in and of itself reveals the extent to which McCarthy is a product of the football culture of the coloured Western Cape. This is, as was demonstrated in Chapter 4, a region heavily impacted by the influence of the English game, a community where the consequences of Liverpool and Manchester United results are—to invoke Bill Shankley again—"more important than a matter of life and death." In this historic instance, McCarthy showed himself to be culturally different from his black and white teammates. If "Shoes" Moshoeu or Helman "Midnight Express" Mkhalele had scored the goal against the Danish 'keeper, the resonances would have been different: The fact of the goal would have taken clear precedence. Schmeichel would not have figured so largely in the after-match event.

That the thickset Dane was assigned a place of prominence speaks of the disjunctures within McCarthy that could not be kept out of public view in so vital a moment in his own life. Up to this point, McCarthy had fulfilled the terms of the postapartheid public transcript, he had represented himself as a "new" South African, emblematic of the nation, product of the racially indistinct townships. In the moment of his greatest triumph, however, his "cultural" essence articulated itself as coloured. After years of trying to make like his Manchester United idols on the dusty fields of Hanover Park with his friends, McCarthy had gone one better: He had beaten the man who minded the net at Old Trafford. In the "theatre" of international football, he had realized an unlikely "dream."

As much as McCarthy's "bifurcated" response to his historic goal reveals an ideological split between his interpellation into the South African nation and the depth of his immersion in the coloured experience, so his status as Bafana Bafana star provided a point of national identification for his community. Much like McCarthy's coded (and racialized) ambivalence speaks of a complicated relationship to the nation, so the township communities on the impoverished Cape Flats have struggled with their place in the postapartheid society. With the unbanning of the black liberation movements and the release of political prisoners in February 1990, the coloured working class on the Cape Flats has become increasingly fearful and uncertain of their place in a nation governed by the predominantly black ANC. Recognizing themselves as too black for the apartheid regime and too white for its successor, they have once again been compelled to situate themselves in that precarious middle ground, tied tenuously to both but anchored by neither—frequently dismissed by the ANC and cogniscant of how expediently they are being interpellated by the NP, they see little evidence of a serious engagement on the part of either organization with the ideological complications of their hybridity. All of these complex positionings, this conflicted, ambivalent history, is underscored by a latent, and sometimes not so latent, antiblack racism, a troubling sense of racial superiority, a not coincidental by-product of the apartheid era. A combination of these factors, and a whole range of others, no doubt, contributed to working class coloureds returning the NP to power in the Western Cape. With that vote, their place in the new nation became tendentious, alienating them in substantive ways unimagined by Nortje and Rive. In pledging their "allegiance" to the Nationalists, they were implicitly understood as disloyal to the black majority. Within the new South Africa, the price of hybridity is alienation.

What Benni McCarthy offered this community was, more than anything, the opportunity to partially reintegrate themselves into postapartheid society. When he scored his goals against Namibia in the Nation's Cup or that memorable one against Schmeicel in France, he enabled—if only for a moment—township coloureds to affiliate with the nation, to transiently name themselves "South African." Through him they were partially affiliated with the society, seeing themselves represented—often quite splendidly and spectacularly—in and by him. Although township coloureds, men more than women, have a passionate interest in football, after the Namibia game (January 1998) and from the start of the World Cup some six months later, they exhibited a palpable rise in that interest. The "Benni phenomenon" marked the conjucture at which township coloureds could, though how permanent or transient a development is debatable, transcend their ambivalence and their "discrepant" voting tendencies and make themselves a part of the national cultural fabric. Cultural affiliation enabled them to cast aside, if not off, their problematic but not inexplicable, allegiance to the NP and become South Africans.

Township coloureds related to McCarthy as they could not to Radebe or Moshoeu. Talented though they are, neither of these could be claimed as "their boys," to invoke the experience of American immigrants—Italian-Americans used to say of Jimmy Durante's cultural accomplishments, "that's my boy." Through this gesture, they distinguished themselves from mainstream WASP culture and made a distinct place for themselves in it. "Their boy," Durante, symbolized at once their difference and their commitment to (as well their partial) integration into this "new" society. McCarthy is the township's "boy"—not so much theirs exclusively, but as a marker of potential. They can make like Benni, not only in terms of young boys imagining themselves as lethal strikers, but as a community integral to the functioning of postapartheid society. "Their boy" proffers a model of how to be "everybody's boy," of how they can become, if only tentatively and cautiously, part of the South African "everybody"—the body politic as incorporative and accommodating to coloureds, as being composed of, in part, the coloured body. But that is not the juncture signaled by the African Nation's Cup or the World Cup. At this point McCarthy was claimed more fully, less presciently, a symbol of the fractured present rather than the reimagined future. Born and nurtured in the townships, his repertoires of representation (the flashy jewelry, the dyed hair, the imperfect English, the grandiose celebration after scoring a goal, the unapologetic showman), made him indisputably "theirs." His public prominence, as opposed to the comparative obscurity of Fortune, implied a desire for a spectacular national recognition. Fortune is superb at his position, but his contributions are lost in the clamor of the game. "Benni's" goals garner a publicity that Fortune's tackles or passes cannot; McCarthy is a showman, Fortune is a skilled craftsman—a man appreciated, if undervalued, by his community.

By embracing McCarthy more fully than Mark Williams or Shaun Bartlett, however, the township community inadvertently articulates a desire for its own future incorporation into postapartheid society. "At 20 he is," as an American journalist so aptly put it, "the future of the sport in his country."[13] Whether or not the township community can achieve the same level of (problematic, uneven) interpellation that McCarthy has (Jomo's "son" and Schmeichel fan), is questionable. But it is clear that this constituency is rethinking its own location on the nation's political landscape, contemplating whether it can retreat into marginality or whether it can convert its partial affiliation into full(er) identification with the new nation-state. As the country's demographics change and more black citizens move to the Western Cape, this process of reevaluation will become increasingly crucial—unable to position themselves as a region of coloured domination, they will have to imagine how to retain a sense of their history, their traditions, their embattled, hybrid sense of self, in the midst of a transforming political environment. The more McCarthy, or other "Bennis" like him, succeed and are represented (and misrepresented, in part) as national icons, the more the township may see itself as literally, and not in some abstract rhetorical way, becoming—it is always a process—part of the postapartheid dispensation. Black South Africa offers more of a cultural home in football than the National Party. Culture, however, is only a starting point, the dynamic beginning of an ideological journey, and it can only be efficaciously deployed if its political import is seriously engaged and fully comprehended. After all, "what know they of football (or morality) who only football know?"

Notes

1. It is absolutely clear that, following the first democratic elections of 1994, South Africa is a legally (and legislatively) different society. However, it is highly questionable, despite the adulation that followed President Mandela's victory, as to whether or not post-1994 South Africa is a substantively "new" society. The legacy of apartheid inequity has endured, exacerbated in ways all too reminiscent of other postcolonial elites—after the rapid ascension to power of this new black governing class, those Frantz Fanon dubbed the "national bourgeoisie."

2. Inigo Gilmore, "Bright Spark Saved from Mean Streets," *Times* (London), 12 June 1998.

3. Peter Auf der Heyde, "World Cup Was 1998 Highlight for South African Football," *Deutsche Presse-Agentur*, 29 December 1998.

4. "One Day I'll Be Rich Like Them," *Mail and Guardian* (South Africa), 12 June 1998.

5. Mohen Govender, "Coach Hoists Benni 'the Flag,'" *Cape Argus* (Cape Town), 10 June 1998.

6. Joseph Aranes, "Benni Wants to Have Fun . . . ," *Cape Argus* (Cape Town), 15 May 1998.

7. "Rags to Riches Story of South Africa's Star Striker," *Hull Daily Mail* (Yorkshire), 23 June 1998. See Gary Rathbone's article, "Rise of the New McCarthyism," *Sunday Times* (South Africa), 14 June 1998, Sunday Life section.

8. See Gary Rathbone's article, "Rise of the New McCarthyism," *Sunday Times* (South Africa), 14 June 1998, Sunday Life section.

9. The ideological contradiction in the black community, the participation in "normal" sport and the intense opposition to the apartheid regime, has not been fully explored or explicated. Because of the black community's status as the dominant disenfranchised group, it has not been subjected to a serious critique about

its cultural implication in the system of apartheid. By broaching the subject in this chapter, of which it is not the focus, *Midfielder's Moment* wants to open up the question of "black cultural collaboration" to fuller inquiry.

10. "Sport's New Generation," *Cape Argus* (Cape Town), February 1998.

11. Govender, "Benni 'the Flag.'"

12. Steven Goff, "McCarthy's 'Great Game' Lifts South Africa's Spirits," *Washington Post*, 23 June 1998.

13. Graham L. Jones, "This Benedict Ready to Defend His Country's Honor," *Los Angeles Times*, 12 June 1998.

Index

171